AFTER THE WHITE HOUSE

After
THE
WHITE HOUSE

*Former Presidents
as Private Citizens*

MAX J. SKIDMORE

First published 2004 by
PALGRAVE MACMILLAN™
175 Fifth Avenue, New York, N.Y. 10010 and
Houndmills, Basingstoke, Hampshire, England RG21 6XS.
Companies and representatives throughout the world.

PALGRAVE MACMILLAN is the global academic imprint of the Palgrave Macmillan
division of St. Martin's Press, LLC and of Palgrave Macmillan Ltd. Macmillan® is a
registered trademark in the United States, United Kingdom and other countries. Palgrave
is a registered trademark in the European Union and other countries.

ISBN 0–312–29559–6 hardcover

Library of Congress Cataloging-in-Publication Data
Skidmore, Max J., 1933-
After the White House : former presidents as private citizens / Max J. Skidmore.
    p.   cm.
  Includes bibliographical references and index.
  ISBN 0–312–29559–6
  1. Ex-presidents—United States—Biography.   2. Presidents—United States—
Biography. I. Title.

E176.1.S613 2004
973'.09'9—dc22

[B]
2003068939

A catalogue record for this book is available from the British Library.

Design by Letra Libre, Inc.

First edition: July 2004
10 9 8 7 6 5 4 3 2 1

Printed in the United States of America.

CONTENTS

In Memory of
Betrenia Watt Bowker
"Aunt Teeny"
who nourished
the habit of thought

PRESIDENTS OF THE UNITED STATES

George Washington, born February 22, 1732; died December 14, 1799
 President: April 30, 1789–March 4, 1797

John Adams, born October 30, 1735; died July 4, 1826
 President: March 4, 1797–March 4, 1801

Thomas Jefferson, born April 13, 1743; died July 4, 1826
 President: March 4, 1801–March 4, 1809

James Madison, born March 16, 1751; died June 28, 1836
 President: March 4, 1809–March 4, 1817

James Monroe, born April 28, 1758; died July 4, 1831
 President: March 4, 1817–March 4, 1825

John Quincy Adams, born July 11, 1767; died February 23 1848
 President: March 4, 1825–March 4, 1829

Andrew Jackson, born March 15, 1767; died June 8, 1845
 President: March 4, 1829–March 4, 1837

Martin Van Buren, born December 5, 1782; died July 24, 1862
 President: March 4, 1837–March 4, 1841

William Henry Harrison, born February 9, 1773; died April 4, 1841
 President: March 4, 1841–April 4, 1841 (died in office)

John Tyler, born March 29, 1790; died Jan. 18, 1862
 President: April 4, 1841–March 4, 1845

James K. Polk, born November 2, 1795; died June 15 1849
 President: March 4, 1845–March 4, 1849

Zachary Taylor, born November 24, 1784; died July 9, 1850
 President: March 4, 1849–July 9, 1850 (died in office)

Millard Fillmore, born January 7, 1800; died March 8, 1874
 President: July 9, 1850–March 4, 1853

Franklin Pierce, born November 23, 1804; died October 8, 1869
    President: March 4, 1853–March 4, 1857

James Buchanan, born April 23, 1791; died June 1, 1868
    President: March 4, 1857–March 4, 1861

Abraham Lincoln, born February 12, 1809; died April 15, 1865
    President: March 4, 1861–April 15, 1865 (died in office—assassinated)

Andrew Johnson, born December 29, 1808; died July 31, 1875
    President: April 15, 1865–March 4, 1869

Ulysses S. Grant, born April 27, 1822; died July 23, 1885
    President: March 4, 1869–March 4, 1877

Rutherford B. Hayes, born October 4, 1822; died January 17, 1893
    President: March 4, 1877–March 4, 1881

James A. Garfield, born November 19, 1831; died September 19, 1881
    President: March 4, 1881–September 19, 1881 (died in office—assassinated)

Chester A. Arthur, born October 5, 1830; died November 18, 1886
    President: September 19, 1881–March 4, 1885

Grover Cleveland, born March 18, 1837; died June 24, 1908
    President: March 4, 1885–March 4, 1889 (also served March 4, 1893–
    March 4, 1897)

Benjamin Harrison, born August 20, 1833; died March 13, 1901
    President: March 4, 1889–March 4, 1893

Grover Cleveland (see above)
    President: March 4, 1893–March 4, 1897 (also served March 4, 1885–
    March 4, 1889)

William McKinley, born January 29, 1843; died September 14, 1901
    President: March 4, 1897–September 14, 1901 (died in office—assassinated)

Theodore Roosevelt, born October 27, 1858; died January 6, 1919
    President: September 14, 1901–March 4, 1909

William Howard Taft, born September 15, 1857; died March 8, 1930
    President: March 4, 1909–March 4, 1913

Woodrow Wilson, born December 28, 1856; died February 3, 1924
    President: March 4, 1913–March 4, 1921

Warren G. Harding, born November 2, 1865; died August 2, 1923
    President: March 4, 1921–August 2, 1923 (died in office)

Calvin Coolidge, born July 4, 1872; died January 5, 1933
    President: August 2, 1923–March 4, 1929

Herbert Hoover, born August 10, 1874; died October 20, 1964
    President: March 4, 1929–March 4, 1933

Franklin Delano Roosevelt, born January 30, 1882; died April 12, 1945
    President: March 4, 1933–April 12, 1945 (died in office)

Harry S. Truman, born May 8, 1884; died December 26, 1972
    President: April 12, 1945–January 20, 1953

Dwight D. Eisenhower, born October 14, 1890; died March 28, 1969
    President: January 20, 1953–January 20, 1961

John F. Kennedy, born May 29, 1917; died November 22, 1963
    President: January 20, 1961–November 22, 1963 (died in office—
    assassinated)

Lyndon B. Johnson, born August 27, 1908; died January 22, 1973
    President: November 22, 1963–January 20, 1969

Richard M. Nixon, born January 9, 1913; died April 22, 1994
    President: January 20, 1969–August 9, 1974 (resigned)

Gerald R. Ford, born July 14, 1913–
    President: August 9, 1974–January 20 1977

Jimmy (James Earl) Carter, born October 1, 1924–
    President: January 20, 1977–January 20, 1981

Ronald Reagan, born February 6, 1911–
    President: January 20, 1981–January 20, 1989

George H. W. Bush, born June 12, 1924–
    President: January 20, 1989–January 20, 1993

William Jefferson Clinton, born August 19, 1946–
    President: January 20, 1993–January 20, 2001

George W. Bush, born July 6, 1946–
    President: January 20, 2001–

INTRODUCTION

They Had it All—But Then What Happened?

INTRODUCTION

INTRODUCTION

BILL CLINTON WAS ONLY 54 AND STILL YOUTHFUL AND VIGOROUS, WHEN HE LEFT the White House in January 2001. George W. Bush, replacing Clinton, was the same age going into office as Clinton was when he departed after serving for eight years. What does a relatively young man whose résumé includes two terms as president of the United States do?

At one time Clinton had been the country's youngest sitting governor. He had been only 46 when he was inaugurated as president, which made him the third youngest president in history, behind only Theodore Roosevelt, who succeeded to the office at 42, and John Kennedy, who assumed office at 43. Clinton is among the youngest former presidents as well, but since he served a full eight years, there were five others who were younger when they left office.

Theodore Roosevelt, at 50, was the country's youngest former president (and he had served all but six months of two full terms because of William McKinley's assassination). Grover Cleveland left office at 51 and Franklin Pierce at 52, after completing one term each. Both James K. Polk, who had one term, and Millard Fillmore who served somewhat fewer than three years, became former presidents at 53. Like Clinton, Ulysses S. Grant was inaugurated at 46, but he turned 47 the following month, while Clinton was in office approximately seven months before reaching that age. Also like Clinton, John Tyler was 54 when his term (in Tyler's case, a single term) came to an end, but he was within a few days of his fifty-fifth birthday.

Very few presidents, then, have found themselves out of office at such a young age, and none have been in this position after serving two full terms. Certainly the most active former president was the youngest, Theodore Roosevelt, but he lived slightly less than a decade after leaving the presidency. He and Fillmore, another very young former president, each ran for the presidency again on third-party tickets. TR's race changed the course of American history, while Fillmore's was inconsequential. Fillmore did live, though, for more than two decades after leaving office. Two of Clinton's other predecessors also ran again. Both influenced history, and one even regained the office.

The first former president to run for the office again was Martin Van Buren who had been elected in 1836, but who lost his 1840 bid for re-election. He attempted to regain the Democratic nomination in 1844, but failed because of opposition from Southern delegates. In 1848, he became the candidate of the Free Soil Party. He won enough votes as a minor party candidate to cause the Democratic candidate, Lewis Cass, to lose in key states, thus enabling Zachary Taylor, a Whig, to become president. The second, Grover Cleveland, lost his race for re-election in 1888. He received more popular votes than his Republican opponent, Benjamin Harrison, but lost in the electoral college. In 1892, he returned to the presidential political arena to defeat President Harrison, becoming the only former president ever to be re-elected to the office.

Because of the 22nd Amendment, ratified in 1951, re-election to the presidency is not a possibility for Clinton. That amendment prohibits any person from being elected president more than twice. And nothing is assured (the presidency often takes its toll on the health of the person holding the office). Polk left the presidency at an age younger than Clinton, and died within three months. Still, Clinton's age, vibrancy, and robust health suggest that he will have a lengthy post-presidential career and will be a major force in American politics for years to come. He was the dominant political presence as the twenty-first century began even after leaving office (causing great anguish among his opponents, including his successor) until the attacks of September 11, 2001, brought the new administration of George W. Bush to the forefront. It is highly unlikely that Clinton will permit himself to fade permanently from the limelight.

Certainly no one can predict what contributions Clinton and the second Bush will make during their lives after the White House. While each post-presidential experience is unique, as is each presidency, the experiences of former presidents may yet offer insights into the possible roles that current and future ex-presidents may play. Former presidents do not necessarily attract sustained attention except from their biographers. Post-presidential influence upon

American political development tends to attract even less attention, although at times it has been substantial. As Clinton himself put it, "when you leave the presidency, you lose your power but not your influence."[1] Because that influence can be significant, it is important that it not be ignored.

To be sure, Stanford University historian Thomas A. Bailey did provide a lively chapter dealing with former presidents in his 1966 *Presidential Greatness*. His chapter, though, was brief and it paid less attention to ex-presidents' influence than to their reputations.[2] Studying reputations can have a value of its own (a concern for restoring a reputation battered by a troubled presidency may have impelled John Quincy Adams and Jimmy Carter to reach great post-presidential heights, or to have motivated the later careers of Herbert Hoover and Richard Nixon) but it is former presidents' influence that most needs examination. Another writer, historian Marie B. Hecht, also dealt with post-presidential lives before Carter, but she emphasized influence less than biography.[3]

Presidents who are relatively young when leaving office of course are more likely to remain active and influential than their older fellows, but not even this is an absolute principle. There was no more reason for the country to remember a rather youthful Franklin Pierce fondly in retirement, for example, than there had been to approve of him as president. At the other end of the spectrum, John Quincy Adams left office at 61 and went on to another political career in the U.S. House of Representatives that not only was distinguished, but was in fact exemplary.

Whether or not a president was highly active, or had a reputation of success when he left office apparently has little relation to a post-presidential career. There was, for example, little or no aura of success surrounding Carter, Herbert Hoover, or William Howard Taft when they left office, but this did not prevent each one from launching a career of considerable public service. Fillmore had been a lackluster president, but still came back later to be nominated again—albeit not by a major party. Andrew Jackson, Dwight Eisenhower, and Ronald Reagan come to mind as presidents who left office with varying reputations for success, and all were relatively inactive thereafter, although Jackson and Eisenhower did continue to exercise some political influence. It may be significant that these were the three oldest former presidents (Reagan was older by far than any other). Richard Nixon and Lyndon Johnson were among our most active presidents, but like the very active Jackson both were less active in retirement. Both during and following his presidency, Theodore Roosevelt was enormously active.

The kinds of influence former presidents are likely to wield surely will prove at best to be only suggested—not determined—by their performance in office. Nevertheless, former presidents frequently remain persons of power and substance.

More often than not they continue to influence public affairs; such influence can come in several different forms. Among the four broad categories of ways in which former presidents remain influential, the one that seems most obvious—former presidents who exercise influence by seeking to regain the presidency—in all probability will never occur again because of the Twenty-second Amendment. Another category of continuing influence consists of former presidents who secure another political office, either appointive or elective. Former presidents who have made contributions to education and to public understanding constitute a third category of influence. Finally several presidents after leaving office have become active in humanitarian causes. Several former presidents, of course, fall into more than one of these groups, and there are additional miscellaneous post-presidential careers that taken together could become yet a fifth category.

In order to provide a seamless historical narrative, this book will deal with former presidents in chronological order. Here, however, I offer an overview by grouping the more outstanding figures into the categories. Four former presidents, as mentioned previously, sought to regain the office. Additionally, there have been two more instances—historical footnotes—in which a former president almost became a major-party candidate for president. U. S. Grant nearly was nominated for a third, and non-consecutive, term in 1880. In 1920, every indication is that Theodore Roosevelt would again have been the Republican nominee for president had he lived—and that he would have won. A bizarre situation emerged in 1980, in which former president Gerald Ford was considering accepting a nomination for vice president!

Although these are the only instances in which former presidents have run again for the presidency, some ex-presidents have served in other governmental offices. George Washington emerged briefly from retirement to command the U.S. Army in 1798. John Adams was a presidential elector in 1820, and also that year was a delegate to the Massachusetts Constitutional Convention. James Madison was a member of the Virginia Constitutional Convention in 1829. James Monroe also was a member of that convention and served as its chair. John Quincy Adams had a distinguished career as a member of the U.S. House of Representatives from 1831 until he died in office in 1848. Martin Van Buren was a presidential elector in both 1852 and 1858. Andrew Johnson became a U.S. senator in March of 1875 and died in office in July of that same year.

John Tyler was the only former president who worked against the Union that he had headed. After failing to gain acceptance for Southern demands, he ultimately threw in his lot with the secessionists, and in 1861 became a member of the Provisional Congress of the Confederate States of America. He was elected to the Confederate House of Representatives late that year, but died in January of 1862, before taking office.

General Ulysses S. Grant had resigned his military commission to accept the presidency. Former President Grant received reinstatement as general of the army in March of 1885. William Howard Taft during World War One became co-chair of President Wilson's National War Labor Board, serving 1918–1919. In 1921, President Warren Harding appointed him to be chief justice of the U.S. Supreme Court. He remained chief justice until he resigned for reasons of health in 1930.

In addition, Bill Clinton is the only president or former president whose wife has been elected to political office. Hillary Clinton was the first presidential spouse even to run for office, so the Clinton family has achieved a first. She is the only member of Congress who ever has been First Lady—and in fact she briefly was simultaneously First Lady and U.S. Senator.

Altough Senator Clinton is unique among first ladies in having achieved her own political career, there have been several family members of other presidents who achieved high office. Former President John Adams observed the inauguration of his son, John Quincy Adams, as president, as did former President George Bush when his son George W. Bush was inaugurated. President William Henry Harrison no longer was alive (in fact, he had died in 1841 within a month of his own inauguration) when his grandson Benjamin Harrison became president in 1889. President John F. Kennedy's brother Robert, became U.S. attorney general during the Kennedy administration. He continued in that post into the administration of Lyndon Johnson and then became a U.S. senator. Another brother, Edward M. Kennedy, also became a U.S. senator, and in fact has had a career there of great distinction. He remains in the Senate after some four decades.

Former presidents who have served as college or university administrators or members of governing boards include Thomas Jefferson (who also founded and designed the University of Virginia), James Madison, James Monroe, John Tyler, James Buchanan, Rutherford B. Hayes, and Grover Cleveland. Those who have become faculty members are Cleveland, Benjamin Harrison, and William Howard Taft. Others who have engaged in a variety of educational activities include Lyndon Johnson, Gerald Ford, and Jimmy Carter. Herbert Hoover, Richard Nixon, Gerald Ford, and Jimmy Carter have represented the United States officially or have headed government commissions. Rutherford Hayes and especially Jimmy Carter have been noted for their exceptional humanitarian activities. Perhaps the most unusual semi-official activity for a former president was Richard Nixon's mediation in 1985 of a baseball umpires' strike.

Numerous former presidents have made substantial public contributions in various ways. Thomas Jefferson provided the nucleus for the Library of Congress, and he and John Adams greatly enhanced political philosophy through their extensive correspondence. During his retirement, James Madison published the only official record of the Constitutional Convention.

Former President John Quincy Adams, when a member of the U.S. House of Representatives, not only opposed slavery, but he argued the *Amistad* case before the Supreme Court, and won freedom for its slave "cargo." In the House, he supported scientific endeavors, and helped secure approval for acceptance of the grant from James Smithson that established the Smithsonian Institution. His contributions were literary, as well. The remarkable diary that he kept throughout his political career is one of the most important resources for the study of the period.

In the decades following Martin Van Buren's defeat in 1840, he and his son John (who was a member of the U.S. House of Representatives), spoke out increasingly against slavery. Before, during, and following his presidency, Van Buren was probably the major architect of America's two-party system.

James Buchanan produced his memoirs, *Mr. Buchanan's Administration on the Eve of Rebellion* in 1866, in an attempt to convince historians to judge him well. They have not done so. In contrast, former President U. S. Grant produced in his own memoirs a literary masterpiece that critics as diverse as Gertrude Stein and Edmund Wilson have lauded. The *Personal Memoirs of U. S. Grant,* is not only a classic account of the Civil War, but one of the most valuable.

Other former presidents have authored worthwhile memoirs. They include Harry Truman, Dwight Eisenhower, Lyndon Johnson, Richard Nixon, and Jimmy Carter. Theodore Roosevelt, in 1913, brought out a complete autobiography, praised widely; it was one of a huge number of books on a wide variety of subjects that he wrote both before and after his presidency. It remains popular today. Along with TR, other former presidents produced regular articles, among them Grover Cleveland, Benjamin Harrison, and Calvin Coolidge. Coolidge's syndicated columns were titled, "Thinking Things Over with Calvin Coolidge."

Although former President Gerald Ford accepted high pay for corporate board memberships, he engages in civic and educational activities as well. He has participated in lecture series and seminars, and also worked with People for the American Way, Norman Lear's organization created to counter influence from the religious right, including from Jerry Falwell's "Moral Majority."

Former President George H. W. Bush, according to numerous news reports, has at least occasionally played a major role in his son's foreign policy. Although he has distanced himself from his son's administration (at any rate in the public's eye) the first President Bush has accepted at least one formal role in that administration. George W. Bush dispatched his father to London as his personal representative to a memorial service for British subjects who were killed in the 9/11 attack on the World Trade Center. There have, however, been hints of some serious disagreements regarding foreign policy between father and son.

For most Presidents there has been a vigorous life after the White House, but for a substantial minority there was none at all. Nine presidents (more than one fifth of the total) failed to complete their terms, and eight of these died in office. William Henry Harrison was the first. He died on April 4, 1841, one month to the day of his inauguration. He became ill shortly after participating with no hat or coat in the lengthy outdoor inaugural ceremonies on a cold, windy day. Next, Zachary Taylor died suddenly in 1850 after barely more than 16 months in office. He was stricken with severe gastroenteritis, apparently from contaminated food. Abraham Lincoln was the third president to die in office and the first to be assassinated. Death came to him on the morning of April 15, 1865, after having been shot from behind in the head the previous evening. The next two presidents to die in office also were the victims of assassins, James A. Garfield in 1881, six months after his inauguration, and William McKinley in 1901, six months after beginning his second term. Warren G. Harding died of natural causes on August 2, 1923, not quite two and a half years into his term. Franklin D. Roosevelt died on April 12, 1945, also of natural causes. He was beginning his fourth term as president. The final president thus far to have died in office was John F. Kennedy, assassinated on November 22, 1963, in his third year as president.

Many of those who had careers after their presidencies exercised considerable influence on American political history. At times, that influence has been dramatic. There is no way to tell whether Clinton or the younger Bush will remain potent political forces as former presidents. Examples from history suggest, however, that they may—especially Clinton, in view of his unusual youth, energy, and talent. It was his departure from office at the peak of his influence, dominating the political scene, that suggested considerable future influence, and thus inspired this book.

Lengthening life spans and the achievements of modern medicine suggest that in the future it will become increasingly common to have several active and vigorous former presidents on the scene. They will have much to offer, if our society can determine ways to use their talents and experience. In any event, many will undoubtedly remain major influences. We should be aware of that influence. The first step in developing such an awareness will come from studying how former presidents have continued to affect society.

One

GEORGE WASHINGTON

*The First President,
the First Former President*

THE FIRST PRESIDENT OF THE UNITED STATES, GEORGE WASHINGTON OF Virginia, finally left office on March 4, 1797, at the age of 65. He was eager to retire—as he had been after having led the Continental Army to victory in the Revolution. He had in fact hoped to leave after his first term, but agreed reluctantly to stay for a second. Efforts to persuade him to run for a third time failed. His desire to return to his home, Mount Vernon, was too strong.

Washington's retirement itself influenced the course of American politics. The effect was immediate. It "eased somewhat the Jeffersonians' concerns about the dangerous aggrandizement of executive power. In fact, as scholar Leonard White noted, Washington's example converted Jefferson from his original belief that the president should serve only one term."[1]

Ironically, though, there is no evidence that the "Father of Our Country" intended his tenure in the presidency to set a two-term limit; quite the contrary, in fact. As he indicated in a letter to the Marquis de Lafayette, he saw no wisdom "in precluding ourselves from the services of any man who on some emergency shall be deemed universally most capable of serving the public."[2] He opposed a limit. Modern advocates of term limits should pay heed to Washington's thoughts on the matter, as term limits are now beginning to cause mischief

in states around the country. Legislature after legislature is now finding its sea-
soned members forced into retirement, to be replaced by enthusiastic but inexperienced people who—however well-meaning—have none of the skills or
prudence required to produce sound public policy. Only in America, and only
in politics, is inexperience considered to be a qualification. Washington's successors nevertheless followed his lead, rather than his ideas. As a result, the two-
term limit became the custom if not the law until 1940 when Franklin D.
Roosevelt won election to a third term, and then went on to win a fourth.

Washington was bothered in his life as a farmer with some of the same demands upon his time that had caused him to be strict in regulating visitors when
he was president. People constantly came to "pay their respects." Some no doubt
genuinely wished to praise the former president, but others surely imposed upon
him simply to satisfy their curiosity. There was no Secret Service in those days,
and thus no agents to protect even sitting presidents, let alone those who had
left the office.

Still, he threw himself into his agricultural tasks, and into restoring Mount
Vernon. His managers had performed poorly, and the estate had deteriorated
greatly in his absence, sorely needing his attention. Washington remarked in ex-
asperation that there was "scarcely anything," including all buildings and his
fields as well, "that does not require considerable repairs."[3] One example of the
disrepair he discovered "more by accident than by design" was that the main supporting girder of his banquet hall had deteriorated so much that "a company only
moderately large would have sunk altogether into the cellar." Historian James T.
Flexner noted that Mount Vernon, so long forsaken, was "dilapidated everywhere." Washington immediately ordered so many repairs that he complained of
having "scarcely a room to put a friend into or set in myself without the music
of hammers or the odoriferous smell of paint."[4] The former president spent hours
each day overseeing his crops. Although he grew corn and wheat, Mount Vernon
was essentially a tobacco plantation. His "farms were in an even worse situation
than his buildings." When he obtained Mount Vernon, its lands already had been
depleted. He had worked diligently "to enrich the land with crop rotation and
fertilizers," he had installed drainage ditches to guard against erosion, but he
found that it all had become "a shambles."[5] Despite the attention that Mount
Vernon required and his desire for retirement, it would have been too much to
expect the father of our country to abandon public affairs altogether.

He was of course grateful to have achieved the retirement that he had so
long sought. Settling passively into the life of the landed gentry might have
seemed attractive to him at the outset, but did not suit his active nature. He
found himself not only turning his attention to his plantation, and dealing with

the constant stream of visitors and guests—Mount Vernon had become "so inundated with guests that Washington complained that his home was more like a public inn than a private residence"[6]—but also continuing to keep a keen interest in affairs of state.

Before he left the capital, Washington had asked Secretary of War James McHenry to keep him well informed, and McHenry did so. Washington biographer Douglas Southall Freeman noted that McHenry did so "within, of course, the bounds of official propriety."[7] Among those affairs was increasing friction with France, leading to the "quasi war" on the high seas. President Adams was concerned that full-fledged war might result, and moved to establish an effective national defense for the unprepared country. Washington applauded Adams's concern for the country's protection, and took issue with the Republicans who thought that any concern for military preparation on Adams's part meant that his administration was seeking war.

The worse the international situation became, the more restless the former president became. Gone were the attractions of simply turning to the land and relaxing. As ship after ship fell victim to French seizure in the Caribbean, Washington informed McHenry that he might accept command of a "New Army." In a crisis, he indicated, a "sense of duty" would leave him no choice.[8] He did insist, though, that he be allowed to choose his top officers—and therein lay trouble for President Adams.

Congress authorized Adams to raise an army—in fact it gave him much more than he had asked for or wanted—and the president without consulting Washington submitted his name to the Senate. Within 24 hours, the Senate "unanimously designated him lieutenant general and commander in chief of all armies to be raised within the United States."[9] Washington agreed to accept the renewed commission, and to raise and command the forces. Thus he not only had been the first president, but after leaving office he regained active command of the military, the only former president ever to do so.

Secretary of War McHenry delivered the commission personally to Washington at Mount Vernon. He also delivered something else: "a letter from Hamilton about which Adams was told nothing."[10] One wonders how this might come within Freeman's category of "official propriety." Here was a member of John Adams's own cabinet secretly carrying word to his new military commander urging that he make his own decisions about the army rather than deferring to his superior, the duly-elected president. Washington read that "the judgment of the President ought not to be a consideration" in regard to the army, because Adams was not competent to decide on matters of national defense.[11]

Washington's new duties required him to leave Mount Vernon, which he re-gretted, in order to spend some time at the capital in Philadelphia. He arrived there on November 10, 1798, "with full military flare, on horseback and in uni-form, and accompanied by cavalry."[12] Following his dramatic entry, though, Washington

> was rarely seen. He was working seven days a week with Hamilton drawing up plans for the army, reviewing applications, and choosing qualified officers for twelve new regiments that were all still largely on paper. Satisfied with what had been accomplished, Washington departed the city for the last time on De-cember 14.[13]

Fortunately—owing in large part to the actions Adams had taken (he had adhered strictly to neutrality and had patiently employed diplomatic means)—the threat passed with no requirement for Washington actually to lead troops. In the meantime, however, there had been action aplenty—political action. Washington had chafed at the politics involved in selecting the general staff, but to his relief he had been able to conduct most of his duties from Mount Vernon.

This did not necessarily make it easy for him. When Washington had said that he insisted upon the authority to select his top officers, the communication had not been made clear to President Adams. Taking the Constitution seriously, Adams had every intention of making the selections himself. He would be happy to take Washington's preferences into consideration, of course, but as president of the United States the choices would be his—and they would not in-clude putting the scheming Alexander Hamilton into the top position under Washington, as the new commander wished.

There was to be much huffing and puffing on all sides, if such terms can be applied to our august Founders, but sentiment favored Washington. Adams could not bear up under the weight of the former president's prestige, to which was added vast pressure from Hamilton's Federalist supporters. Even more pow-erful was a threat from Washington to resign if his wishes were not heeded. Adams's resistance crumbled, and he agreed to let Washington order the rank of his top subordinates. Washington then gave precedence to Hamilton over the others.

Historians Stanley Elkins and Eric McKitrick have noted, perceptively, that "many historians, beginning with Charles Francis Adams, have wanted to be-lieve that Washington was not primarily responsible for Adams's humiliation, and have ascribed it instead to the plotting of Adams's cabinet." (That cabinet, which was the same as it had been under Washington, by and large was loyal to Hamilton, not Adams.) If this is literally true, they wrote, it was only literally.

"Just about everyone ganged up on Adams, Washington among them, and had it not been for Washington's influence—direct, indirect, and hanging in the very air—the order of the Major-Generals, and probably even their names, would have been quite different."[14]

Much of Washington's attitude had been shaped by his increasing alarm at what—under Hamilton's urging—he perceived to be the inability of the Adams administration to deal with France, and by his own increasing partisanship. He had held himself above party politics until the last year of his life, "but by April of 1799 he finally emerged as a Federalist." The Jeffersonians in Virginia had so grown in power that "by late summer, Washington was helping to scour the state for Federalist candidates. He was working to persuade talented men who eschewed public life to run for office."[15] He even donned his military uniform to meet with John Marshall and cajole him into running for a seat in Congress.

To his considerable relief, the military action turned out to be limited to naval engagements. It could hardly have been otherwise. Britain and France were at war, and Britain controlled the seas. It would have been highly unlikely that the French could have landed troops in America—which was why Adams threw his support behind the creation of an effective American navy, and why he was lukewarm regarding an army. The crisis soon passed, and Washington returned to his retirement, this time permanently. As the crisis subsided, Washington withdrew from public life. He drew up a will that ultimately would free his slaves, and one that he hoped would encourage the creation of a national university. He believed that such a university would help foster a spirit of national unity.[16]

So the first president came out of retirement to provide unique service—once again—to his country. In the end, that service had not actually been needed. In fact, its effect if any was considerably more negative than positive.

Nevertheless, while the experience no doubt reflected Washington's concern for his own image, it also reflected his willingness to sacrifice his own comfort for what he perceived to be the public good. That devotion to the public good characterized his entire career, and was as important as any of the many legacies he left to his country. He died on December 14, 1799, of a severe throat infection.

Washington's significance is enormous. As the first president of the United States, everything he did established a precedent. The presidency, and in fact, the entire U.S. government came to function as it did to a considerable extent because of the practices he initiated. That means that the country as it developed owed much to the foundation that his presidency provided. The importance of his reputation for honor and integrity cannot be overestimated. It is doubtful that any other figure could have had the prestige or the ability to hold together the infant nation, consisting as it did initially of 13 (and soon more) disputatious states that could have broken apart at any time. Even the manner in which he left the presidency set the tone for the future. He voluntarily relinquished power and returned to private life—something few, if any, rulers in world history had done before him. His example became the pattern, not only for the United States, but for much of the rest of the world as well.

Two

JOHN ADAMS AND
THOMAS JEFFERSON

Friends, Enemies, and Ultimately Friends

JOHN ADAMS

John Adams, the second president of the United States, was the first president to be defeated when he ran for re-election. He was bitter at his defeat, and the election that he lost was equally bitter. It was a strange election in many ways, one of only two in American history that required the House of Representatives to choose the winner—and John Adams at that point was no longer among those being considered. Tongues wagged when he failed to attend the inauguration of his successor—his friend turned political enemy and also his vice president—Thomas Jefferson.

Tongues still wag figuratively among certain historians—pens anyway—at his lack of sportsmanship, having slipped away at four in the morning. Indeed Washington had stayed to participate in Adams's own inauguration. Even historian David McCullough, Adams's very friendly biographer, wrote:

> To his political rivals and enemies Adams's predawn departure was another ill-advised act of a petulant old man. But admirers, too, expressed disappointment. . . . By his presence at the ceremony Adams could have set an example

of grace in defeat, while at the same time paying homage to a system whereby power, according to a written constitution, is transferred peacefully. After so vicious a contest for the highest office, with party hatreds so near to igniting in violence, a peaceful transfer of power seemed little short of a miracle.[1]

McCullough proceeded to add that in fairness, despite appearances, we should concede that we do not know the real reason for Adams's absence from Jefferson's inauguration. Perhaps, as many have concluded, it really was bitterness—pique—that kept him away. But there are other possible explanations. Washington, it is true, attended Adams's inauguration, but then Washington had expressed a strong desire to retire. Possibly Adams had been made to feel that as a defeated president who was the political enemy of the new President Jefferson, he would not have been welcome. "There was no tradition of a defeated president appearing at the installation of a winner." Moreover, after Adams became aware that he had been defeated he and Abigail had invited Jefferson to dinner. "Jefferson had responded graciously," and they had a cordial evening.[2]

Possibly, also, it was simply a matter of scheduling. In order to get to Baltimore that day, he had to take the stage that left at four o'clock in the morning. Of course, one may wonder why he had to leave that day, but fairness again requires that one note that the departure was not a sudden flight from the District of Columbia. He had planned his departure for more than a week.[3]

According to legend, Adams spent his final night as president "furiously signing appointment letters for Federalist friends and cronies, thereby defying the will of the electorate and the wishes of Thomas Jefferson, his former friend and successor to the presidency."[4] His biographer Joseph Ellis concedes that this "unflattering picture of Adams contains some accurate features," but points out that "like all legendary renderings, and more especially like all attempts to fit the boisterously unorthodox character of Adams into the conventional categories of democratic politics and popular psychology, it misses the essential truths." Such a description, he says, "even at the mundane level of factual accuracy . . . distorts more than it describes," because the evening before he left office, the only official business that Adams conducted was to appoint three lower court judges in the District of Columbia and two minor officials in Pennsylvania. His key appointments, including that of John Marshall as chief justice, took place "soon after the passage of the Judiciary Act in February of 1801," and his last night in office was two months later, on March 3.[5]

One thing about which it seems we can be reasonably confident is that Adams was indeed bitter at his loss. McCullough seems to doubt this. "Downcast, bitter, Adams may have been," he wrote, "but there is no evidence to support such a description. Adams loved the start of a new day, loved being on the move. Conceivably he felt immense relief to be homeward bound."[6]

Perhaps so, but both he and Abigail blamed Hamilton for causing a split among the Federalists and sealing his defeat. Among other disruptive actions from Hamilton had been a powerful crowning blow: his wide distribution just before the election of a "letter" (actually a 54-page pamphlet), titled, "A Letter from Alexander Hamilton, Concerning the Public Conduct and Character of John Adams, Esq., President of the United States." As McCullough aptly put it, "nothing that Hamilton ever wrote about Jefferson was half so contemptuous,"[7] and it was Jefferson, after all, who was Hamilton's political enemy; he and Adams were fellow Federalists who were supposed to be on the same side. He charged Adams with "great intrinsic defects of character," with "disgusting ego-tism," with "eccentric tendencies," with having an "ungovernable temper," and, among other things, with having "bitter animosity toward his own cabinet."[8] Hamilton failed to mention that it was a cabinet largely loyal to him, rather than to its president, John Adams. Adams charged that "Hamilton not only had sought his defeat but also that the disappointed inspector general had wrecked the Federalist Party with his mad designs," and then had tried to blame Adams for the carnage.[9]

Abigail's biographer, Lynne Withy, wrote that "after the election returns were tallied, life in Washington was painful for Abigail and John."[10] Both would have preferred to stay. Although she had been ambivalent about John's political career, "like him, she felt the bitter sting of rejection and ingratitude."[11] In some ways, Withy wrote, Abigail found it easier than John to adjust to retirement at their farm in Quincy, Massachusetts. She had her tasks as wife, mother, and homemaker to occupy her time, but "John, by contrast, for the first time in his life had no specific task in front of him. He would continue to write, of course, but the contemplative life never really appealed to him. He felt useless."[12]

Eight years after Adams had slipped away, Jefferson's own time in office as president ended. Both men journeyed to their respective homes to stay for the rest of their lives. Jefferson had retired voluntarily and Adams had not, but there were nevertheless some similarities. After a triumphant first term that had as its crowning achievement the enormous expansion of the United States by the Louisiana Purchase, Jefferson's second term had been little short of a disaster. He had sought, unsuccessfully, to secure Florida for the United States. In the name of economy and egalitarianism, he had almost eliminated American military forces while bequeathing to his successor conditions that encouraged the War of 1812. He had thought he could prevail over European powers simply by deny-ing them American goods. There was massive civil unrest and even calls in New

England for secession because of his embargo policies and his enforcement of those policies by a "fifteen-month reign of oppression and repression that was unprecedented in American history and would not be matched for another hundred and ten years, when Jefferson's ideological heir Woodrow Wilson occupied the presidency."[13] In truth, the only real accomplishment of that term was the highly valuable Lewis and Clark Expedition. However voluntarily, Jefferson left office as had Adams, a dejected man. As historian Forrest McDonald described it poignantly:

> Embittered and exhausted, Thomas Jefferson . . . remained in Washington about a week, packing his belongings, before quitting the place forever. Then the sixty-five-year-old Father of American Liberty mounted a horse, to ride through snow and storm for three days and nights, until he regained the sanctuary of his home at Monticello. In the seventeen years that remained of his life, he never again left the foothills of the Blue Ridge Mountains.[14]

Jefferson did not ride with Madison in his carriage to the inauguration. Madison had invited him, but he "declined, saying all the honors of the day belonged to" the new president.[15] He had, however, in contrast to his predecessor, "been at Madison's side," as the new president received the oath of office from Chief Justice John Marshall—the political world then was small, and the Virginia elite loomed large within that world. Marshall was himself both a distant cousin and a political enemy of the outgoing president. As Jefferson left office, the soon-to-be former president could at least take pleasure in Madison's victory. He could rely on the new president, his close associate, to continue sound Republican policies.

However ungraciously Adams left office, he did peacefully turn power over to his political opposition, the first such instance in American history—and perhaps in world history. Such a thing is commonplace today, but in Adams's time it was a rarity—if not a unique occurrence. Power tended either to remain with the same faction, or to shift by coup or revolution, usually accompanied by great violence as in the French Revolution. For the first 40 years of the new country's existence it took place only once. Not until 1829, when John Quincy Adams left office and Andrew Jackson succeeded him, did such a shift happen again. Ironically, it was Adams and his son who became the first and second American presidents to be put in such a situation. In neither case was there any question whether the change would be peaceful.

Consider the importance of the precedent John Adams set in 1801. Two centuries later, even after the bitter and disputed election of 2000—with the popular vote clearly on the side of the loser, with reports of Supreme Court justices making partisan statements, and with the Court itself intruding to declare electoral victory in an unsure situation, thus acting inconsistently with its own often-expressed preference for state authority—the country reacted peacefully. That the American political infrastructure can survive normal changes of power—such as, for example, those resulting from the elections of 1992, 1980, 1968, and from the razor-thin Kennedy victory of 1960—should suggest that America owes tribute to John Adams. The system he helped design and then upheld provided a firm and stable basis, and his example in 1801 encouraged commitment to that system.

The debt to Adams becomes even greater when seen in connection with the country's ability to survive transfers of power that are *not* normal. America's political institutions have remained intact even after elections that handed victory to those who lost the popular vote, such as those of 1824 and 1888. Most impressive of all, it has taken in stride even elections that deny victory to the popular-vote winner when the electoral vote itself has been unclear. Fortunately, there are only two such examples: the election of 1876 and the aforementioned election of 2000. Of the two, the election of 1876 was the more extreme. The least favorable interpretation would class it simply as stolen. Regardless, the country survived with its political system intact. For this invaluable stability of its institutions, John Adams deserves more credit— even though he did fail to attend the inauguration of his successor—than he normally receives.

Both Adams and Jefferson retired to their bucolic retreats. Adams, perhaps giving some credence to McCullough's denial that the former president had left the capital in bitterness, was in good spirits when he arrived home to Abigail's greeting.[16] But if his spirits were high, the onset of boredom soon weighed them down. Within a month, he wondered about returning to the practice of law. "There I should forget in a moment that I was ever member of Congress, or foreign minister, or President of the United States," he said.[17] He decided, however, that it was impossible. He had lost so many teeth that he could not speak clearly. "That left his fields and books to occupy him for what the sixty-six-year-old ex-president" assumed would be the little time he had left, but "John Adams still had a full quarter century of life before him."[18] In fact, when he died he was well into his 90th year, the longest-lived of all former presidents except for Ronald Reagan. In a sense, Adams continues to have the record for longevity, because he remained alert and mentally vigorous until his death. Reagan, by contrast, tragically became the victim of Alzheimer's disease. He ceased to function mentally many years ago, although physically he had not reached the end of his life as of early December 2003.

Unlike Washington and Jefferson, Adams had retired to a modest Massachusetts farm and lived simply. Also in contrast to Washington, whose Mount Vernon home had become a magnet for visitors of all sorts, for a long time Adams "seldom saw anyone from the outside world," although he was moved to tears when a delegation from the Massachusetts legislature came to his home to express their appreciation for his contributions to the public. "It was the first occasion upon which a public body had actually honored him. But unlike Washington's experience, few visitors came thereafter.

The contrast grated upon Adams. Ever the realist pricker of balloons and debunker of romanticized reputations, he "consistently bemoaned 'the pilgramages [sic] to Mount Vernon as the new Mecca or Jerusalem.'"[19] He considered Washington a "great man," but said, "I totally despise the miserable catch-penny tricks by which he is represented in situations where he never stood & as the author of measures in which he had nothing to do."[20] Or, as he graphically described the tendency as he saw it for Virginians to preen and exaggerate their status, he said one must remember that when considering Virginians, "Virginian geese are all swans."[21] He may have had Jefferson in mind as well.

Although Adams was "a marvelous letter writer," his formal writings tended to be stilted and legalistic. Adams biographer Ferling wrote that

> He was never a match for the better writers of his age. Franklin appeared to write effortlessly, and his pen was graced by a habitual wit; Tom Paine, a master of the catchy phrase, wrote in a manner easily understood by every reader; Jefferson's sentences flowed clear and untroubled as a placid summer stream; Hamilton's systematized thought enabled him to marshal argument after argument and to march his ideas across the landscape, deftly and briskly devouring everything in their path. To read Adams, by contrast, is to submit to a painstaking struggle with disarray.[22]

Sporadically from 1802 until 1807 when he gave up on it, Adams worked on an autobiography. It was "less like a well-crafted work of literature than an open wound," in which he "got down to the serious business of eviscerating his enemies," foremost of whom was Alexander Hamilton.[23] Subsequently he engaged in a controversy with his friend Mercy Otis Warren. She had depicted him in her *History of the Rise, Progress, and Termination of the American Revolution* as having been corrupted by his long tenure in Europe, thus succumbing to ambition and sacrificing his republicanism to become a monarchist.[24] He was outraged and vigorously denied her charges. A bitter exchange with her ensued, and Adams even took his case to the newspapers. "The letters finally stopped, and by all signs the lifelong friendship between the Adamses and the Warrens had ended, which was deeply troubling on both sides. In time, however, the break would heal, and correspondence between them would resume."[25] As though there were any doubt, the "episode had shown that Adams was quite as capable as ever of furious indignation. The old lion could still roar."[26] For several years he continued to write letters to newspapers justifying his entire administration. He wrote some 130 letters for publication between 1809 and 1812 in an effort to defend his career, but they had little effect then or later.[27]

Nevertheless, Adams was mellowing. He delighted in his family. Through the years of his retirement he had cause to grieve at the deaths of grandchildren. The deaths of two persons even closer to him were especially wrenching. In 1813, his daughter, Nabby, died of breast cancer—months before she had undergone the agony of a mastectomy in those days before anesthetics, but the malignancy had returned. And on October 28, 1818, just three days after their 54th wedding anniversary, Abigail died.

She had been his lifelong companion. Theirs was a relationship of passion and intelligence. Abigail had served as John's eyes and ears at home during the many times he was away in official positions. He trusted her completely. She had been inherently conservative, yet an enthusiastic supporter of the American Revolution and of republicanism. She admired independent women, yet never challenged the prevailing social order. She and John were partners in every sense of the word.

John carried on. Politically, he had moved steadily away from the Federalists. After 1804 he never again endorsed a Federalist candidate for office. "He had drifted to the Republican party, the party of Jefferson, but also the faction of Samuel Adams and Elbridge Gerry and, eventually, of his son John Quincy,"[28] in whose political rise he took special pride. In 1817, the new president, James Monroe and his wife Elizabeth, visited New England. They stopped to pay their respects to John and Abigail Adams, who were pleased that their son, John Quincy, was the new secretary of state. When Monroe successfully ran for re-election in 1820, he received every electoral vote except for one. Because he disliked Monroe, "William Plumer of New Hampshire unexpectedly cast his vote for John Quincy Adams, while Monroe received the votes of 231 electors."[29] Among those voting for Monroe was John Adams. The former Federalist president headed the Massachusetts slate of electors. He also served, that year of Monroe's re-election, as a delegate to a constitutional convention for Massachusetts. At the age of 85, he was helping to revise the state's constitution; a document that he had "drafted some forty years before."[30]

Eight years after John and Abigail had received President Monroe at their home, John Adams became the first former president to witness the presidential inauguration of his son. Sadly, the great event came after Abigail's death. The Adamses were the only father and son presidents in American history until 2001, when the second President Bush took office.

⋄

By 1812, the noted physician Dr. Benjamin Rush, a mutual friend of both Adams and Jefferson, had succeeded in encouraging the two former presidents to put aside their differences and rekindle their old friendship. Neither required much urging, and both were delighted. The resulting correspondence between these two giants of the Revolution and the early Republic was not only a source of joy and comfort to them both—the rekindled friendship was a warm one—but it became the greatest contribution to their country that each man produced in his post-presidential years.

THOMAS JEFFERSON

Like Washington, Thomas Jefferson had returned to his home to find a spacious plantation, but one that had deteriorated seriously. Also like Washington, he began to receive a constant stream of visitors. "Monticello became a tavern, as the President's House had been,"[31] and that added to his troubles. He was deeply in debt. As president, he had continued—even accelerated—his habit of entertaining lavishly and living beyond his means.

Adams was no doubt quite aware—and for a time was quite resentful—of the ironic twist regarding his reputation and that of Jefferson, an irony that likely escaped Jefferson entirely. As McCullough put it:

> Jefferson, the Virginia aristocrat and slave master who lived in a style fit for a prince, as removed from his fellow citizens and their lives as it was possible to be, was hailed as the apostle of liberty, the "Man of the People." Adams, the farmer's son who despised slavery and practiced the kind of personal economy and plain living commonly upheld as the American way, was scorned as an aristocrat who, if he could, would enslave the common people.[32]

Jefferson's role regarding slavery changed little after his presidency, and it is the least praiseworthy aspect of his legacy. Although he detested the institution, recognized its injustices, and hoped to see it die, he took no concrete action at any time in his career to seek to end it where it existed. His conviction that blacks were inferior conditioned his belief that they could never live together with whites on a basis of equality. His one suggestion for slavery's elimination was exceedingly cruel, even when compared with the harsh view of children's rights then prevailing: he proposed that slave children at the age of five be taken from their parents, reared and educated by the states, and then shipped away to colonies outside the United States. They would then be prepared for their new lives, and proceeds from their labor while they were being trained and awaiting exile would be used to pay the transportation costs and to reimburse their masters.[33]

Jefferson's extravagance, on the other hand, perhaps had a beneficial side. Indirectly, his debts probably enriched the country. The British had burned the capitol during the War of 1812, and the fire destroyed the Library of Congress. He offered to sell his private collection to the government to replace the destroyed Library. As McCullough put it, "it was both a magnanimous gesture and something of a necessity, as he was hard-pressed to meet his mounting debts." The two former presidents had to struggle financially, as had Washington and as did many others to come. It was a century and a half after the Republic's founding before Congress saw fit to provide a pension— or any regular form of support—to those who had served as president. Then, a plea from former president Harry Truman that there be some allowance for office expenses, led Congress finally to provide a pension as well (see Chapter 12).

———◆———

When Adams heard that Jefferson's collection was to become the new Library of Congress, he wrote, "I envy you that immortal honor." Jefferson in April 1815 had catalogued and packed his 6,707 volumes in pine boxes that filled ten wagons, and sent them off to Washington. Immediately, he began to collect books again. Adams understood perfectly when Jefferson told him that he could "not live without books."[34]

———◆———

Almost as soon as Jefferson had returned home in 1809, he had begun to write. "He wrote literally thousands of letters, on every conceivable subject, some of them masterpieces of the epistolary art, and all with his own hand until the last years of his life."[35] It was his correspondence that was his greatest contribution as a former president. The same is true for Adams, who himself was a prolific letter writer. The renewed dialogue between two of America's greatest leaders provided their country with an unparalleled legacy of wisdom and insight.

Few thinkers and statesmen—certainly few Americans—have inspired as many works as Jefferson has. Nevertheless, one of his most innovative ideas has aroused relatively little comment. The source of that contribution is his post-presidential correspondence. He appears to have developed the idea for "ward republics" most fully after he left the presidency, mentioning it first in a letter of May 26, 1810, to John Tyler, and in several others through the years, including one to John Adams on October 28, 1813.[36] His concern was political partici-pation, which he suggested to Adams could enable people to act as they did in New England town meetings.

Jefferson's idea was to structure the entire country into a system of hierar-chical units. Autonomous wards, or "ward republics," would be at the base. They would be self-governing. All issues that could be handled locally would be under their jurisdiction. He remained committed to this idea, ending many let-ters with "divide the country into wards," as late as 1824 (as in his letter of June 5 to John Cartwright).[37]

To Adams, he wrote that the wards should handle "those portions of self-government for which they are best qualified, by confiding to them the care of their poor, their roads, police, elections, the nomination of jurors, administra-tion of justice in small cases, elementary exercises of militia," and in fact to make them "little republics with a Warden at the head of each, for all those concerns which, being under their eye, they would better manage than the larger re-publics of the county or the state." He mentioned that at one time, shortly after the Declaration of Independence, he had introduced such a proposition into the Virginia legislature, but that it had not passed.[38] Perhaps because of the offhand manner in which he mentioned the idea, it elicited no response from Adams in his reply.[39]

Even among those who know of Jefferson's idea for "ward republics," most have reacted no more than Adams did. Political philosopher Hannah Arendt, one of the exceptions, said that his idea has been "utterly neglected by statesmen, historians, political theorists," and even by the "revolutionary tradition itself."[40] This is largely true, even though it is a slight exaggeration. Historian Adrienne Koch called the wards one of Jefferson's "most significant and original ideas for implementing representative democracy,"[41] and later political scientist Richard K. Matthews took them quite seriously, analyzing the idea in a study of Jeffer-son's radical politics.[42] Arendt argued that Jefferson was suggesting a new form of constitutional order. He was vague regarding the wards' specific functions, but that vagueness, she contended, was intentional and was evidence that he was suggesting a new form of government rather than advocating reform of an ex-isting one.[43]

Vague or not, it is clear that Jefferson had in mind enhancing the power of each citizen, rather than that of the majority. Arendt noted that he sought "small republics," within which every citizen would be "an acting member of the Common government, transacting in person a great portion of its rights and duties, subordinate indeed, yet important, and entirely within its competence. . . . These little republics . . . would be the strength of the great one."[44]

———◆———

One would certainly expect Jefferson to maintain his interest in politics after he left the presidency, but more than one visitor to Monticello as the years progressed commented on how ill-informed he had become with respect to current affairs. George Ticknor, for example, a young Harvard professor journeyed to Monticello in December 1824 and marveled at the 81-year-old former president. Jefferson's keen intellect led him to continue to study Greek and Anglo-Saxon, and to keep abreast of the progress of knowledge far better than Harvard students, he said. Nevertheless, he was disturbed that Jefferson read only one newspaper, often was misinformed, and in fact was "singularly ignorant and insensible on the subjects of passing politics."[45]

In the years following his presidency, Jefferson took great care not to be seen as interfering with Madison's administration. He was well aware that Madison had been in his shadow, and sought to offset the opinion that he secretly was directing the new chief executive. He made it clear that he would offer advice only when sought. Without doubt, Jefferson did render an "important political service by helping to restore the friendship of Madison and Monroe."[46]

Monroe had been alienated from Madison, and there seemed no office available for him. Jefferson weaned Monroe away from the anti-Madison group, and set about cementing relations between the two who were both his old friends. He was successful. Just when Monroe again had stepped into office, the governorship of Virginia, Madison offered him the position of secretary of state. With the Republicans dominating government, and the virtual evaporation of the Federalists, the holder of the foremost cabinet position was in line to become president. "From that moment, barring misadventure, Monroe's eventual succession to the presidency was assured, to Jefferson's enormous satisfaction."[47] Thus, even after he left the presidency, Jefferson continued to affect the direction of the executive branch.

Jefferson also tried, with varying success, to influence the judicial branch. President Madison had difficulty finding an appropriate appointee to the

Supreme Court to replace the elderly Associate Justice William Cushing, who had died in office. Madison offered the position to three men, including John Quincy Adams; each declined. Madison then turned to a figure Jefferson opposed, Joseph Story. "Much to Jefferson's chagrin, Madison ignored his old colleague's negative opinion of Story and nominated him."[48] Story took office in 1811 and went on to become a distinguished member of the Court, but Jefferson had been correct in his assessment: The new associate justice was much too close to Chief Justice John Marshall to suit the former president.

Former governor of Virginia from 1808 to 1811, John Tyler (the father of the future president), had asked Jefferson to recommend him for appointment to the next federal court vacancy, and Jefferson did so. Madison appointed Tyler to the U.S. District Court. The recommendation had at least an appearance of impropriety, because Jefferson at the time was defending himself against a lawsuit brought by Edward Livingston—a Republican politician later to be secretary of state under Andrew Jackson—having to do with an action that he had taken as president, and the new judge would be sitting on that case. Livingston had claimed some river-bottom land near New Orleans, and Jefferson prevented him from developing the land in order to avoid interference with navigation.

Tyler, who was an old friend, had in fact approached Jefferson before the lawsuit. "Jefferson almost certainly would have sent the same letter of support for Tyler to Madison" if the suit had not existed, but Tyler's appointment "had an added virtue."[49] As for the suit itself, the two-judge panel—Tyler and John Marshall, sitting on circuit—dismissed it for lack of jurisdiction over territory near New Orleans. This was especially fortunate for Jefferson because of his chronic financial difficulties. "Later, Tyler wrote Jefferson that he had persuaded a reluctant Marshall to come to that conclusion."[50]

◆―◆◆◇◆◆―◆

Jefferson's lifelong concern for education led him, after five years in retirement, to found the University of Virginia, design its curriculum, design its buildings, select its faculty and serve as its first rector. He rightly considered the long struggle to create the University as among his outstanding contributions. He said that encouraging public education would be the greatest service he could render to his country.

> When he came to write his epitaph, reflecting on his varied services, he chose for inscription on his tombstone, "Author of the Declaration of Independence,

of the Statute of Virginia for Religious Freedom, and Father of the University of Virginia," because by these, as testimonials that I have lived, I wish most to be remembered.[51]

He did not include having served as President of the United States.

When Dr. Benjamin Rush persuaded the two old statesmen to bury the hatchet, he set in motion a contribution to posterity that would far over-shadow in importance any of their other post-presidential accomplishments: the Adams–Jefferson correspondence. They remained well qualified to produce such a contribution to American thought and letters. Near the end of their lives, when an Italian traveler, Count Carlo Vidua, visited the sitting president John Quincy Adams and his four predecessors, both John Adams and Jefferson charmed him. He commented on the "precise and vivacious" answers to his questions that he received from the ancient John Adams, and upon the "brilliance" that he found in Jefferson.[52]

The editor of the first full collection of the letters—including those from their earlier friendship—Historian Lester Cappon, wrote in the preface to the collection that "no correspondence in American history is more quotable or more readily recognized for its historical significance than that of John Adams and Thomas Jefferson."[53] He spoke of the "richness" of the correspondence, of the "mental vigor of the two men," and noted that:

> During their years in public office they gave close attention to the daily problems that pressed upon them, with occasional reflections revealing the statesmanship behind their decisions. Later, as elder statesmen in retirement, they sat in judgment on the world which had passed through two revolutions, on their country which had won independence and confirmed it, and on themselves; and they did so with an open-mindedness and a feeling of conviction that subsequent generations cannot fail to admire.[54]

The result of their judgment, a substantial contribution from their post-presidential careers, is to be found in their correspondence—as is the genuine affection for one another that the second and third presidents of the United States carried with them to their graves.

> They wrote of old friends and their own friendship, of great causes past, common memories, books, politics, education, philosophy, religion, the French, the British, the French Revolution, American Indians, the American navy, their families, their health, slavery—eventually—and always, repeatedly, the American Revolution.[55]

Each had been in declining health. Jefferson had turned 83 and suffered from a painful prostate enlargement. Adams, 90, had been developing heart trouble, and had contracted pneumonia.

The fiftieth anniversary of the Declaration of Independence took place on the Fourth of July, 1826. On that day, John Adams died. His last words were, "Thomas Jefferson survives." He did not know that on that same day, that same Fourth of July, Thomas Jefferson also had died.

Three

JAMES MADISON
AND JAMES MONROE

The Last of the Virginia Dynasty

JAMES MADISON

JAMES MADISON HAD BEEN JEFFERSON'S SECRETARY OF STATE, AND FOLLOWED him into the presidency to continue the "Virginia Dynasty." Eight years later, he followed Jefferson into retirement. Both men have been honored less for their presidencies than for the entirety of their careers. His fellow citizens likely would have agreed with Henry Adams's comment more than a half-century later that the circumstances when Madison left office were exceptionally agreeable—the War of 1812 was over, Madison had preserved civil liberties, and the constitutional system was strong—but the irony would have escaped them. Madison biographer Ralph Ketcham said that the later Adams "noted with glee that Madison had become a friend of 'strong government.'"[1] Historian Garry Wills pointed out that what Madison did was rather to accept modernity.[2]

Biographers have had little success in softening the rather harsh view that most historians of the Madisonian presidency—following Adams—have presented to later generations.[3] His initial cabinet was largely incompetent, he led the country into a war that he might have prevented, and perhaps worst of all he did so when the nation was totally unprepared. Still, the fourth president should be honored for his commitment to the Constitution and to civil liberties both while he was president and later. He set an example of avoiding authoritarianism in wartime that to this day has been too seldom followed.

Jefferson is honored, above all, as the author of the Declaration of Independence, while Madison remains revered as the "Father of the Constitution." Charles Jared Ingersoll, a member of Congress from Pennsylvania, "first bestowed [the title] on Madison, in those precise words, in an 1827 public address."[4] Certainly his contemporaries thought the title fit him, even though Madison himself stressed that the Constitution was the product of many minds. Wills agreed with Madison's contemporaries, and remarked in his brief but excellent biography that the fourth president deeply deserved the title on many accounts. He defended the call for the Annapolis convention (which was the first gathering that led ultimately to the Constitutional Convention), persuaded George Washington to attend, conducted careful research into the nature of governments and confederacies, worked on the final draft of the Constitution, defended it in Congress and in *The Federalist,* and by defeating Patrick Henry who opposed the Constitution he won the crucial ratification from Virginia.[5]

As for the people, they widely admired him for his role as a Founder. They were well aware of his leadership at the Philadelphia convention, his contributions to *The Federalist,* "and his magnificent triumph over Patrick Henry at the Virginia ratifying convention,"[6] without which the Constitution of the United States might never have survived. Long after he left office, Madison continued to defend that constitution and the government resting upon it.

Upon his departure from the presidency, however, like his predecessors he turned his attention initially to home and agriculture. This, of course, was to have been expected. Congress provided former presidents with no support, and Madison had to make a living. Moreover, like Jefferson he had always identified the good life with the soil. "His earliest letters from Orange [County] after his retirement are filled with talk of field crops, market prospects, and the weather, marking his absorption in the concerns of a farmer."[7]

Returning to rural life did not prevent Madison from keeping in close touch with public affairs. He read avidly, and "almost as if from force of habit," President Monroe "consulted Madison on Latin America, Florida border disputes, the tariff, internal improvements, and other matters." Madison was especially interested in the new revolutionary movements in South America, and urged Monroe to support democratic reforms there whenever possible.[8]

Adams had returned to New England to his Massachusetts farm. Madison followed the course of Washington and Jefferson, each of whom returned to his native Virginia. In the case of all these Virginia patriarchs, the end of their journey was no modest farm, but rather a plantation. For Madison, it was Montpelier, his plantation home in Orange County.

Also like his presidential predecessors, he was delighted to be leaving the burdens of office. Unlike them, his mode of transportation reflected how things were rapidly changing. Until they reached Acquia Creek, 40 miles south of Washington on the Potomac, the Madisons traveled by steamboat. James K. Paulding, secretary of the Navy Board and future secretary of the navy, accompanied them on the boat. He wrote of the journey that "if ever man sincerely rejoiced in being freed from the cares of public life," it was Madison. "During the voyage he was as playful as a child; talked and joked with everybody on board, and reminded me of a schoolboy on a long vacation."[9]

Washington and Jefferson had been dismayed at the rundown conditions they discovered when they returned to Mount Vernon and Monticello, respectively. Madison's situation was better. He had followed markets and adjusted his crop production accordingly, and his absence was less damaging. "Jefferson himself had declared, John Quincy Adams wrote in 1807, that 'the person who united with other science the greatest agricultural knowledge of any man he knew was Mr. Madison. He was the best farmer in the world.'"[10] For several years Madison's prudence, his careful management of his land and crops, and the reserves that he had accumulated permitted him to prosper. The economy nevertheless continued to become progressively worse for planters, ultimately causing Madison difficulty along with others. As if that were not enough, he spent huge amounts to keep his stepson, Payne Todd (a compulsive gambler and worse) out of trouble—often shielding his wife Dolley from knowledge of her son's irresponsibility.

Madison's views on agriculture were intimately entwined with his views on nature and society. He had accepted an invitation from an organization of farmers and planters concerned with scientific agriculture, the Albemarle Agricultural Society, to serve as its president, and in May 1818, delivered a lengthy speech condemning poor environmental practices. The printed speech filled 31 pages, and was widely distributed throughout the United States and abroad. The journal *American Farmer* reprinted it, which provided even greater distribution.[11] Madison's admonition went beyond criticism of Virginians' "carelessly exploitative approach to the land and to nature more generally,"[12] and remains relevant even to modern Americans. He pointed out the necessity of "the fertile activity of a free people, and the benign influence of a responsible government."[13]

The audience for Madison's speech included Jefferson and the Board of Visitors of the University of Virginia as well as local planters. He speculated about the way civilization developed, and about why human beings changed from hunting to farming. What balances of plants and animals, he asked, were the best for human progress, and what features of nature must humanity be careful not to injure? He pointed to the necessity of adequate space, pure air, and periodic restoration of the soil. Delving deeply into economics and agricultural technology, the former president stressed the effectiveness of human reason and will working in concert with natural harmonies.[14]

The appearance of the University's Board of Visitors at a meeting of an agricultural society reflected a commitment to the view that Madison and Jefferson shared regarding the proper connection of human beings with the soil. It also was symbolic of the commitment that Madison had to the University. He became a member of the Board in 1816, along with Jefferson and James Monroe[15]—surely the only time in American history when a university governing board included three presidents.

In 1819, he participated when the Board chose Jefferson as the university's rector (its chief officer), and upon Jefferson's death, he succeeded him in that position. "Though Madison's role in founding and sustaining the University of Virginia was in no sense comparable to Jefferson's, he provided constant support during Jefferson's lifetime, and he served much longer as rector of the university with students in attendance than did Jefferson." He remained as rector until poor health forced him to resign in 1834,[16] and he also worked with numerous other educational institutions.[17]

Madison again accepted elective office in 1829, when he became a member of the convention called to draw up a new constitution for the Commonwealth of Virginia. The gathering was enormously distinguished, including two former presidents, James Monroe as well as Madison, Chief Justice John Marshall, and future President John Tyler. Madison worked diligently to make the new constitution more representative, and to lessen the influence of slavery. The convention rejected his efforts at compromise. Most of the delegates "were loathe to admit that slavery and republicanism were the strangest of bedfellows."[18]

In 1833, he accepted the presidency of the American Colonization Society, an organization devoted to eliminating slavery and colonizing the freed slaves in Africa or elsewhere. It was a reflection of his opposition to slavery—an opposition that he shared with Jefferson. Madison, however, was taking concrete steps that he hoped would contribute to the elimination of slavery in the South—something that Jefferson had never troubled to do. Sadly, Madison's effort reflected his assumption—shared by most of those in the

South and many of those outside—that blacks could never live in a predominantly white society on a basis of equality. Historian John Chester Miller's classic examination of Jefferson and slavery, *The Wolf by the Ears,* remains the best study of this tragic and complicated issue, and it considers Madison's situation also.[19]

An English visitor, writer and social critic, Harriet Martineau, stopped at Montpelier in February 1835 to see the diminutive former president, who by then was in his 80s. She was struck by the intellect and energy of this small man who had been born a decade before the reign of George III and was still living near the end of Andrew Jackson's presidency. He captivated and charmed her. "Never have I seen so much mind in so little matter," she wrote.[20]

But it was the very keenness of Madison's mind that created a mystery for her. She found it impossible to understand how a man with so powerful an intellect, one who admitted the evils of slavery and felt strongly that it should be eliminated, could believe in such an unrealistic remedy as colonization—could believe, in fact, that it was the only solution. Why, she asked, did he assume that blacks could not remain in the United States after they had been freed? Madison conceded that his own slaves expressed "horror" at the thought of going to Liberia, but he nevertheless considered colonization to be the only practical answer to the tragedy of slavery.[21]

As concerned as Madison was about slavery, his retirement found him preoccupied with another issue, one that he feared would tear apart the country that he had worked so hard to built and protect. Words that he had written in the Virginia Resolutions in 1798—those defiant responses to the harsh Alien and Sedition Acts making it a crime to write or speak against the government that John Adams had enforced—came back to haunt him. He "would spend the rest of his life trying to back away from the Virginia Resolutions."[22] Even worse were Jefferson's words in the Kentucky Resolutions. Worse still were the words that the impetuous Jefferson had originally intended to use, but had changed pursuant to wise advice from Madison.

When Jefferson had sought to prescribe the curriculum of the law school at the new University of Virginia, Madison felt required to offer some words of caution. Jefferson had sought to require several texts, including some from Locke and Sydney. "With particular reference to the United States," he included "the Declaration of Independence, *The Federalist,* and Madison's Virginia Report" on the Alien and Sedition Laws.[23] Madison took immediate issue with use of the report. It had arisen from arguments he offered in 1799 in Virginia's legislature when he was protesting the infamous laws. The next year his arguments formed the basis of "a lengthy pamphlet called the *Report of 1800.*"[24]

The report initially had no effect except to arouse criticism, but the increasing movement in the South to claim the right of states to nullify federal laws—that is, to make them null and void within a dissenting state—found much in Madison's arguments to use as support. Garry Wills wrote of Madison's embarrassment at his own "overreaction" to the "spirit of '98.'" By 1825, he said, Jefferson had persuaded himself that the report reflected the will of the people. "Madison had evident misgivings about the use of his own words, but his task in replying to the proposed list of texts was a delicate one." He wished both to distance himself "from his contradictory past," and to point out to Jefferson— tactfully, of course—that the report and *The Federalist* contradicted one another. He suggested that Washington's inaugural and farewell addresses be included in the curriculum instead.[25]

Madison had never advocated nullification—although it is hard to conclude that Jefferson had not done so. He did, however, refer to interposition, the doctrine that a state could shield its citizens from a federal law of which it disapproved. "By the late 1820s, the secret of Madison's and Jefferson's involvement in the drafting of the Virginia and Kentucky Resolutions, respectively, had been exposed, and Madison's authorship of the Report of 1800 was common knowledge. Much to Madison's chagrin, in short, the nullifiers posed as Madisonians and Jeffersonians of the first order."[26]

He insisted that he had remained consistent in his views, and that those who cited him as providing support for nullification were misinterpreting his position. He even defended Jefferson from the charge of nullification—which was even more difficult to do. The firebrands such as Robert Hayne and John C. Calhoun in turn praised Jefferson, claiming him (with some justification) as one of their own, and many scoffed that Madison had become senile. As he saw increasing threats to union from a South determined to substitute state authority for that of the federal government, it is safe to assume that he regretted ever having used the word "interposition." As for nullification, he considered it to be a violation of the principles of representative government and of majority will.

In 1833, Madison erupted at news from South Carolina that secession would be in order if there were any federal attempt to interfere with slavery. He wrote to Henry Clay that the North had every reason to preserve the Union, and that it was "*madness* in the South to look for greater safety in disunion. It would be worse," he said, "than jumping out of the frying-pan into the fire; it would be jumping into the fire for fear of the frying-pan."[27] Time proved him absolutely correct.

Madison clearly discounted the fear that haunted Jefferson late in his life that the country was threatened with unlimited government. He reluctantly accepted the Missouri Compromise of 1820. It admitted Missouri and Maine to the Union, Missouri with slavery and Maine without it. It specified that in the Louisiana Territory, except in Missouri, slavery would exist only south of 36° 30′ latitude, Missouri's southern boundary. And even though he argued that it was not sound policy, he supported the constitutionality of a protective tariff to safeguard American producers. The militancy of President John Quincy Adams's opponents disturbed him, and he scrutinized the debates of the conventions in the states that ratified the Constitution for insights into constitutional interpretation. In the elections of 1828, he decried the extreme partisanship that swept the country. He was apologetic about his own one-time role, recognizing that he had been guilty of "partisan zeal," and that he had "served as a principal catalyst in the political conflagration of the 1790s."[28] Madison remained preoccupied with the nullifiers as his own life drew to a close, and continued to be defensive about the consistency of his record.

As much as he had accomplished before and during his presidency, however, one of Madison's greatest contributions to his country came later in his life. He had been the only participant at the 1787 Philadelphia Convention who had been authorized to keep a journal of the secret proceedings. In the early 1820s, he had begun organizing the huge volume of his papers—including his convention notes—for eventual publication. His papers became the burden of his retirement, which, as biographer Drew McCoy has noted was really not a retirement at all.[29]

Madison had a good reason to increase his attention to his papers. In 1821 a report of the Constitutional Convention by Robert Yates appeared in print. Yates was a New Yorker, who at the time of his death in 1801 had risen through the state judicial system to become chief justice. He had attended the convention only for 7 of its 16 weeks, leaving in protest because of his determined views against a strong central government. His notes became the first report of the Constitutional Convention's proceedings to reach the public.

Madison found so many errors in the Yates report that he was impelled to work on his own more comprehensive, and more accurate, record. He warned that his own report would not come soon. In fact, it would be posthumous. To offset the earlier report, though, Madison produced "an immensely revealing retrospective commentary on both the history of the republic and his understanding of the Constitution." What Madison and his contemporaries did not know was that while Yates's notes themselves were incomplete and inadequate, the Yates report was a deliberate distortion of what Yates had written. Edmund ("Citizen") Genêt had edited the material "for the express purpose of embarrassing Madison."[30] Genêt was the son-in-law of Madison's disloyal first vice president—who had also been Jefferson's second vice president—George Clinton. Clinton had died during the last year of Madison's first term, but while in office had opposed the administration. He had been known for casting tie-breaking votes in the Senate against Madison's positions. Clinton had been disappointed in not having succeeded Jefferson as president.

Madison had served his country in many ways, not the least of which flowed from his collaboration with Jefferson. Dolley resented the view, prevalent then and later, that Madison was a mere pawn of Jefferson, who had been in Paris during the Constitutional Convention. She wrote that Jefferson's knowledge of the Framers' intentions came from Madison, who guided him. "Madison's best efforts," though, "could not prevent Jefferson from indulging in dangerous constitutional aberrations. Jefferson was sounder than Madison as to the basic need of a Bill of Rights; Madison was infinitely superior to Jefferson in the application of those guarantees to specific circumstances."[31]

In the spring of 1825, when Carlo Vidua, the worldly Italian count, visited the sitting president and the four living former presidents, he found President John Quincy Adams, he said, to be the most cultivated. John Adams, despite being nearly 90 years old, was "precise and vivacious" in answering questions. Of the others, he found that "Jefferson's intellect seemed . . . the most brilliant, Madison's the most profound, Monroe's the least keen. . . ."[32]

Representative John Quincy Adams, former ambassador, former secretary of state, and former president of the United States, eulogized James Madison, openly preferring him to Jefferson. He concluded that Madison was a man of more reason, that he had greater sensibility, and that his judgment was the sounder of the two.[33] Supreme Court Justice Joseph Story agreed. He remarked of Madison that "in wisdom I have long been accustomed to place him before Jefferson."[34] Among those who met both statesmen, such views—although apparently the exception—were more common than one would likely expect.

In his later years, Madison suffered a series of illnesses. By the time of his death in 1836, he had prepared his report of the Constitutional Convention for posterity. He willed the manuscript to his wife, Dolley, and directed that it be published under her "authority and direction." Ultimately, Congress purchased the *Notes of the Debates*. America's constitutional history and our understanding of it are vastly richer as a result.

JAMES MONROE

Four of the first five presidents were Virginians. The final three, Jefferson, Madison, and Monroe were the Republican "Virginia Dynasty." James Monroe was the final member, and also the last president to have been prominent in the Revolutionary generation.

Monroe left office with no great triumph, such as the Louisiana Purchase, nor a perceived triumph such as the end of the War of 1812. Neither, however, had he presided over a great failure, such as Jefferson's disastrous embargo. His presidency was less momentous—or memorable—than any that had preceded his, and of the first five presidents, only Washington's post-presidential life was briefer than Monroe's. Of these five, it was the least memorable—except for its sadness—and the least influential.

Monroe's time in office ended with the inauguration of President John Quincy Adams on the March 4, 1825. He delayed his departure from Washington because of the illness of his wife, Elizabeth, who had been in poor health throughout his presidency. After some three weeks, they journeyed to Loudoun County, Virginia. He continued the tradition set by his Virginia predecessors by returning to a plantation where he had lived since he was a young man. Thomas Jefferson had designed their new home there, Oak Hill.

Monroe continued his public service as long as he was able. Along with Jefferson and Madison, he became a member of the Board of Visitors of the University of Virginia. In 1829, he was chosen to chair Virginia's constitutional convention, where he served with Madison.

Elizabeth's already poor health became worse the year after the Monroes returned to Virginia when she fell into a fireplace during a seizure, and suffered severe burns. Monroe was shattered when she died in 1830. In his grief, he burned all their correspondence.

He had left the presidency deeply in debt and Congress had been reluctant to reimburse many of his expenses. Despite stringent efforts, he succeeded only in obtaining a portion of the amount he believed to have been rightfully his. He thus continued the line of presidents who went into debt while working for their country, and found little help from Congress after leaving office.

Monroe in common with many others who had been—or would be—presidents, suffered from a sentiment that many members of Congress held against pensions or any assistance to former chief executives. They argued that "since Monroe had known what his salary would be for all the posts he held," why should he receive anything more simply because he had been president?[35]

Because of ill health, debt, and loneliness, Monroe—alone among the Virginia presidents—abandoned his state. Virginia had passed its days of glory, and had fallen on hard times. No longer was it wealthy and confident, but rather it had become poor and backward. Monroe put his plantation up for sale, and moved to New York to live with his daughter. His health had been deteriorating, and he died soon after, in 1831. In what might have seemed to be a last symbolic demonstration of his commitment to his country, he became the third president of the United States to die on the Fourth of July.

Four

JOHN QUINCY ADAMS

Old Man Eloquent

JOHN QUINCY ADAMS HAD BEEN THE SIXTH PRESIDENT OF THE UNITED STATES. He was the second to be turned out of office after one term, the other having been his father. He also was one of only three living presidents in the entire sweep of American history not to attend the inauguration of his successor, the others being his father, who departed Washington before Jefferson's inauguration, and Andrew Johnson, who had become so bitter at Ulysses S. Grant's support of civil rights for the freed slaves that he refused to attend Grant's.

Also like his father, John Quincy Adams's career prior to his presidency had been one of enormous distinction. In contrast to his father's, though, the second Adams presidency was not memorable. The controversial way that Adams had won office—coupled with strong opposition from Andrew Jackson's supporters who were convinced that his appointment of Henry Clay as secretary of state was evidence of a "corrupt bargain" as payment for Clay's support—greatly hampered his effectiveness as president. On the other hand, his post-presidential accomplishments matched anything in his past—even if those accomplishments came while he held an office of less stature than a number he had held previously. It is rare for a president to accomplish more after leaving office than in it, but John Quincy Adams is a prime example of one who did.

On both sides the election of 1828 was one of the most vile and disagreeable in American history. Each side hurled venomous and irresponsible charges at the other. After it was over, not only did Adams refuse to attend his successor's inaugural, but all but one of his cabinet members agreed that he ought not do so after the incoming president failed to make the traditional courtesy call on him.[1] Under the circumstances, it may have been just as well.

Victory had gone to the popular war hero, General Andrew Jackson. In the election of 1824, Adams initially had been only the runner-up. Jackson had been in that race too, and had won a plurality of both the popular vote and the electoral vote. Despite his strong showing, he lacked the majority in the electoral college required for victory. The House of Representatives therefore had to decide the winner.

The speaker of the House, Henry Clay, threw his support to Adams the insider instead of Jackson the outsider, and the House chose him to be the new president. All was well until three days later when Adams chose Clay as his new secretary of state. Although no evidence supports the charge, Jackson and his forces screamed "corrupt bargain," which effectively doomed the Adams presidency.

Its abrupt end came four years later in an election that contained the beginnings of an emerging two-party system. Jackson's Democratic-Republicans (or Democrats) were cohesive and dedicated. Most states had eliminated property requirements for voting, and all but South Carolina had begun to permit voters, rather than legislatures, to choose presidential electors. The anti-Jacksonian National Republicans could not re-elect Adams in the face of the popular enthusiasm for the rising democracy—later to become the Democratic Party. They "rightfully credited their defeat to the absence of a fully organized party."[2]

After four years of hostility, even though he was bitter at his defeat, Adams was happy to leave the misery of the office. His wife Louisa Johnson Adams had loathed living in the president's house and was equally happy to leave it behind. John Quincy was decidedly not happy at the opposition, ridicule, and defeat he had received at the hands of his enemies. Nor was he happy that he had been unable to achieve anything of the broad and ambitious program he had urged upon Congress to improve the infrastructure and intellectual attainment of the United States. His pleas for roads, bridges, canals, a national astronomical observatory, a national university, and much more not only went unheeded, but were met with derision. When friends asked him shortly before he left office what he planned to do in retirement, he "gleefully predicted" that he would devote the rest of his life to the vindication of his reputation.[3]

As it turned out, he attained considerably more than that goal. Adams "achieved more after he left the White House," wrote biographer Leonard Falkner, "than most men accomplish in a lifetime." In his "second career," he became a "pioneer advocate of civil rights. . . . No other President, before or after, has a comparable distinction."[4] Fortunately, also, he was a "world-class journal keeper.[5] The extensive diary that he kept throughout his long political career constitutes a multi-volume record that continues to provide historians with a wealth of information on the period.

Just before the end of his administration, the disappearance of their eldest son, George Washington Adams, devastated JQA and Louisa. On April 30 1829, the younger Adams had taken a steamboat to New York, only to vanish before it docked. A month later, shortly after Adams had departed his presidency, the body of the troubled, alcoholic, and probably suicidal young man washed ashore.

"Mostly, JQA spent the summer and autumn of 1829 trying to absorb the punishment of losing both a son and the presidency. Much of the time he spent alone in the old Adams mansion."[6] Unpacking his books rekindled his old reading habits, and he continued writing as well. A spark that would re-ignite his political career came when friends—and an editorial in the Boston *Courier* designed probably to clear a presidential path for Henry Clay—urged him to run for a seat in the United States House of Representatives. He did, and on November 7, 1830, he was announced the victor. "No election or appointment conferred upon me ever gave me so much pleasure," he wrote."[7]

In those days, a year elapsed between the election and the meeting of the new Congress, so Adams had an extensive period to wait. He journeyed to Washington, where he and Louisa stayed until they returned to Massachusetts for the summer. From Baltimore on toward the capital, he risked danger by riding the new and dramatic—yet still unreliable—conveyance, the railroad.

While in Washington, along with politics he occupied his time with literature, and of course with his diary. His dour demeanor notwithstanding—one might expect that he would occupy himself with legal briefs or diatribes at his enemies, rather than seek beauty, feeling, and deep meaning from words—he was a fairly prolific poet. The Adams personality, though, did defeat his attempts to write comic verse. The result of his "natural sliding into gravity" meant, as he put it, that all of his "attempts at humor evaporated in the first canto." He also studied the newly available letters and memoirs of Thomas Jefferson, happily concluding that the Sage of Monticello wrote nothing but "what redounds to his own credit." The entire Jefferson career, he took pleasure in saying, reflected a "perfidy 'worthy of Tiberius Caesar.'" Upon their return to Quincy, Massachusetts, he stopped in New York City "to call at the bedside of the dying James Monroe," for whom he had been secretary of state.[8]

That summer in Quincy as he waited for his term in Congress to begin, he encountered a rising tide of opposition to Freemasonry. The Masons are a secret society, bound by oath, and appeared to be powerful, and to be working as a bloc to elect their members to office. Moreover, there was a national outcry against the organization as a result of the kidnapping and probable murder in western New York of William Morgan, a former Mason who was attempting to expose the secret of Masonic ritual. According to a widespread perception, Masonic judges and law enforcement officers combined with Masonic jurors to permit the guilty to get off with light sentences or to evade justice entirely. Although Adams had earlier resisted efforts to recruit him into the Anti-Masonic Party, it had become powerful in his district, and he ultimately accepted membership. Andrew Jackson's status as a Mason no doubt helped entice Adams into the new party, which in any event endured only a few years until most of Jackson's opponents, Adams included, affiliated themselves with the new Whig Party.[9]

Also that summer came the news of James Monroe's death. Like two of his illustrious predecessors, Monroe died on the Fourth of July. At the request of the Boston Commonwealth Council, Adams gave a lengthy and much admired address in Monroe's memory. The next few weeks "went mostly to revising the Monroe oration for what proved a very popular publication."[10]

Adams began his congressional career at the age of 64. Accounts of his health generally refer to numerous ailments, but he exercised vigorously and displayed extraordinary stamina. "Historians are fond of telling the story of how Adams as President skinny-dipped in the Potomac. What they often neglect to point out is that the old man swam against the tide for over ninety minutes at a stretch."[11] He continued to take long walks and to swim after he returned to Washington to serve in the House, and in more ways than one he continued to swim against the tide.

Adams took the chairmanship of the Committee on Manufacturing where he fought unsuccessfully on behalf of the Bank of the United States. He was more successful in his work to lower the tariff, but the revisions failed to settle the abrasive South Carolinians who were attempting nullification. Despite his pleasure at being elected to Congress, Adams soon discovered that Southern recalcitrance was reminiscent of the frustrations of his presidency. This did not stop him from vigorous participation in House debates, where he was sharp-tongued and quick-witted. He warned over and over against sectionalism and the dangers of nullification. But it took its toll. He almost gave in to despair, heightened by Jackson's re-election, by serious financial difficulties, and by the deep slide into alcoholism of another son, John.[12]

On the way back to Washington in November, his train derailed in New Jersey, and Adams was nearly killed. He wrote of the excruciating scene: "men, women, and a child scattered along the road bleeding, mangled, groaning, writhing in torture, and dying."[13] His despair continued, made worse by John's death, until he had to admit that he must depend upon his remaining son, Charles Francis, to manage his financial affairs. With this burden lifted, and with the joy he found when Charles and his wife presented him with his first grandson, John Quincy II, he began to conquer his depression.

Adams set aside his sensitivity regarding lack of appreciation by the public, and became more aggressive than ever on the House floor. "He suddenly seemed to enjoy the attacks and taunts of enemies incurred as the House debated national banking, the tariff, and the behavior of the executive branch." He also now and then found himself, unexpectedly, on the side of Andrew Jackson. Principle, for example, required him to support the executive by opposing the politically motivated John C. Calhoun and Daniel Webster when they attempted to interfere with Jackson's efforts to deal with a dispute with the French—France had owed large sums to Americans for violating their rights as neutral shippers in the Napoleonic Wars; Jackson achieved settlement of the claims. Calhoun by that time had resigned the vice presidency after an open break with Jackson, and had assumed a seat in the Senate.[14]

After Congress adjourned in the spring of 1835, Adams found peace and renewal at home. He pruned his trees and took care of his grounds. He took seriously his new duties as an overseer at Harvard. He went fishing and took his customary long walks and swims. He joyfully took under his wing the surviving two daughters of his deceased son, John. And he gathered strength for the coming battle of his life that he may have sensed would come when the new Congress assembled.

He did not enter Congress as an abolitionist. In fact, in common with most white Americans of his day, he had little sympathy for that group of "extremists" who through the years made so many historians (none of whom would justify slavery; certainly not) uncomfortable for so long. Many historians—following neo-Confederate interpretations—long treated the abolitionists, rather than Southern extremists who demanded slavery's expansion, as the villains of the Civil War. Rather, he sought to enhance knowledge and education on the one hand, and on the other, to counter that which he considered to be a "general depravity in behavior that produced men like Jefferson, Jackson, Crawford, Calhoun, and others whom Adams scorned or despised. Consequently, when he began militantly to oppose the South, it was mainly because he believed the region's representatives were unprincipled, and thus a threat to the health of the country."[15]

Success in countering the Southerners and in fostering learning was long in coming, but the death of an Englishman who had never been to the United States, and who apparently had no ties here, created an opportunity—literally a golden opportunity—for the former president. The Englishman was James Smithson, an illegitimate son of the Duke of Northumberland, and a distinguished scientist. Smithson willed his estate to a nephew, but with an unusual proviso: in the event the nephew, Henry James Hungerford, died without children, the estate was to go to the United States to found a "Smithsonian Institution, an Establishment for the increase and diffusion of knowledge among men." Hungerford died, childless, in 1835. President Jackson had doubts about the constitutionality of accepting the bequest, but left it up to Congress to decide.[16]

Adams seized the opportunity. He had been interested in scientific research, especially astronomy, throughout his life. "In his first State of the Union message as President he had deplored that the country had no astronomical observatory. . . . Unfortunately, he called it a 'lighthouse of the sky.' His opponents had changed 'of' to 'in,' and laughed it off."[17] Later, he had attempted to create an endowment at Harvard to establish an observatory, but nothing came of it. Smithson's bequest was another chance to boost America's lagging scientific research.

The estate was more than a half million dollars in gold, which was a huge amount at the time. Adams knew that he would have to struggle to keep it from being "wasted upon hungry and worthless political jackals."[18] Congress showed little interest in research, but the House appointed JQA chairman of the committee to determine what might be done. In the Senate, Calhoun argued that it would be undignified for the United States to accept a bequest from an illegitimate foreigner. Always fearful that any federal authority could lead to the elimination of slavery, he also argued that the federal government had no authority to establish a university or any other research institution.

Adams kept consideration of the Smithson bequest alive through Congress after Congress. President Van Buren ignored his appeals for the project, as did Presidents Harrison and Tyler. Ultimately, Congress agreed to accept the funds, but could not agree on what to do with them.[19] On April 28, 1846, just three months before Adams turned 79, the House again debated the issue.

He found himself "quickly embroiled with the agrarian opponents of 'this gift horse.'" Alexander Sims of South Carolina asked Adams to cite the portion of the Constitution that would permit Congress to accept and administer the fund. He retorted that he would answer when the South Carolinian would demonstrate where the Constitution permitted the annexation of Texas. After ten years of effort, Adams finally saw his bill pass both houses. It would establish the Smithsonian Institution, destined to become a world leader in research and preservation. At the time, though, it attracted little attention. President Polk had just sent General Zachary Taylor into Texas to contend with Mexican forces—a move that Adams strongly opposed.[20]

Today, Adams is probably best known for his fervent opposition to the "gag rule" that the House adopted—despite a constitutional guarantee of the right of petition (that is, a right to submit to Congress a request that it consider and take action on an issue)—to prevent the receipt of petitions regarding slavery. He was furious when the House in May 1836, bowing to the demands of Southern representatives, adopted a rule that it would accept no petition or memorial that in any way related to the South's "peculiar institution." This rule prevented any debate on the subject. Under that rule not only would the House refuse a petition dealing with slavery from a citizen or a private organization, it would refuse such a petition even from a state legislature or other official body.

Late in his life, the restless former president had found his calling. He became the talk of the country. His biographer Paul Nagel remarked that "his cause transformed him into a debater so impassioned, so mischievous, so stubborn, and so radical that his foes and even some friends wondered at times if he had lost his sanity." Louisa wrote in her journal a hope that he might leave a fame to posterity and awaken the justice of this nation to record his name as one of the fairest midst the race of man."[21]

In the meantime, he was triumphantly delivering public addresses. At the request of Boston's leaders, he gave a eulogy for James Madison, who had died on June 28, 1836. Researching his topic, he was astonished at what he discovered. He considered it to be evidence of Jefferson's "craft and duplicity." He remarked privately that on issue after issue the Sage of Monticello had been "double-dealing, treacherous, and false beyond all toleration."[22] One of his best speeches came on April 30, 1839, when he addressed the New York Historical Society on the occasion of the fiftieth anniversary of Washington's inauguration. His "Jubilee of the Constitution" stressed that America put itself on the road to greatness when the Founders "put aside the irresponsible despotism of state sovereignty," and created a Constitution built upon the "self-evident truths of the Declaration of independence. In this manner, he introduced the inflammatory issue of universal human rights." Nagel pointed out that Adams had produced "one of the most influential statements concerning the nature of the federal Union. It would continue to be quoted," he said, "on the eve of the Civil War and afterward."[23]

In 1841, Adams created a furor among the Southern pro-slavery extremists, the "fire-eaters," by taking up his first case before the U.S. Supreme Court since 1809. Making it even worse for their piece of mind, he won. Thirty-nine Africans had taken control of the slave ship *Amistad,* which had been transporting them between ports in Cuba, then under Spanish rule. Under the leadership of a kidnapped African named Cinqué, they killed the captain, captured the officers, and demanded that the ship sail for Africa.[24]

The officers, however, guided them instead to the United States. Ironically, they landed in Long Island Sound, rather than in a port in the slave-holding South. American officials arrested the mutineers and took them to New Haven for trial. The noted abolitionist (and one of the founders of the American Anti-Slavery Society) Lewis Tappan began publicizing their situation, the Spanish minister registered protests, and Southern newspapers were filled with lurid stories of cannibals on American soil.

The U.S. district judge in charge of the case, Van Buren appointee Andrew T. Judson, was known for his hostility toward abolition and toward blacks. Nevertheless, his ruling in 1840 favored the Africans and ordered their return to Africa. An angry President Van Buren, seeking to curry favor with the South in hopes of being re-elected, ordered the U.S. attorney to appeal. A year later, the case appeared before the U.S. Supreme Court. Tappan had persuaded Adams to join attorney Roger Baldwin in representing the Africans.

Baldwin's legal arguments were cogent and persuasive, and the former president's "nine-hour appeal for justice left its mark." Justice Joseph Story called it "extraordinary, for its power, for its bitter sarcasm, and its dealing with topics far beyond the record and points of discussion."[25] The Africans had their victory and were freed. Both Tappan and Adams distributed copies of the verdict widely. One Virginian responded to Adams: "May the great Eternal God in his wrath curse you at the last day and direct you to depart from his presence to the lowest regions of Hell!"[26]

In 1844, President Tyler urged Congress to review the case and pay reparations to the slaveholders. Adams fought the proposal and it failed. In 1846, President Polk's Secretary of State James Buchanan again urged reparations. Again Adams fought the proposal and again it failed. "So it went, until long after

Adams's death, as one President after another between 1844 and 1860 tried to satisfy the South and reverse the outcome of the *Amistad* case."[27]

All along, Adams kept attempting to present petitions from constituents regarding slavery. "In January 1842, Adams presented several petitions that so angered Southern representatives that they tried to censure him. And that set off a furor that shook the nation."[28] The fire-eaters had stepped into Adams's trap. He had to be given the floor to defend himself and he used the occasion to flay the slaveholders. He read the situation and was confident that he likely would prevail. If, however, he were censured, he would resign and his constituents would immediately re-elect him. "His public repute was becoming that of a hero."[29]

People across the North had begun to call him "Old Man Eloquent." After eight long years, his diligent efforts brought him victory against congressional suppression of debate in the interests of the slaveholding South. On December 8, 1844, by a resounding vote of 108 to 80, the House approved his resolution to rescind "the hated gag rule."[30]

On the afternoon of Monday, February 21, 1848, Adams collapsed from a stroke and died on the floor of the U.S. House of Representatives, the institution that had given him back his life. Nagel noted that the former president had hoped to be known for some significant contribution to the world's literature, to science, or to philosophy, but he knew that in this, he had failed. His strengths lay elsewhere. The year he died, two U.S. senators, John Davis of Massachusetts and the formidable Thomas Hart Benton of Missouri, edited and published a collection of Adams's poems. Other collections of his writings followed, but his literary efforts are barely remembered. Nagel thinks of it as a "bittersweet truth" that Adams's fame has resulted not from these contributions, but from his thirst for political vengeance.[31]

Be that as it may, Old Man Eloquent contributed far more to humanity than all but a few persons in history. For the most part, he did it not as president, but afterward. The cause of human rights worldwide took a step forward when the former president, late in life, became—in the words of Virginia's Henry Wise—"the acutest, the astutest, the archest enemy of Southern slavery that ever existed."[32]

Five

THE JACKSONIANS

Jefferson's Heirs and Beyond

Andrew Jackson, "Old Hickory," was the first president to come from outside the ruling elite, and the first to owe his election to popularity with the people. The 1820s brought a great expansion of the electorate. Property requirements for voting fell, which brought more people into the process. These were all white men, of course, but it was nonetheless a step forward and was a move toward eventual universal suffrage. In addition, except for the lone holdout (typically) of South Carolina—which still empowered its legislature to select them—states had begun to choose their presidential electors by popular vote. This gave the expanded electorate a significant role in presidential selection.

That great surge of popular vote swept Jackson—the Old Hero, the victor of the Battle of New Orleans in the War of 1812—all the way to the presidency. As president, he was a whirlwind of activity. He faced down South Carolina when it attempted to nullify federal law. He killed the Bank of the United States. With the skillful assistance of Martin Van Buren—his secretary of state, later his vice president, and still later his successor as president—Jackson built a party structure that laid the basis for the development of America's two-party system. He was the first president who used the veto "as a carefully calculated political move,"[1] casting his veto 12 times, more than all of his predecessors combined. Previously, presidents cast vetoes essentially to turn back measures they considered unconstitutional. He energized the presidency in a manner not seen since the times of Washington and Jefferson, and succeeded in converting it into an institution of the people. He produced his lengthy list of accomplishments without becoming what opponents of a strong executive so feared: a demagogue.

Jackson rode a popular wave so forcefully, and so skillfully, that it took his name: Jacksonianism. The movement was based on the old republican principles of limited government, states' rights, and political equality (for white men), but by stressing the capabilities of the "common man," rather than emphasizing an educated elite, it introduced a populist element that previously had been absent. It also modified old principles to accommodate the new political reality: It openly accepted parties, it recognized that sensitivity to the states could not be permitted to infringe upon national supremacy, and it frankly brought forth the executive as the source of energy in government.

Jackson was the first, but other Jacksonians followed: Martin Van Buren, John Tyler (despite his discomfort with Jackson and his election to the vice presidency as a Whig), and James K. Polk (Young Hickory) carried on the principles. Of these, Jackson and Polk were the most active in office. In their post-presidential careers, however, it arguably was Van Buren who had the greatest influence on the direction of the presidency, and it was Tyler who was most notable for the direction his career was to take—arguably the most perverse direction of all former presidents' careers.

ANDREW JACKSON

Jackson left office on the March 4, 1837. He was tired, ill, and would turn 70 on March 15—the oldest person to have served in the presidency until Dwight Eisenhower, a century and a quarter later. In view of his age and health, when he took office in March 1829 many observers doubted that he would survive a term as president. He surprised them. He not only survived, despite illnesses and a body damaged by bullets from duels, but went on to serve two highly active terms. He surprised them again by living more than another eight years in retirement, dying on June 8, 1845.

The outgoing president had strongly endorsed his vice president, Martin Van Buren, to be his successor. Van Buren won, and was the last sitting vice president to be elected president until Vice President George H. W. Bush won the presidential election in 1988, over a century and a half later. Jackson happily attended Van Buren's inauguration.

Shortly thereafter, he embarked upon a slow journey home to Tennessee, to his plantation, "The Hermitage," near Nashville. He traveled for several weeks, stopping in various locations along the way to visit friends. He received the cheers of crowds everywhere, touching the Old Hero's heart. He wrote that he had been opposed throughout his administration "by the talents, wealth and money power of the whole aristocracy of the United States, but nobly supported by the Democratic republicans—the people."[2]

When he arrived home, he discovered that he had something immediately in common with his predecessors Washington and Jefferson: His plantation had deteriorated in his absence. His adopted son had proven to be a poor manager, and had lied about The Hermitage's condition. Nevertheless, Jackson stood by his son, accepted responsibility for his debts, and even purchased another plantation, for him to manage, "encouraging him to begin again, hoping he had profited by his mistakes."[3]

Although the country's deep financial troubles that began shortly after he left office made it difficult for Jackson to recover economically, he continued to follow politics and to advise Democratic leaders, writing letter after letter recommending various courses of action. Consistent with his objection to banks—reflected in his success in destroying the Bank of the United States, and in his veto of the bill to renew its charter—he endorsed Van Buren's proposal for an independent treasury. When it ultimately passed, private banks no longer had federal deposits for their use.

He was stunned when Van Buren lost the election in 1840 to a Whig, but the new president, William Henry Harrison, died a month after his inauguration. No president had ever before died in office, and there was confusion as to what should be done. The Constitution was rather vague. Did the vice president merely act as president until there could be a special election, or did he truly become president? Vice President John Tyler settled the issue; he insisted that he was the new president. Despite jeers from those who called him "your accidency," the country accepted him.

Tyler had been a Democrat, but broke with Jackson whom he thought to be a dictator. He ran for vice president on the Whig ticket with Harrison without changing his opposition to the Whig program of a national bank and extensive internal improvements, and without accepting the Whig view of a very limited presidency. He also remained a strong advocate of states' rights. As president, he began vetoing Whig legislation, and set about governing as a pure Jacksonian. Jackson was delighted. "A kind and overruling providence has interfered to prolong our glorious Union," he remarked.[4]

Jackson was all the more delighted when Congress voted to reimburse him for a fine that he had paid in 1815 for contempt of court—as a general in the War of 1812, he had established martial law in New Orleans, and had ignored a court's writ of habeas corpus. "Senator Linn of Missouri introduced the legislation early in 1842, and while the Whigs fought it out of a sense of revenge, it finally passed on February 15, 1844."[5] This was personal vindication. It also had practical benefits, since he was struggling to pay debts.

On the other hand, he was shocked and saddened when his old friend and colleague, former President Martin Van Buren, in 1844 came out in opposition to the annexation of Texas. Van Buren was attempting to secure the Democratic nomination once again, but as a result of his disappointment with his former vice president, Jackson threw his support to the eventual winner, James K. Polk. In the eyes of Polk's Jacksonian enthusiasts, he had become "Young Hickory."

Death came to Andrew Jackson from multiple causes, including chronic tuberculosis, on June 8, 1845, nearly three months after Polk had assumed the presidency. He was 78. Jackson, as an ardent expansionist, had been able to take pleasure not only in Polk's victory, but also—just as the Tyler administration came to a close—in the annexation of Texas. As the old duelist, war hero, slaveholder, Indian fighter, man of the people, and vigorous president of the United States lay dying, among his last words were, "my dear children, and friends, and servants, I hope and trust to meet you all in heaven, both white and black."[6]

MARTIN VAN BUREN

Martin Van Buren journeyed far, intellectually speaking, after he lost the election of 1840 and left the presidency in March 1841 at the age of 58. As president, he had enforced Jackson's Indian removal policy vigorously, and with tragic results. He had demonstrated no concerns whatever about the morality of slavery.

In the famous *Amistad* case, captive Africans aboard a Spanish slave ship from Cuba seized the ship and attempted to sail it back to their homeland in Africa, but had been tricked into landing on American soil. Van Buren ordered the Africans returned to Cuba, only to find his order reversed by order of the Supreme Court—before which the elderly U.S. representative and former president, John Quincy Adams, had argued on behalf of the Africans. In this and other ways, although Van Buren was never an expansionist, he had attempted—in an unsuccessful bid to win a second term—to curry favor with the slaveholding South. His post-presidential career saw him change markedly, and enabled him ultimately to change the course of the American presidency.

Van Buren left office showing no bitterness. He graciously greeted the man who defeated him, General Harrison, and entertained him in his final days as president. He even offered to vacate the executive mansion early for the new president's convenience, and he attended the Harrison inaugural. It was the first time that a defeated incumbent had done so—of course, there was not an extensive precedent. The only incumbents previously defeated had been John Adams and his son, John Quincy.

After the new president's inauguration, Van Buren returned to his farm, "Lindenwald," at Kinderhook, New York. "In 1844, after turning down President Tyler's politically motivated offer of a seat on the Supreme Court," he once more tried for the Democratic presidential nomination.[7] It was the first time a former president had attempted to regain the office.

Van Buren was the leading contender. His opposition to the annexation of Texas—fearing that it would lead to sectional strife—had cost him the support of Jackson and of the Southern expansionists. Nevertheless, he had a majority of the delegates and led on the first ballot, but the party's two-thirds rule—ironically the very rule that had secured his vice presidential nomination in 1832—thwarted him. Ultimately, he lost to the first "dark horse" candidate—one who had little or no support at first but who came from behind to win the nomination—James K. Polk.

Four years later he tried again, but this time not as a Democrat. The Mexican War had come and gone, and sectional controversy had become bitter and divisive. The South was furious over the "Wilmot Proviso," even though it failed. David Wilmot, a Democratic representative from Pennsylvania, had proposed that slavery be prohibited in any territory acquired from Mexico. Van Buren not only supported the Proviso, but accepted the 1848 nomination of the Free Soil Party. It was the only party in the race that took a clear position absolutely opposing the expansion of slavery into the territories. He had concluded that slavery and freedom could not coexist, and wrote "a moving appeal for adoption of a commitment that all future states would be admitted only when they banned slavery."[8]

Once again, he was a candidate. It was the first time that a former president had received a party's nomination to try again for the presidency. Van Buren presented the party as the "plain republicans of the North," and ran a vigorous race. He carried no state, and thus received no electoral votes, but he did garner 10 percent of the popular vote. His showing was impressive for a third-party candidate, and was enough to deny victory in several states to Lewis

Cass, the Democratic nominee. Van Buren's role was decisive. His candidacy resulted in defeat for Cass, and victory for the Whig, Zachary Taylor.

Van Buren's 1848 candidacy thus changed the history of the presidency. Taylor was the last Whig elected president. There was, in fact, only one other, Harrison. He and Taylor each died in office. Harrison's vice president was the former Democrat, John Tyler, who as president immediately proceeded to antagonize the Whigs; they quickly read him out of the party. Taylor's vice president was Millard Fillmore, who replaced him as a Whig president. Thus, there were only three Whig presidents (or four, if one insists on counting Tyler), only two of whom were elected—and one of those barely had a chance to serve. Therefore, except for Harrison's one month in office there was only one four-year period of Whig administration, the Taylor–Fillmore years of 1849–1853. Without Van Buren's attempt to regain the presidency in 1848, there effectively would have been no Whig administration at all.

During the 1850s, Van Buren traveled to Europe for an extensive, two-year trip.[9] He "poked around ancestral Dutch towns," and "during a sojourn in Italy the seventy-one-year-old former chief executive wrote his autobiography, which still interests scholars because of the author's inside knowledge and candor."[10] Unfortunately, he did not complete it, failing to carry his narrative beyond 1834.

Back in Lindenwald, he had given up on third parties and gradually returned to his beloved Democrats. In the election of 1852 he was chosen as an elector, and cast his vote for the victorious Pierce. In 1856, he again cast an electoral vote for the winning Democratic candidate, James Buchanan. Nevertheless, as his writings indicate, he was greatly disturbed over the pro-Southern policies of both administrations.

Van Buren remained a Democrat, and did not vote for Abraham Lincoln in 1860. In that election he cast his ballot for Stephen Douglas, hoping that the Democrat could bring unity to a dividing country. But when South Carolina seceded he declared that the Constitution was "a perpetual and irrevocable compact." He proclaimed his confidence in Lincoln, and called upon the Democratic Party of New York, the party that he had been instrumental in building into a powerful force, to support the Republican president's policies. The war that Martin Van Buren, the eighth president of the United States—and later Free Soil presidential candidate—had worked so hard to avoid, came despite his efforts. He did not live to see the successful conclusion to this most bloody of America's conflicts, which ultimately had been necessary to save the Union. He died of respiratory and heart failure at his home while the battles raged, on July 24, 1862.

JOHN TYLER

John Tyler, "His Accidency," had been the first vice president to fill the position of a president who died in office. William Henry Harrison's death came on April 4, 1841, one month to the day after he had been inaugurated as president. He had participated in all the lengthy inaugural ceremonies, which were outside in a brisk and chilly wind. He wore no hat or coat, and sometime later he developed a severe cold that worsened, probably into pneumonia.

Tyler had begun his time in office boldly—it had not been at all clear that a vice president under such circumstances actually *became* president, but he established the precedent for all time. He also had been highly controversial for other reasons, many of them far from praiseworthy.

Tyler had been a Jacksonian Democrat, but broke with Jackson over Jackson's threat to use force against South Carolina's attempt to nullify national laws, and over his fiscal policies. Tyler then joined the opposition party, the Whigs. In the 1836 election, the Whigs ran several different candidates for president in various regions, and Tyler had been one of the candidates for the vice presidency. Whig leaders had hoped to throw the election into the House, but their strategy failed as Jackson won decisively. In 1840, the Whigs chose General William Henry Harrison as their national candidate, and put Tyler on the ticket to run for vice president. They chose Tyler in the hope of attracting Southern states'-rights voters to their ticket. They got those votes, but more as well—considerably more than they had bargained for.

When Tyler became president, he defied the Whigs who had put him on the ticket in the first place, vetoing their enactments and destroying their program. As a result, they expelled him from the party. As president, he had been stubborn, proud, and independent. The Whigs should not have been surprised. Tyler's views had never been compatible with theirs, and he had been rigid and unyielding throughout his entire political career. Also as president, his pro-slavery and expansionist policies contributed greatly to the tensions that developed so rapidly and that ultimately almost destroyed the country.

Tyler may have hoped for another term, but without a party he had no chance to remain as president. Just before he left office, he and his young wife, Julia Gardiner (whom he had married while he was in office, after his first wife's death) gave a huge ball, entertaining Washington society lavishly. He remarked at the time that no longer could anyone say he was a "President without a party!"

Tyler, at 51, had been the youngest person yet to occupy the presidency. He had been 53, however, when he married Julia, who was three decades his junior—leading to many jokes that had nothing to do with his politics. He had come into office with eight children, and he and Julia, while in retirement at their Virginia estate, Sherwood Forest, had seven more. His 15 children set a record among presidents that remains standing today. In addition to becoming the first vice president to step into a presidential vacancy, he also was the only president who had been read out of his party, and the first to face serious discussion of impeachment. Some Whigs were incensed that an "acting president" would veto a tariff bill, but their discussion of impeachment led to nothing.[11]

He set another record that one hopes will remain forever. John Tyler became the only former president in American history to give open aid and comfort to, and to affiliate formally with, an enemy of the United States of America. After departing the presidency, Tyler settled again, apparently happily, into plantation life. He rejoined the Democratic Party, and continued to hope for preservation of the Union—with, however, a secure place for the South with its slavery system intact and protected.

In all probability, he was no more happy with the Republican victory in 1860 and with Abraham Lincoln's forthcoming presidency than were other Southerners, but he was not among the fire-eaters. He made a last attempt to achieve the unity that his counterproductive presidential policies had made even less likely. In February 1861, before Lincoln's inauguration in March, Tyler was the moving force—and in fact, the presiding officer—of a Peace Convention in Richmond. The convention passed several resolutions, hoping to achieve a national "compromise" that nevertheless would provide for slavery's expansion. Among them, one proposed extending the Missouri Compromise line all the way to the Pacific, dividing the country into a slaveholding region south of the line and a free region above it.

Tyler journeyed to Washington to meet with President-Elect Lincoln at Willard's Hotel and presented him the Richmond Convention's resolutions. Lincoln may have appreciated the effort, but was under no illusion that they would satisfy the extremists who had seized control of policy in the South. When the president did not act upon the proposals, John Tyler, former president of the United States of America, at last threw up his hands and lost hope. He joined other Virginia leaders in recommending that they proceed to destroy the Union. Virginia, he asserted, should secede.[12] He went so far as to take a seat in the Provisional Congress of the Confederacy and accepted election in November to the new House of Representatives of the Confederate States of America. He died, however, on January 18, 1862, before he could serve. No other person who had been an American president accepted an official position among the Confederates who, after all, were seeking to supplant the Constitution of the United States and its Union.

Although there were official ceremonies in the Confederacy marking Tyler's passing—his flag-draped body (with a Confederate flag) lay in state in Richmond—there were no such ceremonies in Washington. It should be no surprise that many people outside the South considered him a traitor. Union troops vandalized his plantation during the Civil War, and not until 1915, some half-century following the close of that war, did Congress authorize a memorial at Tyler's gravesite—which lies next to that of another former president, James Monroe.

Tyler left an ironic legacy for one who at one time had favored the Union. It was a legacy of Confederate activism and Southern vindication. His son, Lyon Gardiner Tyler—the fourteenth child of this most prolific of all presidents—long after Tyler's death and almost as long after the Confederacy's, embarked upon an anti-Lincoln crusade. It began as a reaction against an editorial lauding Lincoln in *The New York Times*.[13] The 1917 editorial had said that the South declared war when the North resisted the spread of slavery, and then had the effrontery to call the war defensive. Tyler fumed that it was Lincoln who misused the Constitution and then claimed necessity.

Lyon Tyler's ire intensified more than a decade later when the House of Delegates of Tyler's own state, Virginia, adjourned in honor of Lincoln's birthday. Lincoln merited no such honor, Tyler sulked. "*Time* magazine fired back that Tyler's father . . . was a dwarf in stature and accomplishments compared to Lincoln." Tyler's rejoinder, *John Tyler and Abraham Lincoln: Who Was the Dwarf?*, demonstrated that the Tyler family—at least this representative of it—still was fighting the Civil War as late as 1929.[14] This Tyler, whom *The New York Times* declared to be a "perverse political thinker," died, ironically, on February 12, 1935, the "126th birthday of his archnemesis, Abraham Lincoln."[15]

JAMES K. POLK

James Knox Polk was the first "dark horse" president—a long shot at the beginning, but the ultimate nominee—in 1844. Initially, he was seeking the vice presidency. The leading presidential candidate was former President Martin Van Buren. When Van Buren's bid for the nomination faltered, however, and Van Buren found that even his friend and mentor Andrew Jackson had turned away from him, the way had become clear for Polk.

Among the four Jacksonian presidents, only Jackson had been more of an activist than Polk. "Young Hickory" had been strikingly successful in achieving his agenda. It had been an ambitious one and included such enormous accomplishments as statehood for Texas, settling the Oregon boundary question with Great Britain in favor of the United States, and—however much it is subject to criticism—obtaining territory from Mexico that eventually brought war with that country. The war brought to the United States a huge amount of additional territory (in addition to the already annexed Texas) that ultimately became all or most of the states of Arizona, California, Colorado, Nevada, New Mexico, Utah, and Wyoming. Polk was also an efficient administrator. He streamlined processes and maintained much tighter control of the federal budget than any of his presidential colleagues until the twentieth century.

As a former president, though, Polk, for reasons beyond his control, wielded the least influence of the four. He had not enjoyed being president. From the outset, he had determined to serve only one term, and did not run for a second. He was only 53 when he left office and his diary revealed that he was glad that his presidency was over.

As his term ended, "Polk handed the reins of government over to Zachary Taylor with as much graciousness as he could manage, given their stormy relationship during the recent war. What satisfaction Polk felt upon being relieved of the burdens of public life was no doubt tempered by the fact that the electorate had repudiated the Democratic party at the polls."[16] The new president, General Zachary Taylor, was a Whig. General Taylor's identification as a Whig had led to friction with the highly partisan Democratic President during the 1846–1848 war.

Polk and Taylor rode to the inauguration together in a carriage, where Taylor allegedly said to him that he hoped California and Oregon would form independent governments, because they were too far from the rest of the country to be governed effectively by the United States. Polk did not argue, but later expressed dismay. As for Taylor's inaugural address, a "very critical and somewhat arrogant Polk could find nothing to laud" about it. He criticized Taylor's delivery, and wrote that "Gen'l Taylor is, I have no doubt, a well-meaning old man. He is, however, uneducated, exceedingly ignorant of public affairs, and, I should judge, of very ordinary capacity." A scholar of the Polk presidency, Paul Bergeron, noted that although this judgment was not entirely fair, it might have been expected given the quarrels between Polk and Taylor since the beginning of the Mexican War.[17] At the end of Taylor's inaugural address, though, Polk simply shook the new president's hand, and said, "I hope, Sir, the country may be prosperous under your administration."[18]

The former president, his wife Sarah Childress Polk, their nieces, and some friends then set out the day following the inauguration for the Polk home in

Tennessee. This was March 6, because the normal inaugural day at the time, March 4, had occurred on Sunday, which delayed the inauguration until the following Monday. The party left Washington by train, transferring at various times to steamboats and carriages. Instead of taking a direct route, they journeyed leisurely through Virginia, the Carolinas, and Alabama to New Orleans. Then they went up the Mississippi to Memphis, and on to their home in Nashville.

Polk's health had never been robust and he was ill off and on throughout the trip. Fearing cholera, he was terrified at each intestinal upset. He escaped the cholera that was prevalent along his journey and enjoyed an enthusiastic reception at Nashville. For the next few weeks, he "visited with family and friends, superintended construction work at Polk Place, his increasingly elegant Nashville home, and arranged his papers and books." The "temporary rejuvenation" that he experienced, though, was deceiving. "Suddenly, in June, he was stricken for the last time,"[19] by an intestinal ailment, which probably was indeed cholera.

On June 15, 1849, three months after he left the presidency, James K. Polk died. He still was but 53. His four-year presidency was probably the most momentous of any single-term president's, but the brevity of his three-month retirement denied him the chance to influence the course of his nation beyond his time in office.

Six

A BIZARRE
HISTORICAL FOOTNOTE

Zachary Taylor

ALTHOUGH ZACHARY TAYLOR DIED IN OFFICE AND HAD NO POST-PRESIDENTIAL career in the traditional sense, he in some ways did have an interesting posthumous role in American history. Taylor died on July 9, 1850. His 16 months in office meant that he served the third shortest time of any president. Only William Henry Harrison's one-month term and James A. Garfield's six months were shorter.

On the Fourth of July, Taylor had watched Independence Day ceremonies, sitting all afternoon in the hot sun. As he sat, he ate and drank. Exactly what he consumed is not certain—nor is it important—but most accounts describe it as sour cherries and cold milk. At any rate, shortly thereafter he developed extreme gastroenteritis, and died a few days later.

As president, Taylor had been fiercely independent. He stood on principle and resisted political pressures from all sides. Some historians say, unfairly, that he refused to cooperate with anyone and accused him of standing in the way of sectional compromise. What is fair to say is that he was a Louisiana slaveholder whose election had pleased the South. His actions in office, however, were anything but pleasing to the Southern slaveholders who were threatening secession if they were not permitted to expand slavery into the territories.

Taylor stood firmly for the Union and threatened to use force against any attempt to dissolve it. Although he supported slavery where it existed, he resisted efforts to expand the system and stood ready to veto Henry Clay's "omnibus bill," which essentially was the famous "Compromise of 1850" that passed after his death. Obviously the legislation did not prevent the Civil War. The most that can be said for the measure is that perhaps it held war off for a decade or so.

Regardless of that, there were persistent rumors that Taylor did not die a natural death. Americans apparently have always delighted in conspiracy theories, and Taylor's demise lent itself to one of the better ones. A president died in office. He had disappointed Southern extremists who had hoped that he would foster their aims. He (nearly a century before FDR) was "a traitor to his class" (and certainly no "credit to his race"). Some felt that it was obvious that angry Southerners had assassinated him. Clearly, he must have been the victim of poison: Arsenic surely was the agent of his death!

Historians upon occasion may be no less prone to such delusion than the average American. The twentieth century had almost passed with no action on the case. The authorities clearly had failed to exercise due diligence in pursuing the truth. Finally, however, a few persistent historians managed to move the bureaucrats. A forensic anthropologist in 1991 directed the exhumation of Taylor's remains and studied them intensely.

Alas, there was no evidence that Zachary Taylor, the twelfth President of the United States, had died of anything other than natural causes. He had not been poisoned. Southern extremists may have been Taylor's mortal antagonists, but they were not his murderers. Taylor, therefore, rests, and the conspiracy theorists can devote their attention to JFK, or perhaps to Elvis.

Seven

DOUGHFACES

Northern Men with Southern Principles

ALL OF THE JACKSONIAN PRESIDENTS HAD BEEN SOUTHERNERS (OR Southwesterners), except for Van Buren. Prior to the Civil War the party of Jackson—the Democratic Party—tended to cater to Southern interests. Accordingly, the antebellum Democrats tended to be the party of the slaveholders, just as their Jeffersonian predecessors, the Republicans, had been. In both instances, however, the parties were likely to place the Union ahead of sectional interests. Unfortunately, the closer war became—that is, after Taylor's death in 1850—the more likely presidents were to identify the Union with the interests of the slaveholding South.

After the last of the strong Unionist Jacksonians, Polk, came the only four years of Whig rule. Zachary Taylor, who died in office, was a staunch nationalist. His vice president, also a Whig, Millard Fillmore, was another matter—to be sure, he too was a nationalist, but in his view preserving the Union required concessions to increasing Southern demands for the protection and expansion of slavery. Fillmore's two Democratic successors, Franklin Pierce and James Buchanan, also essentially were Jacksonians, but were so weak in office and so prone to cater to the South on every issue that it hardly mattered whether or not they were nationalists. There could be some objection to classing Fillmore's presidency as that of a doughface—a Northern man with Southern principles—but hardly so with regard to the administrations of Pierce and Buchanan. Their post-presidential careers, however, present a considerably more varied picture.

MILLARD FILLMORE

Fillmore declared shortly after he succeeded the suddenly deceased Zachary Taylor that he would not run for re-election. Nevertheless, in response to pressure from supporters, he—apparently with some reluctance—permitted them as the end of his term was drawing near to place his name before the 1852 Whig convention. He should have maintained his resolve. After numerous ballots the convention reverted to the formula that had worked for them in the past—the only one in fact that had worked: putting forth a general. General William Henry Harrison and General Zachary Taylor had been their only two successful presidential candidates. This time it failed to work. Despite rejecting Fillmore and giving the nomination to General Winfield Scott, the party lost badly in the 1852 election. It was never again to elect a president, or even to run another presidential candidate. The Whig Party—created to oppose Andrew Jackson and the Jacksonian Democrats—for all practical purposes evaporated.

Fillmore became one of those anonymous nineteenth-century presidents. His biographers generally believe that he deserves better, as does historian Jean Harvey Baker, but his own lack of judgment is largely responsibility for his having faded from view. Baker, in fact, has noted that his "anonymity [is] such a joke to members of the Millard Fillmore Society that they meet annually on his birthday to celebrate his invisibility."[1]

Fillmore's wife, Abigail Powers Fillmore, had been one of his closest advisers. She was politically astute, and her judgment, in contrast to that of her husband, was sound. Fillmore himself was a capable administrator and a man of integrity, but he had made a series of poor choices. Initially, he had affiliated with what for a time was a major anti-Jacksonian party, the Anti-Masons; by 1836 it had dissolved to be replaced by the next major anti-Jacksonian group, with which he also affiliated, the Whigs. This party eventually also dissolved, since it could not deal with the issue of the expansion of slavery. During his time as a Whig president, Fillmore sincerely worked for sectional accommodation, but against Abigail's advice—even though it seems that he did have some misgivings—in 1850 he signed the outrageous Fugitive Slave Act.

The Act required state officials—and in fact all citizens—to render active support to federal officials on behalf of Southern slaveholders. Its provisions were designed to force all Americans to become agents of slavery. Any black person accused of being a runaway slave according to the law had to be captured and sent to his or her accuser. There was no provision for civil liberties and no court could intervene. Thus, any black person, legally free or not, was subject to enslavement with no recourse. All that legally was required to force any black person into slavery was an accusation. When some states responded by passing "personal liberty laws," Fillmore considered them to be extremist. Ironically, the South that had insisted on states' rights and even asserted the power of a state to resist national laws by nullifying them within its own borders, in this instance, rejected any thought of state's rights. Southern leaders applauded this use of national authority to run roughshod over the states' rights principle.

Fillmore seems to have favored civil liberties, including freedom of religion, but they obviously were not his primary consideration. Unfortunately, he exercised poor judgment in not heeding Abigail's advice on the Fugitive Slave Law. She told him in fact that he would be committing political suicide if he signed it.

Also compounding Fillmore's misery was Abigail's longstanding poor health. She and the outgoing president stood in the cold wind on March 4, 1853, to participate in President Franklin Pierce's inauguration, and she became seriously ill. She developed a fever and died from pneumonia on March 30, mere weeks after Fillmore departed the presidency. Her death was tragic in many ways. "She had been the inspiration of Fillmore's youth and shared his life, thoughts, challenges, problems, and triumphs for twenty-seven years."[2] One biographer has speculated that Fillmore's historical reputation might have been vastly better if she had lived and they had followed their original plans to travel, and then settle into retirement in Buffalo. Unfortunately, "he brooded silently for a year and then returned to the political wars."[3] Sadly, 16 months later his daughter Mary Abigail (Abby), also died, apparently from cholera. Her sudden death occurred after a 12-hour illness, on July 26, 1854; she was only 22.[4] Presidential scholar Elbert Smith said that Fillmore had adored his daughter, who had served as his hostess in Washington when Abigail was ill. Smith speculated that her death—the second tragedy in his life since leaving the presidency—may have driven Fillmore to a resumption of political activity.[5]

Whatever the reason for his re-entry into politics, Fillmore had only his own instincts as a guide. When he had relied on them and had disregarded Abigail's advice in the past, he tended to make poor decisions. Without Abigail, Fillmore's record of poor judgment continued, and contributed considerably to his poor reputation among historians.

In 1854, he took a long journey to the Midwest and the South. In January 1855, he wrote to a friend a letter for publication. In it, he said that Europe's oppressed peoples should continue to be welcome in the United States, and should have the full protection of the law. Because of "the corrupting influence which the contest for the foreign vote is exciting upon our elections," though, only those who had been reared in this country should ever be qualified to hold office. He then accepted membership in the Order of the Star Spangled Banner.[6] The organization was a secret society working to restrict political power to native-born Protestants. It merged with the new American Party, whose members were ordered to reply if questioned about the party that they knew nothing. The new group quickly came to be known as the "Know-Nothing Party." It rapidly accumulated political power, winning a number of state and local elections in 1854.[7] In March 1855, Fillmore set off on a tour of Europe and did not return for more than a year.

While he was in Europe, the Know Nothings nominated Fillmore as their 1856 presidential candidate. He accepted and returned to the United States to share the ticket with Andrew Jackson Donelson, Andrew Jackson's stepson and a former Democrat, as his vice presidential running mate. The new Republican Party, only two years old, nominated General John C. Frémont, while the Democrats choose James Buchanan. Under the circumstances, Fillmore did well. He garnered nearly 22 percent of the popular vote, but carried only the state of Maryland, which gave him eight electoral votes. Buchanan won substantially in the electoral college, but had considerably less than a majority of the popular vote. Frémont came in second, but his vote was highly sectional. He carried states only in the north, with Ohio being the southernmost.

Fillmore's biographers have tended to stress that he was not really prejudiced against foreigners or Catholics. Only rarely did his speeches employ nativist themes. "He saw himself as the best hope for sectional peace among the three candidates," said Smith.[8] "He was no more anti Catholic or anti-foreigner than anyone else," wrote biographer Robert Scarry. The Know-Nothing Party, Scarry said, was merely a convenient vehicle to achieve political power (admittedly, this explanation itself raises some questions, implying that Fillmore would sacrifice principle for expedience).[9] Another biographer, Robert Rayback, similarly presents a softened view of Fillmore's attitudes.[10]

Whatever the merits of these attempted justifications, Fillmore associated himself with some of the worst elements of American society and accepted the candidacy of a movement that even Smith conceded "deserves condemnation."[11] He did himself no good by doing so, nor did he serve his country well. Regardless of the nature or merit of his own convictions—and admitting freely that things always look different in hindsight—Fillmore's judgment clearly was lacking; in fact it was woefully deficient. Moreover, although he did achieve something for the history books and the trivia buffs—the greatest popular vote by a third-party candidate in the nineteenth century, the first third-party candidate to achieve electoral votes, etc.—he failed.[12] He did not alter the election's outcome and did not prevent the Democrats from gaining victory.

After the election of 1856, Millard Fillmore did what he should have done when he left the presidency. He retired to Buffalo, and accepted his position as its most prominent citizen. Although he had no formal education, he worked diligently for education and other worthy causes. He was only 56, but sought no other office. In 1858, he married Caroline Carmichael McIntosh, a wealthy widow. Their generosity, among other things, included supporting "charities, public education, museums, Buffalo's Fine Arts Academy, the incipient University of Buffalo, libraries, the YMCA, the Historical Society, the Buffalo General Hospital, the Orphan Asylum, the Society for the Prevention of Cruelty to Animals, and the Natural Sciences Society."[13]

Fillmore's political judgment, however, remained consistently poor. Although he favored the Union cause, he had reservations about Lincoln's policies. In 1864, he voted for Lincoln's opponent, General George McClellan,[14] who had run on a platform calling for appeasement of the South and an end to the war (McClellan belatedly rejected that part of the platform after the Union forces began to win major battles). Fillmore's reputation as a doughface caused a mob to assemble before his house after Lincoln's assassination and splatter it with ink. He had neglected to drape it for mourning. He hastily confronted the mob, eulogized Lincoln, and apologized for his failure to show adequate respect to the fallen leader. He pleaded with them for understanding, because he had been preoccupied at the bedside of his wife, who was ill. Knowing of her illness, the assembled group accepted his explanation and departed.[15] Even though emotions understandably were at a fever pitch, the mob's actions in threatening the former president because of his presumed political views were a poor commentary upon the degree of popular adherence to America's ideals of freedom.

Fillmore continued to live in Buffalo, and continued to be its most distinguished citizen. He died there of a stroke on March 8, 1874. "His statue still graces the square in front of the Buffalo City Hall."[16] His widow, Caroline, lived in Buffalo until her death from pneumonia in 1881.

FRANKLIN PIERCE

Franklin Pierce, a native of New Hampshire, left office convinced that he had been a successful president, even though his own Democratic Party refused to renominate him for a second term. Pierce's bias in favor of the South and its efforts to expand slavery had been painfully—and to those who disagreed, outrageously—obvious. He was distressed at the formation of the anti-slavery Republican Party during his presidency, and blamed the new party for the increasing sectional discord.

Originally, both sections had agreed upon the Missouri Compromise; slavery's expansion would be limited. It would be kept out of the northern portion of the Louisiana Purchase. As president, however, Pierce had supported the Kansas-Nebraska Act, and its provision for popular sovereignty specifically repealed the Missouri Compromise. At the South's urging, all territory became potentially open for slavery. He considered all who objected to slavery's expansion to be disloyal. Thus it was only natural that he would blame the country's troubles entirely on the Republicans and accept no blame for the mini-civil war that his bungling and biased policies had ignited in "Bleeding Kansas," where pro- and anti-slavery forces engaged in murderous raids and battles.

Pierce and his wife, Jane, had more than their share of personal troubles as well, in addition to his heavy drinking. After he had won the 1852 election but before he took office, Pierce and Jane were riding in a railroad car with their 11-year-old son Bennie. The train derailed and the horrified Pierces watched as wreckage crushed their son. Jane, who had always been fragile physically and mentally, never recovered from the shock. She had always despised politics and resented Pierce's political career. His was not a happy presidency, either personally or politically.

Pierce did manage to save money while in office, however, and investment income permitted him and his wife to travel widely in Europe and elsewhere after he left the presidency. For several years he cared for Jane and they stayed largely in warm regions to escape the bitter New England winters. Her health nevertheless continued to deteriorate and she never recovered from grief over their son's death. In December 1863, she died of tuberculosis.[17]

Pierce did not remain politically active, although he did follow politics and felt despair at the state of the country. He made no secret of his views, including on the rare occasions when he appeared in public. In 1860, for example, he had suggested Jefferson Davis as the Democratic candidate for president.[18] If any doubts remain about his judgment or his attitudes, that should settle them. He was bitter at Lincoln's election, and especially at the Emancipation Proclamation—he thought it "interfered with states' rights and the right of private property."[19]

Pierce was a Unionist and did not support secession, although he saw the South as victim and thought anti-slavery forces had caused the trouble. He especially found it impossible to place any blame upon the Confederate President, Jefferson Davis. Davis not only had been Pierce's secretary of war, but also was his close friend.[20] In 1864 he supported General George McClellan's candidacy, including the Democratic platform that called for giving in to the South's demands and ending the war. As might be anticipated in view of the emotionalism of the time, Pierce's views brought charges that he was a Confederate sympathizer. "An anonymous letter accusing him of belonging to the Knights of the Golden Circle—a mostly legendary secret, pro-Confederate organization—came to him from Secretary of State Seward who asked for an explanation." The accusation hurt the former president and he vigorously denied the charges. His contribution of money to provide aid to ill and injured Union soldiers helped little.[21]

Pierce, along with most Americans including many in the South, was shaken by President Lincoln's assassination, but did not display a flag in mourning. When citizens gathered at his home to ask why not, he said merely that "he did not need to display a flag to demonstrate his loyalty, for his whole public life did that."[22]

In the remaining years of his life, he did little but drink. There was not much that he needed to do, "because he was largely ignored and forgotten."[23] Pierce's health had declined for years. He died of a stomach ailment on October 8, 1869. President Grant proclaimed a day of nationwide mourning. After his burial, historian Larry Gara wrote, Franklin Pierce's name was seldom recalled in New Hampshire or beyond."[24] Pierce's presidency had given Americans little or no reason to remember him fondly. His post-presidential career gave them no further reason to do so.

JAMES BUCHANAN

When James Buchanan rode in a carriage with Abraham Lincoln to the new president's inauguration, he was 69 years old and tired. The outgoing president made a poignant comment that writers repeat time and again. "My dear sir," he said, "if you are as happy in entering the White House as I shall feel on returning to Wheatland, you are a happy man indeed."[25]

Buchanan happily retired to Wheatland, his sprawling Pennsylvania home, and he became a trustee of Franklin and Marshall College. Like his predecessor, Pierce, he was convinced that he had done well in office. Also like Pierce, he left the country in worse shape than it had been before he assumed the presidency. Whether anyone could have helped by the time he became president is doubtful, but Buchanan's consistent bias in favor of the South's efforts to expand slavery made him especially unsuited for the position. Ironically, anyone who picks up any commentary about Buchanan is likely to find a statement that never has a beginning president been so well-prepared—at least on paper—by background and experience but been so discredited by the time he left office.

Shortly before he left office, Buchanan's belated attempts at compromise caused his Southern friends one by one to shun him as a traitor. His opponents outside the South also accused him of treason, and charged him with conspiring to aid the secessionists. Attacks upon him ranged from the serious to the petty. Death threats led fellow Masons to stand guard at Wheatland for his protection.[26] At the other extreme, the pettiness of his foes was astonishing. "Congress abolished the franking privilege of ex-presidents to prevent the free mailing of any pamphlet or letter he might write."[27]

For years, Buchanan attempted to counter the charges and he continued to follow the developments closely. He had been dismayed at the attack on Fort Sumter. At the time, he wrote to his nephew, "the Confederates have deliberately commenced the civil war, & God knows where it may end."[28] From that time on, he "outspokenly supported the war effort." He argued that the Lincoln administration had no choice but to pursue military action. He also supported the draft and contributed funds to the war effort.[29]

Buchanan's effort to vindicate his administration resulted in the publication of his memoirs. They appeared in 1866 under the title, *Mr. Buchanan's Administration on the Eve of the Rebellion*. The work is defensive and unconvincing—he accepted no blame, and continued to believe that abolitionists had caused it all. His reputation as a president remains tarnished and is unlikely to change. Nevertheless, he did produce a valuable record of the period that may have influenced some subsequent presidents to do the same. Moreover, in his post-presidential career he avoided much of the bitterness and extremism that the other "doughface" presidents, his two predecessors Fillmore and Pierce, displayed.

He was the first president to present his detailed and systematic explanation of his administration. Former President Martin Van Buren had set out to do so, but his memoirs remained uncompleted. Buchanan died at home of heart failure and pneumonia on June 1, 1868. He was buried near Lancaster, Pennsylvania, and was 78 years old.

Buchanan was the only American president who never married. Harriet Lane, his niece, served throughout his term as his official hostess. Although historians and popular writers at times have speculated that he was homosexual, no scandal arose during his life—and such an allegation would, at the time, have been especially scandalous. In any case, according to an early biographer he had once been engaged, and was greatly distressed when the engagement ended and when, shortly thereafter, his former fiancé died.[30]

Eight

RECONSTRUCTION PRESIDENTS

The Aftermath of War

ABRAHAM LINCOLN WAS OF COURSE THE FIRST PRESIDENT WHO COULD BE CALLED a "Reconstruction President." His mortal wounding, on Good Friday, April 14, 1865, at the hands of a crazed assassin, and his tragic death at 7:22 the next morning shocked the country into an outpouring of grief. Legends sprang up immediately and continued for years. One was that jewelers set the clock hands on their painted signs at 7:22 in Lincoln's memory. Another, even less plausible, was that the brown thrush refused to sing for a year. The killer, a Southerner named John Wilkes Booth, was obsessed with Lincoln, and driven to fury over the idea that the president would move to provide equality for the newly freed black citizens. He saw to it that it would not happen—Lincoln would not direct reconstruction of the South.

When the Republican National Convention had renominated Lincoln as its candidate for president in 1864, it turned away from the staunch anti-slavery Republican from Maine, Vice President Hannibal Hamlin. Rather than re-nominating Hamlin, the convention decided upon a Union ticket. No doubt it seemed to be a good idea at the time, but in retrospect, it could hardly have been worse.

The convention in its wisdom chose Andrew Johnson to replace Hamlin as Lincoln's vice-presidential running mate. Johnson was a Southerner from Tennessee who had opposed secession and remained loyal to the Union. Lincoln had appointed him Military Governor of Tennessee during the war, a post that brought him the rank of brigadier general. Johnson, a courageous man who was quite skilled in the rough and tumble backwoods politics of mid-nineteenth-century Tennessee, had been vice president for fewer than six weeks when suddenly he became president of the United States.

His presidency at first seemed as though it would be successful, but things quickly fell apart. The blunt, rough, tactics of Tennessee politics did not prepare him to meet the country's needs following the Civil War. His rigid ideology hampered him as well. Johnson was an old Jacksonian Democrat, who shared the Jacksonian commitment to Union, but also to states' rights; he shared the commitment to an activist presidency but also held to the Jacksonians' view of a severely limited federal government; and he shared the praiseworthy commitment to the "common man" of the South in preference to the hated wealthy former slaveholders. The decided downside was that he also maintained a burning commitment to keep the South a "white man's country."

It was a recipe for disaster and disaster came. Johnson was arrogant in his dealings with Congress, adopting a policy of belligerence rather than compromise. He turned his back on the Republican Party and refused to encourage its development in the South. For generations to come no two-party system existed in that region, leaving little chance for Johnson's immediate successors to effect true reconstruction there. His states' rights views caused him to permit the defeated South to reengage its old Confederate leadership. His racism caused him to ignore it when they created the Ku Klux Klan and other terrorist guerilla armies to intimidate the region's black citizens as well as any would-be allies that they might have there. He believed that the South needed no "reconstruction," and his presidency ensured that it would not have one in any enduring sense.

Andrew Johnson held the views of the Jacksonians three decades before, but he had none of Andrew Jackson's ability to change with the times, and none of Jackson's political awareness. Had he held office during earlier days with their different issues, he might have been hailed as a success. Unfortunately for him and even more so for the country, he held office when the country needed not only a skillful and subtle approach—which he lacked—but a depth of understanding that was far beyond him.

Johnson had challenged Congress with intemperate and public language, and was directly defiant. In violation of the Tenure-of-Office Act (later to be repealed) he fired Secretary of War Edwin Stanton without the Senate's approval. The House impeached him and the Senate lacked only one vote of the two-thirds required to remove him from office. He had hoped, as his administration fell apart, that despite his impeachment and near removal, he could put together a coalition of different groups that might be strong enough to return him to the presidency. Failing that, he anticipated that the Democrats might turn to him as their candidate in 1868. Neither happened. Instead, the Democrats nominated a New Yorker, Horatio Seymour, who fell victim to the popular war hero, General Ulysses S. Grant.

Johnson, the accidental president, then embarked upon his post-presidential years. Far from settling in to a quiescent old age, which was not his style, he remained vigorously active. However implausible it may seem, after the White House he accomplished something unique and actually did achieve a true mark of distinction.

ANDREW JOHNSON

General Grant had become his bitter enemy when Johnson, as president, had attempted to undermine him. He tried, for example, to remove the popular general from the scene by sending him on a diplomatic mission to Mexico and giving control of the army to General William T. Sherman, but both Grant and Sherman refused.[1] The outgoing president was anything but happy that the hailed general was to be his successor. There are varied stories today as to what happened when President-Elect Grant proceeded to his inauguration on March 4, 1869, but one thing is certain. For whatever reason, Johnson did not attend. Along with John Adams and John Quincy Adams, he became the third living president in American history—and thus far the last one—who, at the end of his term, did not attend the inauguration of his successor.

Instead of attending the inauguration, he set out to return home to Greeneville, Tennessee. In the course of his journey, first in Baltimore and then in numerous other cities, he stopped for banquets and welcoming ceremonies. Crowds hailed him along the way. He must have been gratified upon arriving to see a huge banner in Greeneville proclaiming him a patriot. When he was military governor of Tennessee, his hometown had flown another banner entirely, calling him a traitor.

Although he had told audiences that he had retired from politics, the old warhorse could not keep away. He immediately set about speaking and working for candidates. Before the year was up, in sharp contrast to most former presidents, he even tried again for public office. He sought election to the U.S. Senate. After an intensive speaking campaign around the state in which he blasted both Jefferson Davis and President Grant, the Tennessee legislature in October 1869, settled on Judge Henry Cooper as the state's new senator (there was no popular vote for U.S. senators until the Seventeenth Amendment, ratified in 1913, provided that the voters, rather than legislatures, would choose them). It was the first time Johnson had lost an election since 1837.[2] He had served in both houses of the Tennessee legislature, as governor of Tennessee, and in both houses of Congress.

In 1872 he conducted another statewide campaign, that time for election to an at-large position to the U.S. House of Representatives (one chosen by the entire state rather than by a district). As he had anticipated, it was not possible to win. With the state's power structure in opposition, he came in third. His vigorous and courageous campaigning, however, had impressed the voters and laid groundwork for another race.[3]

Along with many of his supporters, he had assumed that the legislature that took its seat in 1873 would send him to the U.S. Senate. That year, however, proved to be a trying one for the former president, politically, physically, and financially. Politically, Senator Henry Cooper did not resign, as many of Johnson's supporters had expected that he would, and thus there was no open seat. Physically, Johnson fell victim to a raging cholera epidemic. He recovered, but had come close to death. Financially, he suffered great losses in the panic of 1873— one of the periodic depressions that have plagued America. He was far from bankrupt, as reports alleged—he was, after all, a highly skilled businessman— and still had considerable assets, but they had shrunk alarmingly.

He recovered from these various shocks and began intensive, and skillful, campaigning for a seat in the U.S. Senate. He appealed to varied groups, including former opponents. He courted former Whigs—whom he formerly had disdained—by eulogizing the recently deceased Millard Fillmore. He cultivated the members of the Patrons of Husbandry, or the National Grange, a new group involved in agrarian protest. He stressed his Jacksonian and Jeffersonian principles. Additionally, he promised to be independent, supporting both Democrats and Republicans as his principles permitted. He would never forget, he pledged—apparently ignoring his entire presidency—how much he owed to the Republican Party. After more than 50 ballots, the legislature named Johnson the new U.S. senator from Tennessee. When he received the news, he remarked, "well, well, well, I'd rather have this information than to learn that I had been elected President of the United States. Thank God for the vindication."[4]

Andrew Johnson had achieved something that no former president of the United States had ever accomplished, by winning election to the U.S. Senate. He took his seat in the short session beginning in March 1875. Only two former presidents have ever been elected to Congress—John Quincy Adams to the House of Representatives, and Andrew Johnson to the Senate. Adams had made his post-presidential years the most distinguished part of his distinguished career, and during them he made a substantial contribution. Johnson could claim no such distinction. His election to the Senate was a major achievement, but Johnson did little of note in his second political life. He did give a major speech in Congress, bitterly criticizing President Grant's reconstruction policy, and—by implication—defending his own administration's record. Newspapers across the country, depending upon their own partisan affiliation, praised his speech as courageous or condemned it as intemperate and unjustified. He still had his combative edge.

Senator and former President Andrew Johnson made only that one speech in the Senate. The session ended quickly, and Johnson returned that spring to Tennessee for a vacation. He was comfortable and felt that he had been vindicated.

That summer, he decided to travel to Ohio to defend his record in an election campaign underway there. On the way, he stopped at Carter's Station to visit his daughter, Mary, who had been ill. He had been active all day speaking with travelers on the train and ate a large dinner at Mary's farm. That evening he suffered a stroke. He appeared to recover, but had another stroke on July 30. He died at the age of 66 the following morning at 2:30.[5]

Senator Andrew Johnson, former president of the United States, was buried on August 3, 1875, just outside Greeneville, Tennessee. President Grant issued a proclamation "fulfilling his 'painful duty' to announce the death of the 'last survivor of his honored predecessors,'"[6] and officials draped government buildings in black. Dignitaries came from around the country to pay their respects.

Few doubted Johnson's honesty or integrity. Many doubted his principles— and even more have come to doubt them as the country moves away from its race-obsessed past. Johnson had worked toward a Jeffersonian vision of a country filled with small farms and without large disparities of income characterized by small enterprise, limited government, and a devotion to its workers—long after any possibility of such a Jeffersonian country had passed, if it had ever existed. And, he worked to achieve a Johnsonian vision of white supremacy everywhere—when, belatedly, the notion at last had started to come under question. It is true that in this case he had some success—tragic success. Andrew Johnson had great political skills, but they were sufficient only to achieve and to transmit as his legacy the most destructive of his principles.

ULYSSES S. GRANT

The eighteenth president of the United States, the great Civil War general, stepped out of the executive mansion and into retirement on the March 4, 1877. His administration had been a tumultuous one, but the people of his day tended to understand his presidency better than many of those who looked back upon it from the twentieth century. He was popular and there was a movement seeking to renominate him for a third term, but on May 29, 1875, long before the convention, he sent a letter to *The New York Times* declining to run. *The Times* ran his letter the next day.[7] Despite this, most summaries of Grant's presidency say that he sought a third term, but that the Republicans refused to nominate him.

The tendency has been—similarly, against massive evidence—to write of Grant as a "passive" president, as being politically naïve, and as heading a corrupt administration. Later commentaries marvel at how Grant, who had been so decisive in wartime, had been so incompetent, so innocent, and so ineffective as president. If this had been so, it would indeed have been startling—but this "conventional wisdom" that developed after the fact does not hold up to close scrutiny. Recent historians have begun to recognize this, and have set about restoring Grant's image.

Grant's record alone is enough to invalidate the charge of passivity. He used the veto with great effectiveness and restored it as a powerful executive tool. Andrew Jackson is known as the president who gave life to the veto by using it effectively to influence policy. His opponents bitterly called him "King Andrew," and charged him with executive usurpation. All in all, he cast a mere 12 vetoes. Andrew Johnson had infuriated Congress with his use of the veto, casting a total of 29, of which Congress overrode more than half, fifteen.

Compare this to the "passive" Grant. He cast more vetoes than all his 17 predecessors combined, a total of 93, and he prevailed on all but a mere four. Consider in addition a few selective examples of his actions. Grant used executive power forcefully against the Ku Klux Klan—a terrorist guerilla army that spread violence throughout the South. In the Treaty of Washington that settled claims against Britain for damages to American shipping during the Civil War, he established the principle of arbitration in international disputes and set the United States permanently upon a course of friendly relations with Great Britain. He enforced civil rights for the former slaves and he used executive power swiftly and effectively to break the "gold corner" of robber barons Jim Fisk and Jay Gould. Grant perhaps can be faulted for having associated with them socially, but when he discovered that they had misrepresented their association with him to enhance their strength on Wall Street and were buying up gold to force up the price to unreasonable levels for their own benefit, he flooded the market with massive sales of government gold to drive the price back down and destroy the plot.

Additionally, he appointed the first Indian (Brig. Gen. Ely S. Parker) to be commissioner of Indian Affairs, and adopted policies toward Native Americans that were enormously progressive for the day; moreover, he directed that, for the first time, Indians be dealt with as individuals, not merely as tribes. This was a first step toward providing native peoples with American citizenship. He averted widespread war against the Plains Indians. To be sure, there were military atrocities against tribes during his administration, but these were in violation of his policy. Perhaps most important, and most neglected of all, Grant worked diligently and successfully to secure ratification of the Fifteenth Amendment, which barred race as a criterion for voting.

Most Northerners had been opposed to slavery's spread, but concurred with most Southerners' commitment to white supremacy and with their opposition to political equality for blacks. The leadership that Grant demonstrated in convincing three-fourths of the states to ratify an amendment requiring every state in the Union to recognize black citizenship was nothing short of remarkable. Grant himself proudly issued a proclamation asserting that the Fifteenth Amendment had overturned the infamous *Dred Scott* decision that had denied citizenship to any person of African descent.

Grant certainly made mistakes. He was not a perfect president—it is unnecessary even to debate whether he was a great president. There were severe limits to what he or anyone else could accomplish, especially at that time. Although he remained popular, his policies faced opposition from Democrats, from the Court, from the public, and from major segments of his own party— for example, from "reformers"—such as Senators Charles Sumner and Carl Schurz, or editors E. L. Godkin and Horace Greeley—who wanted "clean politics," but who rejected civil rights legislation and other efforts on behalf of the South's black citizens.

Under the circumstances, what he did manage to accomplish was impressive. The record demonstrates that Grant was far from a passive chief executive or a political innocent. But was he not corrupt? There was corruption in his administration, but none that touched him personally. Nor did scandals "engulf the Grant administration," as critics are so fond of saying.[8] The Crédit Mobilier episode in which members of Congress had been bribed to support legislation favoring the Union Pacific Railroad, although breaking during Grant's time in office, actually took place under Johnson. Others reached into his own cabinet. This was deplorable, but in no way was it unique to the Grant administration.

Perhaps it is fair to criticize Grant for being too public in his defense of his own personal secretary, Orville Babcock. Babcock was acquitted of charges that he had conspired with distillers to defraud the government of tax money in the "Whisky Ring" scandals—but in fact there was little evidence against him.[9] Grant did not use his pardon authority to shield government officials who had been guilty of misconduct. This actually happened under later presidents, and occasioned less criticism than has been directed at Grant.

There is an explanation for the harsh view of Grant's presidency and it has nothing to do with passivity or incompetence—quite the contrary. Prior to the Civil War, Southern leaders knew very well that slavery was the cause of the controversy. During the war, the common soldier no doubt was fighting to preserve his home, but the South's leaders had brought on the war quite clearly to expand their "peculiar institution."

When Robert E. Lee died in 1870, however, a group of former Confederates—including Jubal Early, William Nelson Pendleton, and the Rev. John William Jones—set about consciously to create a pro-Southern myth of the Civil War, the "Lost Cause" interpretation. Early and his followers, mainly Virginians, came to control the Southern Historical Association. They set about refashioning history, and—amazingly—managed to spread their doctrines throughout the country.[10] Their influence grew to be extraordinary.

A flawless and saintly Robert E. Lee became the nucleus of their mythmaking. Slavery? It was regrettable, of course, but was a mere trifle that the South would have eliminated on its own. Constitutional and economic issues were at the heart of the dispute. The war certainly was not about slavery; it was about Northern aggression, about Yankee hostility to the "Southern Way of Life" that had become "the most glorious in the history of the world."[11] This interpretation simply ignored many awkward facts, but it nevertheless was the prevailing opinion among American historians for the first half of the twentieth century.

It was impossible to overlook all facts, though; one was too obvious and too awkward to let lie. If Lee were the perfect general, how could it have been that Ulysses S. Grant defeated him? The answer was simple. Not even the noble Lee, the flawless tactician who conducted himself always with honor, could succeed against overwhelming forces commanded by a butcher who knew no civilized restraint—a savage who then became (rather inconsistently) the most incompetent of presidents.

After half a century of dominance, the notion that slavery had little or no role in causing the Civil War eventually retreated in the face of massive evidence.

Even now, the Lost Cause argument continues to influence countless class-rooms, but historians generally have dispelled it, having restored slavery to its central place as the cause of the war. Not until the twentieth century drew to a close, however, did a resuscitation of Grant's reputation of take place.

The popular press has even taken note of the reconsideration. A *New York Times* article in 2000 cited numerous historians—Gary Gallagher, Lloyd Hunter, Brooks Simpson, Jean Edward Smith, Jeffrey Wert, Joan Waugh—who had asked just how much was it reasonable to have expected Grant to accomplish? The article quoted Waugh, who pointed out that "with the rise of Robert E. Lee and the 'Lost Cause' came the diminution of the Union cause." The North won, but the South for quite some time had, in modern terms, "spun" the interpretation of the war, turning consideration away from slavery, racism, and the South's "shattering defeat."[12]

Grant's contemporaries were too familiar with the facts to have been influenced by revisionist arguments. Grant left the presidency amid acclaim at home and abroad. Travel had always fascinated him, and it was thus first on his agenda. Even as president he had traveled considerably, which for the time was most unusual.

The Grants left the executive mansion and after a few days journeyed to Georgetown, Ohio, where he had spent his boyhood. Then they proceeded to his farm in Missouri near St. Louis, then on to Galena, Illinois, where he had worked as a clerk in his father's tannery, and finally to Philadelphia. Already they had traveled a good deal, but more was to come—much more. He and Julia proceeded on to Europe, and as biographer Jean Edward Smith wrote, "for two and a half years Grant circumnavigated the globe. He left Philadelphia May 17, 1877, heading east. He returned to his starting point, still heading east, December 16, 1879."[13]

Lawyer and Grant scholar Frank Scaturro has described the reception that the Grants received on their world tour. World leaders consulted him, Scaturro said, and he was hailed in countries throughout Europe, Africa, and Asia. The treatment accorded the Grants reflected the "unprecedented respect the U.S. had recently acquired throughout the world," and was in marked contrast to the receptions accorded former Presidents Van Buren and Fillmore.[14]

In addition to friends and relatives, the Grants took with them a reporter for the *New York Herald,* John Russell Young. The *Herald* was "the most popular newspaper in the country and Grant, in office or out, was front-page copy."[15] In England, he and Julia were houseguests of Queen Victoria at Windsor Castle. He spent days in France with Marshal MacMahon, President of the Third Republic. In Italy, he dined with King Umberto, and met with Pope Leo XIII.

In Russia, Tsar Alexander and he discussed the future of the Plains Indians. He met Germany's "Iron Chancellor" Otto von Bismarck, and the two became fast friends. The informal Grant simply walked to the meeting with Bismarck. "It was all very un-European," no salutes or great ceremony, "but for iconoclastic Berliners, Grant was the hero of the hour."[16]

The conversation with Bismarck was especially significant. The chancellor remarked that it was sad that Grant, as a general, had had to fight his own people. Grant replied that it had to be done. Bismarck agreed that yes, it had been necessary to save the Union. Grant responded that war had been necessary not only to save the Union, but to "destroy slavery." Bismarck persisted, saying that he assumed that the dominant sentiment was to save the Union. "In the beginning, yes" Grant said. "But as soon as slavery fired upon the flag it was felt, we all felt, even those who did not object to slaves, that slavery must be destroyed. We felt that it was a stain on the Union that men should be bought and sold like cattle."

Bismarck proceeded to speculate that it would have been a shorter war if the United States had had a standing army. Grant answered that there might have been no war at all. He thought the army might have gone with the South. "In fact," he said, "Southern feeling in the army among high officers was so strong that when the war broke out the army dissolved. We had no army. Then we had to organize one." It was providential, he thought, that the war had taken so long, because a brief war might have left slavery intact. Continued slavery would have been the "germs of a new rebellion. There had to be an end to slavery. Then we were fighting an enemy with whom we could not make a peace. We had to destroy him. No convention, no treaty, was possible—only destruction."[17]

From Germany, the Grants traveled extensively throughout the Continent, and then on to Turkey. The Sultan gave Grant—an expert horseman—two Arabian stallions. Grant shipped them to the United States, where they became "the foundation sires for the Arabian breed in North America."[18]

His most pleasant visit was in Japan. He was impressed with their extraordinary culture, and was convinced that China, also, ultimately would rise. In Japan, he remarked, a foreigner was treated with much more consideration than in the West. He noted the "heartlessness of nations," and predicted that "the day of retribution is sure to come." He also performed a valuable feat of diplomacy while in the Orient, negotiating peace between China and Japan with regard to a dispute over the Ryukyu Islands. His telling point was that war would benefit only the West.[19]

When the Grants returned to the United States, the publicity that surrounded them led to a "Grant in 1880" boom. Quickly, Republican Party stalwarts took control of the movement. At the convention, Grant for a time led in the balloting, but his supporters blundered, and their attempts to "steamroll the opposition," led to Grant's ultimate defeat.[20] Even here, commentators can manage to blame Grant. Ari Hoogenboom, for example, wrote that Grant's supporters had been unable to attract enough allies, partly because of "Grant's record as president." He contradicted himself, however, on the very next page by quoting President Hayes approvingly that Grant's defeat was the result of the "unpopularity of his managers."[21]

Julia urged Grant to go before the convention personally, taking it for granted that his presence would stampede the delegates to his banner. He refused, saying that he would rather cut off his right arm. She persisted, asking did he not want the nomination? He replied that he would rather be nominated, but because he considered it improper to do so, he would do nothing to further his cause.[22] On the thirty-sixth ballot, the convention finally produced a majority for a dark horse candidate, James A. Garfield. Grant immediately pledged Garfield his support.

Grant returned to his home in Illinois. Not for some three-quarters of a century would America's government see fit to award its former presidents with a pension, but he managed to live comfortably because of gifts from wealthy admirers, who provided him with a lavish house and a trust fund. For a brief period, he became president of the Mexican Southern Railroad that was to be built in Mexico and Central America with financing from American investors and a charter from New York State. Grant's responsibilities involved negotiating with the Mexican government, which he accomplished, but the line never materialized.

His biographers have remarked that he did not adapt well to inactivity. He pressed advice on Garfield, and then on President Arthur after Garfield's assassination, but had little influence. For a time, Grant seemed to prosper when he tried his hand at investment banking, putting his money into a restructured firm, Grant and Ward. Some accounts mislead here as well. The "Grant" in the firm's name was his son's, and the partnership had existed before he invested in it, but some accounts describe him as "lending his name" to the firm. In any case, Ferdinand Ward, the managing partner, while keeping the others— including the trusting Grant—completely in the dark, was draining all the firm's assets and maintaining a fraudulent set of books. Grant had never been a good businessman, and had always been careless of his own financial affairs. He suddenly found himself destitute.

The great impresario, P. T. Barnum, at this time offered the former president a huge sum, $100,000, for his Civil War memorabilia. Despite his great need,

Grant turned down the offer as unbefitting for a former president. Earlier, he had been uninterested in an offer by an editor at *Century* magazine, Robert Johnson, to commission some articles on the Civil War. Grant asked Johnson if he were still interested, and received a contract to produce four articles at $500 each. After an abortive first attempt, Johnson recommended that Grant set forth his personal observations, and was stunned by the result. Grant was a natural writer. His prose was clear, concise, and gripping. The articles were a huge success.

Johnson then offered Grant a contract to write his memoirs of the war. It provided for a standard 10 percent royalty, with no guarantee, and no advance. Briefly, Grant's luck changed for the better. Samuel Clemens—Mark Twain, an old friend—had heard of Grant's memoirs and dropped by to discuss his publication plans. When he heard of the offer from the *Century,* Twain was appalled. It was what a firm would offer a complete unknown, he said. Twain had his own publishing house, and offered Grant another contract, either twenty percent of sales, or seventy percent of profits—plus an advance of $100,000, a small fortune at the time.

Twain actually had to persuade Grant to accept, because the former president felt obligated to the magazine. He also recommended that Grant choose the twenty percent of sales option, but Grant chose seventy percent of royalties instead. He said he did not want to earn money if the book made no profit.[23] Another stroke of good fortune brought legislation from Congress restoring his rank and salary as general of the army (he had resigned his commission to accept the presidency). Outgoing President Arthur—as his last official act on his last day in office, and in his last few minutes as president—on March 4, 1885, signed the enabling legislation; as his first official act, President Grover Cleveland signed Grant's commission.[24]

Grant's good fortune was not to last. His health was failing, and he was diagnosed with cancer of the esophagus. Years of smoking strong cigars finally succeeded in burning away the life of the tough old general. He was dying.

Terrified of leaving Julia destitute, Grant threw himself into his work. He steadily turned out page after page as his pain increased. He could no longer talk, and could barely swallow—and then only with unbearable pain. Still, he wrote, his iron will holding death at bay until he was ready to accept it. In some ten months, often through the haze of medication, he had written some 275,000 words, all by hand in those days before word processors or even effective typewriters. With mere days left in his life, he had managed his last act of heroism. He had completed his manuscript.

It not only earned his widow a fortune—$450,000, record royalties at the time—but Grant had produced a literary masterpiece. His *Memoirs* were largely his story of the Civil War. As a former president, he had made a last, immortal, contribution to the United States, and to the literature of the world. Critics as diverse as Edmund Wilson and Gertrude Stein were effusive in their praise. Wilson compared Grant's *Memoirs* to Thoreau's *Walden* or to Whitman's *Leaves of Grass*. Stein said it was one of the finest books that an American had ever written. Twain said it was the "most remarkable book of its kind since the *Commentaries of Julius Caesar.*"[25]

On the morning of July 23, 1885, General Ulysses S. Grant, former president of the United States, died. He was only 63. Julia lived for another seventeen years, during which time she wrote her *Memoirs*[26] (not published during her lifetime) and worked for women's suffrage. She died at the age of 76 on December 14, 1902. The Grants are entombed in the Grant Monument ("Grant's Tomb"), in Riverside Park, in New York City.

RUTHERFORD B. HAYES

The final Reconstruction president, Rutherford B. Hayes, brought reconstruction to an end by withdrawing federal occupation troops from the South. He had firmly believed that the "better elements" there would prevail, and that if freed from federal interference they would ensure civil rights and political equality for the newly freed slaves. He was badly mistaken and ultimately had to concede his error. Nevertheless, Hayes was confident that his administration had restored unity to the Union and that he had been a success. His biographer Ari Hoogenboom wrote that he had been "both a good man and an able president."[27] Certainly he was a good man; all things considered, many reasonable people might agree that he had been a good president as well.

After attending the inauguration of his successor, James A. Garfield, on March 4, 1881, Hayes and his wife Lucy—"Lemonade Lucy," as she had been called while First Lady because of her prohibition of alcohol in the White House—retired happily to their estate, Spiegel Grove in Fremont, Ohio. Enroute, the train in which they were riding collided with another. The Hayeses were unhurt and did what they could to assist the wounded.

Rumors circulated that Hayes had saved a considerable sum as president. He denied it, but fortunately the Hayeses had income from investments in real estate that enabled them to live comfortably.

Spiegel Grove had been enlarged from a simple house to an impressive brick mansion almost twice its original size. The new rooms included a library decorated with portraits of the presidents of the United States, a state dining room, a curio room to house the presidential mementos (called "the Smith-sonian" by the family), and twenty guest rooms. The house was set in a twenty-five-acre park that boasted a miniature ravine and two small lakes.[28]

In retirement, the Hayeses occupied themselves with numerous civic and re-form activities. Hayes served on several foundation boards, especially those that re-flected his concern for education, and was on the governing boards of Western Reserve University, Ohio State University, and Ohio Wesleyan.[29] He also accepted memberships and was highly active on the boards of the Slater Fund and the Peabody Foundation, "both devoted to education, the Slater Fund particularly to education for freedmen in the South."[30] He was especially interested in education for the black population both inside and outside the South. Among the black youth whom Hayes aided through the fund was W. E. B. DuBois,[31] who went on to a distinguished career in literature and political activism, helping to found the National Association for the Advancement of Colored People in 1909.

Hayes retained a lifelong interest in politics. Nevertheless, just as he had re-fused to consider a second term in 1880, he refused to run for any other office, even though party officials urged him several times to do so.[32] He kept in close touch with President Garfield and was stunned at the president's assassination only six months into his term. Garfield's assailant, Charles Guiteau, usually is described as a "disappointed office seeker." Whatever the motive, Guiteau clearly was unbalanced. The immediate effect, though, was to encourage civil service reform. In 1883, Hayes complimented Supreme Court Justice John Mar-shall Harlan, his appointee, for Harlan's vigorous dissent when the Court over-turned the Civil Rights Act and denied that the federal government had the power to protect citizens from state action.[33]

In addition to education, one of Hayes's major interests was prison reform. In 1883 he became president of the National Prison Association, devoted to achieving humane prison conditions and programs of rehabilitation for inmates. He remained an active president of the association for the rest of his life.

A Hayes biographer notes that, "In all of these activities, Lucy Hayes staunchly supported her husband. Indeed, whether the issue was abolition or tem-perance, she was more ardently committed to reform" even than he was.[34] Few for-mer occupants of the White House have contributed so much to worthy causes.

Hayes was devastated when, in June 1889, Lucy suffered a stroke and died a few days later, on the twenty-fifth of that month. After her death, he continued his reform activities, but the zest had gone from his life. On January 17, 1893, he died from a heart attack. The remains of Rutherford and Lucy Hayes rest in Spiegel Grove, which now houses the Rutherford B. Hayes Presidential Center.

Nine

PRESIDENTS OF
THE "GILDED AGE"

THE TIME AFTER LINCOLN'S CIVIL WAR PRESIDENCY UNTIL THE END OF THE nineteenth century, historians tell us, was a time of congressional supremacy. Although generally correct, this analysis ignores the efforts that numerous presidents during those years made to recapture power for the executive, and the successes that some had on this score. Historians in general have hailed no president from that period, tending to treat them as a series of men with beards who are more or less interchangeable—or at least highly forgettable. Only specialists would know that James A. Garfield in his brief time in office would win patronage battles with the Senate, remember that Chester A. Arthur signed legislation establishing a merit-based civil service, that Grover Cleveland approved the creation of the Interstate Commerce Commission, or that Benjamin Harrison signed into law the Sherman Anti-Trust Act. Neither, as one would expect given these circumstances, have writers as a rule noted the often significant accomplishments of some of these men in their post-presidential years.

Almost no one knows of the commitment that led Rutherford and Lucy Hayes to give so fully of themselves to causes in which they believed, that Benjamin Harrison remained prominent in international law, or that Grover Cleveland was active in higher education. As the century drew to a close these former presidents contributed substantially, if usually not dramatically, to their country and to the world after they left their presidencies.

CHESTER ALAN ARTHUR

Chester Arthur was not among those who contributed significantly in his post-presidential career, but this was through no fault of his own. In 1882, he discovered that he had Bright's disease. This severe kidney ailment is fatal if untreated, and in Arthur's day, there was no treatment. Observers during his presidency commented on his lethargic nature. Yet it may have been his disease rather than his nature that slowed his actions.

Arthur had not thought that he ever would be president. He had never held elective office when party stalwarts (from his branch of the party that favored the "spoils," or patronage, system) approached him during the Republican National Convention in 1880 to suggest that he might be James A. Garfield's running mate. Arthur's mentor, former U.S. senator from New York, Roscoe Conkling, urged him to reject the overtures. Garfield, he said, could not win. Yet it was Conkling who could not win. His days as a power broker were behind him. Arthur told Conkling, the ringleader of the Republican stalwarts, that he could not reject the nomination. He said that he had never dreamed of attaining so great an honor.[1] Garfield won and Arthur became vice president of the United States.

Reformers were aghast at Garfield's assassination. Arthur had been part of the Republican machine in New York and a notorious henchman of Conkling's. President Hayes had removed Arthur as Collector of the Port of New York in order to strike at "boss politics." They had not been especially concerned when he became vice president, because they assumed that he would have little or no influence on policy and appointments. Suddenly, after barely more than six months, President Garfield had died of a wound inflicted by an assassin's bullet, and Chester Arthur had become president of the United States.

To everyone's surprise, Arthur no longer catered to his former associates. He would socialize with them, but they found that he would give them no favors. One machine politician remarked that Arthur did less for them than Garfield, or even Hayes. Another explained what had happened: "He isn't 'Chet' Arthur anymore," he complained, "he's the President."[2] Worse, from their point of view, he came out as a strong advocate of civil service reform and signed into the law the Pendleton Act of 1883 that established the basis for today's merit-based civil service. The classic days of the spoils system were on their way out.

Because he had so alienated the machine politicians, he found that they had no intention of permitting his renomination. They did, oddly, offer him the position of U.S. senator from New York, but he refused. Thus he left office at the end of his term, on March 4, 1885, after attending the inauguration of the in-coming president, Grover Cleveland.

Arthur returned to New York and the practice of law. He also became pres-ident of the New York Arcade Railroad Co., but his health had declined so abruptly that he was able to do little. The last few months of his life were spent largely in bed. In a blow to historical understanding, Arthur had seen to it that all his personal papers were destroyed.

His last public appearance was in December 1885, when he attended a cer-emony honoring a New York judge, Charles Daly, who was retiring. Less than a year later, November 16, 1886, he had a severe stroke at his home in New York City. Two days later, on November 18, he died. His funeral took place four days later. Among his pallbearers were General Phil Sheridan, and "Commodore" Cornelius Vanderbilt, the railroad tycoon.

He was buried in Albany, beside his wife, who had died of pneumonia be-fore he became vice president.

GROVER CLEVELAND

After one term as president, Grover Cleveland went down to defeat, losing in the election of 1888 to Republican Benjamin Harrison. Cleveland, like Al Gore, had won the popular vote, but Harrison had won in the electoral college. Un-like the situation in 2000, Harrison had a clear majority of electoral votes, re-quiring no Supreme Court decision to stop vote counting, or to declare him the winner.

Cleveland had been a capable, conservative, Democratic president—the first Democrat to hold the office since the Civil War. He also had been the only bachelor president, excepting James Buchanan. Buchanan had remained a bach-elor through his term, but not Cleveland. To great popular acclaim, the 49-year-old president married in the executive mansion. His new bride, Frances ("Frank") Folsom, was 21. In spite of her youth and the difference in their ages, she quickly became an enormous asset to the president, and handled the duties of First Lady with great tact, charm, and skill.

The outgoing president greeted the incoming president cordially. They rode together to the inauguration. Once there, as President Harrison gave his inau-gural address, former President Cleveland graciously stood by him, and gallantly held an umbrella to shield his successor from the heavy rain.

On their way out of the White House, Frances Cleveland pulled a favorite servant aside. "I want you to take good care of all the furniture and ornaments in the house," she said. "For I want to find everything just as it is now when we come back again." In response to what must have been an inquiring look, she said "we are coming back, just four years from today."[3]

The Clevelands retired to New York City, where he practiced law. According to Louis Koenig, Cleveland became for first former president to argue a case before the United States Supreme Court.[4] Koenig, however, was wrong; he overlooked former president John Quincy Adams and the *Amistad* case.

To their great joy, the Clevelands had the first of their five children, Ruth, in 1891. She became "Baby Ruth" to an admiring public, although sadly she died of diphtheria in 1904 when she was 12. She lives, indirectly, in the public memory, since the Curtiss Company named its new candy bar in her honor in 1921. "Baby Ruth" is still popular today.[5]

Cleveland amused himself by fishing in his limited spare time, but found himself drawn back into politics. When the Democratic National Convention met in Chicago on June 21, 1892, on the first ballot it once again nominated Cleveland. He had no difficulty receiving the two-thirds vote that the Democrats required to choose their nominees until the convention of 1936. It was the only time a former president has been nominated again for president by a major party. When Cleveland won the 1892 election, he became the first and only former president in American history to be elected president again, and thus is the only president to serve two non-consecutive terms. His vice presidential running-mate was Adlai Stevenson, the grandfather of the 1952 and 1956 Democratic presidential candidate who lost both times to Dwight Eisenhower. Frances Cleveland had been right. The Clevelands returned to the executive mansion four years after leaving it—an accomplishment unique among former presidents.

After his second term, Cleveland was appalled when the Democrats nominated the populist William Jennings Bryan to replace him. He was pleased that conservative Republican William McKinley trounced Bryan, and considered it a vindication of his own conservative policies. He and McKinley met cordially at the inauguration.

When the Clevelands left Washington for the second time, they retired to Princeton, New Jersey. They purchased a mansion there, and named it "Westland," in honor of their friend Andrew West who had encouraged them to settle there. West was a professor of classics at Princeton and became dean of the Graduate School. Cleveland became active in the Princeton community and accepted an honorary doctorate in 1897.

The former president contributed to education by lecturing at Princeton and becoming a member, and then chairman, of the university's board of trustees. When Dean West had a bitter controversy with University President Woodrow Wilson over the location of the Graduate School, Cleveland aligned himself with West and against Wilson. Wilson was not one who forgave easily—if at all. Cleveland scholar Henry Graff notes, "The bad blood that this created between Cleveland and Wilson, over what can only be called a minor academic issue, marred the relationship between the only two Democratic presidents elected between the outbreak of the Civil War and the onset of the Great Depression—and the only two such figures to live so close to each other on the grounds of a leading university."[6]

Within universities, a common tendency is to invest even the most trivial matters with enormous importance. In this instance, a stubborn Cleveland encountered a rigid, self-righteous, and unyielding Wilson. Two such figures meeting anywhere are likely to strike sparks; in a university setting, they will inevitably set off an explosion of invective and emotion. Whether the result is tragic, amusing, or just plain silly is a matter of judgment—perhaps it is all three.

Cleveland kept busy and wrote for numerous magazines. He produced a book, *Presidential Problems,* in 1904, offering his views of the issues of his administration. For leisure activities, he continued to hunt and fish with friends, and played billiards and cards. Late in his life he joined the board of the troubled Equitable Life Assurance Association, seeking to reorganize the company around sound and fair business practices. Finally, he became head of the Association of Life Insurance Presidents. Always well-meaning, "he seemed to have become a well-paid front man for the insurance industry."[7]

The former president's health began to fail in early 1908. A heart attack felled him on June 26 of that year. Frances was at his side. He was buried in Princeton alongside his daughter, Ruth. Several years later, his widow Frances married a Princeton professor. She lived on into her 80s.

BENJAMIN HARRISON

Benjamin Harrison defeated Grover Cleveland for the presidency in 1888, even though Cleveland had more popular votes. In 1892, Cleveland returned, this time to become the winner, and turn Harrison out of the White House. Benjamin Harrison—five feet six inches tall, spellbinding orator, brusque and impatient with small talk, stiff, courageous, honorable, lawyer, civil war hero and brigadier general, president of the United States—once more was a private citizen. He was the final Civil War general to serve as president.

In 1892, Caroline Harrison, the wife of the president, became seriously ill. It turned out that she had contracted tuberculosis. On October 25, she died. Two day later, her body lay in the East Room of the executive mansion for her funeral. Shortly thereafter, Benjamin Harrison lost the presidency and retired to Indianapolis.

He had presided over modernization and expansion of the navy and had pursued a vigorous foreign policy developing international trade, sending Secretary of State James G. Blaine to participate in the first Pan-American Conference, establishing a protectorate over Samoa, and attempting unsuccessfully to annex Hawaii.[8] Despite his grief over Caroline's death, he remained active in politics and returned to the practice of law. He wrote numerous articles for magazines and in 1894 lectured on constitutional law at Stanford University.

In a surprising move, the former president astonished the country—and forever alienated his grown children. Despite his impatient nature, gruff demeanor, and colorless personality Harrison, on April 6, 1896, remarried. The new Mrs. Harrison was Mary Lord Dimmick, a widow, and the niece of the deceased Caroline Harrison.[9] In February 1896 they had a daughter, Elizabeth.

As the century drew to a close, Harrison represented Venezuela in its case against British Guiana over their disputed boundary. He devoted enormous time and energy to the case. Although Venezuela lost, his extensive written and oral arguments were extraordinarily precise and displayed deep understanding and comprehensive knowledge of the subject.

When his daughter Elizabeth was four, Harrison contracted pneumonia. He died on March 13, 1901, having lived to see the new century, and to see it begin with a Republican administration. His funeral took place in Indianapolis, and he was buried there next to his first wife, Caroline.

Ten

THEODORE ROOSEVELT

The Bull Moose

THEODORE ROOSEVELT BECAME PRESIDENT OF THE UNITED STATES AT THE AGE of 42, younger than any president before or since. He was the first president who, as vice president, had filled a presidential vacancy and then received the nomination to run for his own term. He had been the first president to win his own term after stepping in to complete the term of another (that now has happened four times; Coolidge, Truman, and LBJ did it as well), and his popular-vote percentage when he did so, in 1904, was the greatest that any president had achieved up to that time. He was the first president to be called, affectionately, by his initials, "TR."

Then, of course, following in his footsteps, came FDR, JFK, and LBJ. Few presidents have been known by their initials. Nixon did sign his memos and name his biography "RN," but it did not become common usage. A simple "W" (sometimes spelled out by his critics as "dubya") now and then denotes the second Bush.

TR was keenly aware of the importance of symbolism. He officially bestowed the name "White House" upon the executive mansion. More important, he revitalized the institution of the presidency.

He was the most vigorous president the United States has ever experienced and its most joyous—no one has taken more delight in the office than he did.

His post-presidential years also were the most active of any president, before or after, and they at least equaled any other president's in significance.

In short, he was a phenomenon. All presidencies have been unique, but Theodore Roosevelt's was such a different species that only those of George Washington, Abraham Lincoln, and his distant cousin Franklin D. Roosevelt can be considered its equal. The only others that even come close would be those of Andrew Jackson and Lyndon Johnson, although one might possibly make a case also for those of Woodrow Wilson and Thomas Jefferson. His all-too-brief years as a former president were also in a different class from those of any other.

Some former presidents have changed history. TR, both as president and former president, did so; he created, shaped, and molded much of what followed. He became a former president of the United States on March 4, 1909. Thereafter, by his own choice, he was to be "the Colonel," or "Colonel Roosevelt," rather than "Mr. President."

The new president, Roosevelt's friend William Howard Taft, had been his secretary of war. TR had chosen Taft as his successor and engineered his nomination. Although TR did have some misgivings about Taft's strength and his ability to handle the challenges that would face him, he was generally confident that he had left the presidency in good hands. Still, the old Bull Moose left the office with much regret.

No one familiar with the period can doubt that he could have been re-elected in 1908. He undoubtedly would have been—thus becoming America's first three-term president—had it not been for a rash promise he made at his electoral victory in 1904. Causing his wife, Edith, to "wince in surprise," he blurted out that he would not be a candidate for a third term.[1] When 1908 approached, there was enormous pressure from those urging him to renounce his pledge and run again. As much as he wished to do so—he had loved being president and remarked that he would give his right arm if he had not made the promise—he refused to go back on his word. But he told William Jennings Bryan that he would miss it all. Take no stock in it, he said to Bryan, when he would see the inevitable items in the press quoting him as welcoming the rest. It would all "be laid aside with a good deal of regret," he said, "for I have enjoyed every moment of this so-called arduous and exacting task."[2]

TR was adept in dealing with the press and was keenly aware of its ways, so he knew well that reporters—and the public—would be more interested in him than in his bland and rotund successor. To avoid interfering with Taft's presidency and to head off the automatic assumptions from the press that he would be dominating the amiable new incumbent, he set off for a year on an African safari.

TR and his son Kermit set sail on the March 23, shortly after Taft's inauguration. The financier J. P. Morgan was supposed to have offered a toast calling upon every African lion to do its duty.[3] TR was an avid hunter, but this time there also was an official purpose for his trip. He collected huge numbers of valuable scientific specimens for the Smithsonian Institution.

Although he attempted to divorce himself from Washington, even in Africa TR could suppress neither his interest in politics nor his political instincts. He had been masterful in dealing with both his party's Old Guard (the conservatives) and its Progressives, the "Insurgents," while leading it in a progressive direction. Taft, on the contrary, as one Roosevelt biographer notes, "did not have Roosevelt's catlike grace in working both sides of the political street without permanently crossing from one side to another. Nor did he have the explosive vitality that Roosevelt had used to keep mutually antagonistic factions subordinate to his leadership."[4] On safari TR periodically received packets of letters and newspapers from home, and these brought him unsettling news. At best, his handpicked successor was inept; worse, TR sensed in Taft betrayal of his Progressive principles.

Taft had replaced several of the Roosevelt cabinet, although he had led TR to believe that he would keep the cabinet intact. Also, because of a controversy between Secretary of the Interior Richard Ballinger and the head forester, TR's close friend Gifford Pinchot, Taft discharged Pinchot. Pinchot had been outraged at Ballinger's questionable sale of certain public lands in Alaska to private interests.

Another indication that all was not well with the progressive cause may be seen in Taft's tariff policy. Although Taft had favored lowering the tariff—a progressive measure—he did little to influence Congress when it was considering the new Payne-Aldrich measure. The result was a confused mix that actually raised many rates while it lowered others, yet Taft not only defended the new law, but praised it extravagantly. Roosevelt feared that the network of progressive—and aggressive—measures that he had used to recast government was unraveling.

The following February—1910—TR's wife Edith and their daughter Ethel set forth on a journey to Sudan to meet him and Kermit in Khartoum. The reunion found them all in excellent condition. The Roosevelts traveled in Egypt, and then proceeded to the Continent for an extensive European tour. Any thought of privacy for a lengthy reunion evaporated.

As TR biographer Kathleen Dalton noted, "TR's fame as a historian and scientific writer coupled with his presidency had brought him invitations to receive honorary degrees and give speeches at the University of Berlin, the Sorbonne,

Cambridge and Oxford, and to receive in person his Nobel Prize in Christiania"[5] (now Oslo). The Roosevelts' travels took them from one city and country to another throughout the Continent. Everywhere he was the center of attention, and everywhere he spoke of democracy.

In his Nobel acceptance speech on May 5, TR warned of militarism. He foreshadowed both the League of Nations and the UN by suggesting the formation of a League of Peace. In Germany, he mentioned arms limitation to a kaiser uninterested in the subject. In Britain, he served as official representative of the United States at the funeral of King Edward VII and delivered the Romanes Lecture at Oxford.[6] Oxford welcomed him enthusiastically, but seemed less interested in his topic, "Biological Analogies in History." His thoughtful critique of social Darwinism deserved more careful attention there and at home than it received.

The travels were valuable and he made an immensely favorable impression throughout Europe. Instead of the rude frontier manners that many Europeans expected from Americans, they found the former president to be skilled in French, German, and Italian, to have "wide literary and historical knowledge," and to have "high standing among scientists."[7] As a matter of fact, no president, not even Jefferson, excelled TR in breadth of intellect. The Roosevelts, however, were more than ready to come home. The trip had tired them all—even TR, who remarked that if he saw another king, he thought he would bite him! In spite of their yearning for privacy, when they landed in New York on June 18, 1910, not even the huge and boisterous crowd that welcomed them could dampen their spirits.

He continued to write as always and in 1910 published *African Game Trails.* The public received it enthusiastically, and royalties were substantial. In 1911 he became an editor for *Outlook* magazine. He used the journal as a forum to campaign against lynching, working with Booker T. Washington and the leaders of the NAACP. He complained that other reformers were hardly better than indifferent to the issue, which he equated to letting rapists go free with light fines. He also wrote that women should have the vote as they desired.[8]

Although numerous progressive forces were joining in an attempt to persuade TR to run for president in 1912, he resisted and tried to mend the split in the Republican Party. In June, he visited President Taft in Beverly, Massachusetts, where the Tafts—escaping Washington's oppressive heat and humidity—were staying for the summer. They spent several cordial hours together, but however friendly they attempted to be, the conservative Taft could never accept the doctrines that Roosevelt was developing in speech after speech. TR's "New Nationalism" sought to use Hamiltonian means—the power of government—to achieve Jeffersonian ends—the protection of the welfare and liberty of the people.

TR first developed his themes fully in public in an address on August 31, 1910, in Osawatomie, Kansas. Interestingly, the occasion was a memorial ceremony for abolitionist militant John Brown. Dalton called it the "most important speech of his political career." Roosevelt, who always had been resentful of "radicals," then, before an audience of some 30,000, had joined their ranks—although he continued strongly to resist socialism. The Osawatomie speech was, Dalton wrote, "his first post-presidential attempt to place himself at the head of the country's liberal trend and convince it to clean up its politics and provide a larger share of wealth to the worker."[9] He asserted that he continued to stand for the Square Deal—the name he gave to his progressive program—the theme of his presidency, but that it could only come with basic changes in society.

It would not be enough, he said, to have fair play under the rules of the game as they existed. The rules themselves needed to change. As the major chronicler of TR's progressive years writes, "He called for a long list of reforms, including graduated income and inheritance taxes, comprehensive workmen's compensation, conservation, regulation of the working conditions of labor, and extension of federal powers and agencies to regulate business."[10] It was the most progressive program ever set forth by a prominent American figure, and it laid the groundwork for the reforms of the Wilson and Franklin Roosevelt administrations. The *Boston Traveler* reported that TR's speeches from that point on had "roused his followers to enthusiasm and his enemies to frenzy."[11]

Many people believe that the event that ultimately prompted TR to run again came in October 1911, when the Taft administration brought an antitrust action against the U.S. Steel Company. TR had previously been asked to testify regarding the acquisition by U.S. Steel of a controlling interest in the Tennessee Coal, Iron, and Railroad Company. The acquisition took place during the panic of 1907, and TR had specifically assured U.S. Steel that he approved the merger in order to help stabilize the stricken economy. The lawsuit implied that TR "had fostered monopoly and had been duped by clever industrialists."[12] Regardless of whether there was a specific precipitating factor, TR could no longer restrain himself, and broke completely with Taft. On February 21, 1912, he declared his candidacy, coining a new phrase, "my hat is in the ring."

TR was the clear favorite of the Republican rank and file, as even his most hostile biographer conceded.[13] Presidential primaries were new, and he swept nearly all of them—including Ohio, Taft's home state.[14] Primaries then, however, did not choose enough delegates to secure the nomination. Taft's forces controlled the convention and renominated the president. Taft had said that he was a man of peace, but that he would fight. "Even a rat in a corner will fight," he said,[15] reflecting the limitations of his skill in public relations.

TR and his forces pulled out of the convention, and held a rump session of their own. The result was the formation of the Progressive Party, which chose Roosevelt as its candidate with California Governor Hiram Johnson as his running mate. "I feel as strong as a Bull Moose," TR said, and thus in the public's mind the Progressives had formed the Bull Moose Party.

TR addressed the Progressive Convention, electrifying the overcrowded hall with his 20,000-word "Confession of Faith." The date was Tuesday, August 6, 1912. The audience interrupted him with applause 145 times. He spoke of many reforms and regulations that he had advocated before, but "now he went further and called for the creation of a full welfare state by advocating social security insurance to cope with the 'hazards of sickness, accident, invalidism, involuntary unemployment, and old age. . . .'"[16] Not until Franklin D. Roosevelt's New Deal more than two decades later did any of these come to pass; not until Lyndon Johnson's Great Society more than four decades later was there any progress on health care. Today, nearly a century later, government provision for health care remains limited primarily to the elderly and the indigent—and conservatives continue to fight to keep it limited.

However much politicians may appeal to Theodore Roosevelt as a symbol, even a Republican symbol, it would be a rare public figure in early twenty-first-century America who could speak out with such courage. There are very few who dare to counter the prevailing appeals to selfishness. Instead, we hear "I'll lower taxes and let you keep more of your hard-earned money; you can spend it better than the government can." Even after the attacks of September 11, 2001, the public appeal to civic duty was to go shopping—and to accept restrictions on civil liberties.

The lack of the kind of courage that TR displayed over 90 years ago should give pause to anyone who might still believe that progress is inevitable. FDR and LBJ, especially, helped achieve much of TR's dream, as did Dwight Eisenhower and even Richard Nixon. Since LBJ, however, no president except Bill Clinton has sought to provide a comprehensive solution to the problems with health-care delivery that TR saw developing nearly a century ago—and Clinton, of course, failed. To be fair, Nixon did seek to expand health coverage but not in a comprehensive manner.

Fierce partisans, the self-interested, and various ideologues charged—hysterically, inaccurately, but effectively—that Clinton was attempting to "socialize medicine," or even more nonsensically attempting to "socialize one-seventh of the U.S. economy." His plan was overly complex, but it required either a fevered imagination or much misinformation to have seen it—or to continue to portray it—as "socialism." Its goal was simply to require employers to provide *health insurance through private companies* to their employees.

⎯⎯◈⎯⎯

TR in 1912 displayed physical as well as moral courage. While campaigning in Milwaukee, a madman shot him in the chest as he was on his way to give a speech. TR noted that he was not bleeding from the mouth and concluded that he could delay treatment. He insisted—unwisely, to be sure, but impressively nonetheless—upon proceeding to the auditorium where, in his bloodstained shirt, he delivered his full speech. He stood and talked for more than an hour. The would-be assassin, John Schrank, reportedly had declared that the ghost of William McKinley had directed him to kill TR.

Schrank spent the rest of his life, more than three decades, in a mental hospital. Surgeons were unable to remove the bullet from TR's chest—a folded speech, a glasses case, and TR's heavy musculature kept it from penetrating his heart, but it was too near it to risk extraction given the techniques and equipment of the day. It remained in his body the rest of his life.

The Democratic candidate in 1912 was New Jersey Governor and former President of Princeton University Woodrow Wilson. Running with him was Thomas R. Marshall of Indiana. The campaign truly centered on Wilson and Roosevelt. Taft came in a poor third, carrying only Utah and Vermont. Roosevelt accumulated a higher percentage of the vote than any other third-party candidate, over 27 percent, and won 88 electoral votes to Taft's eight. It is the only time that a minor party candidate has come in ahead of one of the two major party candidates. TR did not win, however; he lost to Woodrow Wilson who took just under 42 percent of the popular vote.[17]

Many writers have assumed—or asserted—that TR entered the race out of spite, or ego, when he could simply have sat out for four years and run in 1916 without having split and antagonized the Republican Party. Dalton's excellent analysis puts the Bull Moose race into perspective.[18] She conceded that of course no one can "plumb the inner thoughts of any man, especially one like the Colonel." Many factors, she said, figured into the decision—ambition, boredom, commitment to reform, desire to head off socialism, the U.S. Steel suit— "but the key factor was his keen sense of duty." Actually, he had been reluctant to run. He knew that his chances of victory were slim to none, that he would face abuse, and that he would be "risking his place in history." Dalton wrote that he felt an obligation to prevent Taft's renomination because he had been responsible for his presidency in the first place. "To remain on the sidelines would be irresponsible and craven."

In 1913, only one year following his defeat, TR produced an extensive and detailed autobiography.[19] It not only was a splendid account of his entire life up to that time, but also undoubtedly remains the best discussion of his presidency by any former president. It is an enormously valuable book. That year, he not only continued his extensive publications, but also set off with Kermit at the request of the Brazilian government and the American Museum of Natural History to explore Brazil's uncharted "River of Doubt." It was, he confessed, his "last chance to be a boy."

It also was almost the last of Theodore Roosevelt.[20] To add to the extreme conditions, he injured his leg jumping into the river to save a boat of supplies that had become loose. The leg had been injured years before when a trolley, driven recklessly, had struck TR's carriage, killing one of its occupants. The leg had never been quite the same since and this time developed a serious infection. Weak with fever, he nearly died. Kermit insisted that, dead or alive, he would not leave his father, and they and what was left of their party finally made it back to civilization, where they discovered they had been presumed dead. For 48 days they had faced insects, severe heat, disease, threats from natives and various predators, and semi-starvation; TR had lost nearly 60 pounds. The Brazilians renamed the river "Rio Teodoro," or the "Rio Roosevelt."

Back in the States, at first he favored President Wilson's policy of neutrality in the European conflict that had broken out in August 1914, but he declared the country dangerously unprepared for war. As reports of German atrocities increased, he urged entry into the war on the side of the Allies.[21] Wilson adamantly refused. TR's sharp-tongued daughter, Alice, referred to Wilson as "That sissy in the White House," while TR campaigned ceaselessly, writing and speaking, to alert the country. Wilson was furious.

The Cunard liner, *Lusitania,* sailed from New York on May 1, 1915. The German Embassy in Washington had placed a notice in the newspapers next to the Cunard announcement of the *Lusitania*'s sailing, warning Americans that the liner would be entering a "war zone" around the British Isles, and thus would be subject to attack. The Germans did sink the passenger liner with numerous Americans on board and still Wilson resisted calls for war. An outraged Roosevelt said that if he had been in the White House when the Germans placed their notice in the newspapers, he would immediately have called in the German ambassador, handed him his passport, and hustled him directly out of the country—*on the Lusitania!*[22]

It appeared to many as though TR were devoting his full time to prepared-ness, but in fact he "still fought domestic conservatism with vigor. The sharp re-cession of 1913–1914 had shown him how much the country needed Bull Moose social insurance plans."[23] Dalton dispelled the popular image of a Roo-sevelt who became bitter and reactionary in his old age, motivated largely by loathing of President Wilson.

"His critics (and most later historians)," she noted, "would ignore his call for progressive programs and tell only stories of warmongering and hatred of Wilson in the last years of Roosevelt's life." She demonstrated, though, that they "were missing a story of a determined reformer who despite illness and loss stayed committed to Bull Moose ideas to the end of his life."[24] In 1916, the Pro-gressive Party again nominated him as its presidential candidate, but he rejected the nomination—knowing that another three-party race would again ensure Wilson's victory—and the party disintegrated.

The Republicans, as yet, would have none of the old warrior. He belatedly gave his support to their candidate, Charles Evans Hughes, who resigned from the Supreme Court to run. Wilson won a close election with under 50 percent of the popular vote. By 1918, TR's old popularity had resurged and he received and rejected overtures to run again for governor of New York.

When Wilson finally recognized that U.S. interests were at stake—he had won in 1916 on the slogan "He Kept Us Out of War"—he belatedly took the United States into the conflict. Earlier, the discovery of the "Zimmerman Mem-orandum" startled Americans. The German foreign minister, Arthur Zimmer-man, had sent a secret memorandum to the German representative in Mexico. Germany was offering the Mexicans the return of all lands that had once been Mexican territory if they would attack the United States in the event of an American declaration of war upon Germany. For another month after the Zim-merman revelation, Wilson still resisted. Then German submarines sank three more American vessels. On April 2, 1917, he requested Congress to recognize that a state of war existed and said that the "world must be made safe for democ-racy."[25] The Germans had acted cavalierly toward the United States and appar-ently thought they could win quickly enough that United States entry would be too late to make a difference. They were mistaken.

TR pleaded with Wilson to be permitted to raise and lead a division of vol-unteers. Wilson would have none of it. TR even offered to take a subordinate position, but again, Wilson refused. Not even a public plea from the French premier, Georges Clemenceau, to send Roosevelt because he had "legendary force" in France and would work wonders for morale, had any influence on Wilson. The president's arguments against sending TR were plausible. He was not a military professional, he was 59 and blind in one eye, and Wilson preferred conscripts. Nevertheless, TR was at least as competent as many of the generals who did go, and even the regular army needed more training.

But it was not to be. It was one of the greatest blows to Roosevelt in his life. Wilson's motivation no doubt reflected the cruelty inherent in an attitude that he later expressed when he said "the best way to treat Mr. Roosevelt is to take no notice of him. That breaks his heart. . . ."[26]

Roosevelt urged his four sons, however, not only to go to war but to seek combat. They all did and were all decorated. TR's romantic attachment to war was shattered to the core when his youngest—and arguably favorite—son, Quentin, a fighter pilot, was killed in action. Friends heard TR sorrowfully mutter to himself behind closed doors, "poor Quinikens."

Despite much that has been written about the latter years of TR's life, he worked against the Wilson administration's restrictions on free speech, and "tried much harder than Wilson to stop the racial violence that the war and migration set off."[27] He spoke out against racial violence "more sharply than any other white leader." When labor leader Samuel Gompers defended the lynching of 39 blacks in East St. Louis, Illinois, because they were an economic threat to white workers, TR crossed the stage in fury, and shook his fist in Gompers's face, saying "Murder is murder, whether black or white." Police had to escort him from the hall. The occasion had been "a public gathering honoring Russia's new [democratic and unfortunately brief] Kerensky government.[28]

With regard to free speech, TR was certainly not a civil liberties absolutist, but he strongly resisted the Wilson administration's excesses. In a famous editorial, *The Nation* magazine asked, "Why is Roosevelt Unjailed?" when so many less-famous critics of the administration (including socialist leader Eugene Debs and others known and unknown) had been—simply for speaking out. The editorial concluded that TR had created so much opposition to the administration's autocratic behavior that Wilson had modified his policies. TR, *The Nation* said, had "saved the right of free speech in wartime."[29] As Dalton pointed out, this is exaggerated, but TR did have a healthy influence, especially when he openly courted arrest to make his point.

If TR had not run in 1912, he almost assuredly could have had the Republican nomination in 1916, and would likely have defeated Wilson who won very narrowly. As it was, Republican resentment of his Bull Moose race faded, and his popularity in the party surged. Historian William Harbaugh noted that by 1918 Roosevelt's had become the "foremost candidacy for the presidency" of the Republican Party.[30] Just as Grant almost got the nomination again in 1880, so too in a sense did TR come close in 1920. John A. Gable, the Executive Director of the Theodore Roosevelt Association, echoed Harbaugh's comment. TR, he said, by 1918 "was again the most prominent leader of the Republican Party and the odds-on favorite for the nomination." He had even drawn up a platform and chosen a campaign manager.[31]

The chairman of the Republican National Committee at the time, Will Hays, said that Roosevelt's nomination in 1920 was a virtual certainty.[32] Both TR's *least* critical and his *most* critical biographers agree on this point. The enthusiastic Hermann Hagedorn, a contemporary, wrote in 1919 that the Republican leaders who had "robbed him of the nomination in 1912 and rejected him in 1916" had come to TR by 1918, "hat in hand, to make amends and tell him that the Republican Presidential nomination in 1920 would be his for the taking."[33] Henry Pringle was at the other end of the enthusiasm continuum, but he, too, wrote that had Roosevelt lived, "he might have been elected President in 1920." Moreover—and coming from the skeptical Pringle this is especially important—he wrote that if this had indeed happened, "then there would have been, in all probability, no era of shame and scandal at Washington."[34]

More important even than the likely avoidance of scandal was another possibility. John Milton Cooper raised the intriguing likelihood that another Roosevelt presidency beginning in 1921 "might have chastened the Republicans' love affair with business and material prosperity." Although the party had moved considerably to the right, TR was popular precisely because of his views on domestic reform. He speculated that TR was the likely nominee and that "he could at least have dampened the rampant materialism of the decade and leavened his party's pro-business ardor with a different brand of conservatism." The party might, in fact, have become the champion of governmental action "after the manner of the Tory party in Britain during the next three generations."[35]

Warren G. Harding, the dark-horse Republican choice in 1920, won by the greatest percentage of the popular vote of any president up to that time. It seems certain that TR could have been nominated. It seems equally certain that, had he been nominated, he could have won more resoundingly than the unknown and considerably less competent Harding.

But it was not to be. TR died unexpectedly on January 6, 1919, of an embolism. His son Archie telegraphed his brothers and sisters: "The Old Lion is Dead." His "strenuous life" had taken its toll. He was 60 years of age.

Theodore Roosevelt was buried in Oyster Bay, New York, the location of his home, Sagamore Hill. His widow, Edith Carow, lived until 1948. She, too, died in Oyster Bay; she was 87. Edith is buried beside her husband. Their oldest son, Theodore, Jr., died of a heart attack during World War II, shortly after D-Day, in 1944. His valor at Normandy brought him the Medal of Honor. Kermit, who had accompanied his father on the African and Brazilian trips, committed suicide while in the Army in Alaska in 1943. Ethel Carow (Mrs. Richard Derby), the only daughter of TR and Edith, lived into her middle 80s, dying in 1977. Along with her brothers, she had served with distinction in World War I; she was a nurse in France. Archibald (Archie), also lived into his middle 80s, dying in 1979. TR's oldest child, Alice Lee, Mrs. Nicholas Longworth, was the only child from his first marriage (his wife, Alice Hathaway Lee, died in 1884 of kidney disease after fewer than four years of marriage). Alice Longworth lived until 96, dying in 1980. For decades she had been the undisputed leader of Washington society. A caustic wit, she remarked a few years before her death, after undergoing a double mastectomy, that she had become "Washington's most prominent topless hostess."

Shortly before he left office, President Bill Clinton, pursuant to a unanimous act of Congress, awarded Theodore Roosevelt the Medal of Honor. Numerous generals, fellow officers, and subordinates had recommended him for the medal for his valor in the Spanish-American War. Politics in the War Department and resentment at TR's vigorous actions to bring his troops home quickly to safeguard their health when they no longer were needed in Cuba, prevented award of the medal earlier. Along with Generals Arthur McArthur and Douglas McArthur, Col. Theodore Roosevelt and Brig. Gen. Theodore Roosevelt, Jr., are the only two father-and-son Medal of Honor winners in American history.

Eleven

BETWEEN THE ROOSEVELTS

Retiring into a Changed World

THE PRESIDENTS BETWEEN THE TWO ROOSEVELTS WERE AN ESPECIALLY VARIED lot. In chronological order, they are the judicious Taft, the charismatic Wilson, the amiable Harding (who died in office and thus had no post-presidential career), the indolent Coolidge, and the brilliant but bitter Hoover. Of these five, the first and the fifth, Taft and Hoover, had the most significant careers after they left the White House. Taft's unique post-presidential career was especially important; like John Quincy Adams, his years after leaving the presidency were the most distinguished of his career.

Although these presidents were varied, they share elements in common. Except for Wilson, all were conservative. Again except for Wilson, each had a restrictive view of government. Including Wilson because of his fragile health, each failed to deal adequately with rapid change. Coolidge was aware of his inability to deal with the new world—even Hoover was too radical for him. The overly confident Hoover had no such self-awareness. He lived on into LBJ's presidency, and thus witnessed the greatest changes of them all.

WILLIAM HOWARD TAFT

Big Bill Taft, the largest of the presidents—some six feet two inches tall and weighing at times close to 350 pounds—had been a good baseball player in his youth and was a skillful dancer. He had never wanted to be president. His ambition was to secure an appointment to the U.S. Supreme Court. He was devoted to his wife Helen ("Nellie") Herron, however, and it was clear that she had White House fever. Nellie Taft pushed and prodded her husband to become president.

Among other positions prior to his White House years, Taft had been a lawyer and law professor, a U.S. Appeals Court judge, civil governor of the Philippines under both Presidents McKinley and Theodore Roosevelt, and TR's secretary of war. He had never run for office until his 1908 campaign to become president of the United States.

Taft had been Theodore Roosevelt's handpicked successor and TR skillfully engineered his nomination and election. Nellie never trusted TR, however. Until the day Taft became president, Nellie was suspicious that in some manner Roosevelt would thwart her ambitions. She was so devoted to Taft and his career that she could put her trust in no one else. Despite their close friendship, TR became disenchanted with Taft's presidency and sought to wrest the Republican nomination from him in 1912. When she heard the news that TR would enter the race, she told her husband and the assembled dinner guests, "I told you so four years ago, and you would not believe me."

Paolo Coletta, a student of the Taft administration, wrote that in response to Nellie's assertion, "Taft laughed good-naturedly and replied: 'I know you did, my dear, and I think you are perfectly happy now. You would have preferred the Colonel to come out against me than to have been wrong yourself."[1] She may have been bitter, but by all accounts Taft felt relief. He did work to be reelected, but went down to a massive defeat. He ran third in a race of three, carrying only the states of Utah and Vermont. At the rather young age of 55, William Howard Taft had become a former president of the United States.

In 1913, Taft's alma mater, Yale, offered him the Kent Chair of Constitutional Law. He accepted the position gladly, but quipped that he could not really accept a chair, but that "a sofa of law would be fine."[2] By all accounts, he enjoyed teaching, the students enjoyed him, and he was a skilled and effective professor. He filled his hours not only with his academic duties, but lectured and wrote widely in magazines and newspapers.

He remained active in politics and public affairs and supported Republican candidate Charles Evans Hughes for president in 1916. Hughes actually had been a Supreme Court justice, but had resigned from the Court to run for president. Despite his association with the Republicans, Taft supported Democrat Woodrow Wilson's policies, first to keep out of the European war, and then when Wilson took the country into World War I. In April 1918, Wilson created a National War Labor Board and Taft accepted appointment from him as co-chair.[3] The NWLB operated with varied levels of success to coordinate federal labor policies.

In 1920, Taft supported Wilson's doomed peace treaty—the treaty that called for U.S. membership in the League of Nations—with some reservations,[4] but as a Republican, he campaigned for Warren G. Harding despite Harding's opposition to the League. Harding had nominated Taft at the Republican convention in 1912.[5] Taft did not hold it against Harding that his speech then describing "Taft as 'the greatest Progressive of the age'" received hoots and "derisive howls" from many of the delegates.[6]

Harding had been a dark horse candidate and was not widely known, but the country was tired of war and tired of reform. It handed him an enormous victory. His percentage of the popular vote was the largest ever recorded until that time; he is one of only four presidents in history—along with FDR in 1936, LBJ in 1964, and Richard Nixon in 1972—to achieve 60 percent of the popular vote.

Harding's inauguration took place on March 4, 1921. Shortly thereafter, Chief Justice Edward D. White of the United States Supreme Court died. President Harding appointed Taft to be the new chief justice. Taft thus achieved his long held dream. His years on the Court "were the happiest of his life," and his geniality brought to that body "a spirit of harmony."[7] He wrote in 1925 that in his present life, he did not even remember that he had been president. The fulfillment that had "eluded him in the White House" was present in abundance on the Court.[8]

Taft was an influential chief justice, and as a good administrator, he streamlined the Court's procedures. As Taft aged, he apparently became more conservative. His decisions were considerably further to the right than his presidency would have led one to expect.[9] In general, he reinforced the Court's economic conservatism, its approach to "freedom of contract" that often prevented effective regulation of business, and with some major exceptions its suspicion of federal power over the states. At times, however, hints of his old Progressive connections were apparent.[10] One of his decisions was especially bold and has had historic influence on the presidency.

From the beginning, the president's power to appoint officials with the consent of the Senate has been clear. The power to remove those officials, though, had presented persistent difficulties. Congress and the chief executive have fought periodically over the issue. In its anger at Andrew Johnson, Congress passed the Tenure of Office Act. The law required Senate approval to remove, as well as to appoint, officials. It was Johnson's removal of his secretary of war in violation of the act that became the basic charge of his impeachment. Congress modified the act during the Grant administration and repealed it during Cleveland's first term, but nothing prevented Congress from once again enacting similar legislation.

Then, in 1926, Chief Justice Taft, writing for the majority in *Myers v. United States,* strongly asserted the inherent power of the executive to remove officials. "Taft's opinion on behalf of a divided Court displayed a boldness rarely seen during his tenure in the White House." What was especially astonishing was that the conservative chief justice, even as president, had taken a narrow view of executive power.[11]

Taft stayed on the Court until February 1930, when he resigned because of ill health. President Hoover replaced him as chief justice with Charles Evans Hughes. Hughes had previously been on the Court, but had resigned to run for president in 1916. Taft died the next month from heart failure, on March 8. He was buried in Arlington National Cemetery. His wife, Helen, lived until 1943, and is buried beside him.

William Howard Taft made his mark as a former president in a manner that no other has achieved. He is the only person in American history to have been both president of the United States and a member of the Supreme Court—let alone chief justice of that court. His successor as chief justice is the only person, besides Taft, who has been both a Supreme Court justice and a major party's candidate for president. Only Taft, however, actually achieved both positions.

WOODROW WILSON

Woodrow Wilson as president had legislative achievements that only Franklin D. Roosevelt and Lyndon B. Johnson could equal. He had won the election in 1912 when the Republican Party chose to renominate President Taft rather than to turn to former President Theodore Roosevelt. Roosevelt entered the race as the Bull Moose Progressive and came in ahead of Taft, but his candidacy permitted Wilson to be victorious. Wilson became the only Democratic president since before the Civil War, except for Grover Cleveland. He had been the only president to serve two full consecutive terms since Ulysses S. Grant. Wilson followed Theodore Roosevelt in winning the Nobel Prize for Peace, the second president to do so.

His presidency was one of both huge triumph and tremendous failure. He had presided over great progressive accomplishments and also the most oppressive policies against loyal citizens since those of Jefferson's embargo. He had insisted upon policies of international good will, but had failed to obtain ratification for the treaty with his goal of American participation in a League of Nations.

His post-presidential career was much less dramatic. In fact, it was markedly unimpressive. He had suffered a massive stroke in October 1919. Although his presidency continued until March 4, 1921, he was never the same again. Not only was he physically debilitated and terribly weak, but he no longer had the power to concentrate.

After his retirement, Wilson and his wife, Edith—whom he had married shortly more than a year after his first wife, Ellen, died of Bright's disease on August 6, 1914—continued to live in Washington. He attempted for a time to practice law, with Bainbridge Colby, his former secretary of state. He was too weak both mentally and physically to contribute to the firm, however, so he resigned.

Wilson did manage to make two additional contributions to public affairs. The first, "The Road Away from Revolution," was an article he authored for *The Atlantic Monthly* setting forth his thoughts on government and international relations. It appeared in August 1923. The last was a nationwide radio broadcast on November 10 that same year. Both efforts taxed him greatly, but he had managed again to warn his country against isolationism and to call for commitment to high ideals.

The twenty-eighth president of the United States, Woodrow Wilson died at home on Sunday morning, February 3, 1924, at 15 minutes past eleven. He was buried in Washington, with a simple ceremony. He was 77 years old and is the only president to be buried in the nation's capital.

CALVIN COOLIDGE

When Woodrow Wilson's successor as president, Warren G. Harding, died in office on August 2, 1923, Vice President Calvin Coolidge was catapulted into the presidency. As president, he worked skillfully, and successfully, to get the nomination for himself in 1924. He became the second vice president to win his own term as president after having stepped into the office of a deceased predecessor. Only Theodore Roosevelt had managed to do so before him.

Despite his dour demeanor (TR's daughter, Alice, remarked that Coolidge looked as though he had been weaned on a pickle), Coolidge was enormously popular. He opened his private life to the public, courted reporters, and never failed to take advantage of photo opportunities. He seemed the sound, sensible, no-nonsense supporter of business and American values that the country needed to reassure itself that all was right with the rapidly changing world.

He shocked the public in general, the political community in particular, and his wife Grace especially (he had not told her) when he said simply on August 2, 1927—the fourth anniversary of President Harding's death—"I do not choose to run for president in nineteen twenty-eight." In his last annual message to Congress, President Coolidge, on December 4, 1928, had said, "no Congress of the United States ever assembled, on surveying the state of the Union, has met with a more pleasing prospect than that which appears at the present time." There was, he said, "tranquility and contentment, harmonious relations between management and wage earner, freedom from industrial strife, and the highest record of years of prosperity."[12] Three months later to the day, the Coolidges attended the inauguration of the newly elected President Herbert Hoover; it was March 4, 1929. They then left for Union Station, boarded a train, and headed to their home in Northampton, Massachusetts. Hardly more than a half year later, the stock market crashed, and the Great Depression began.

Coolidge had been noted for being a president who "raised inactivity to an art"[13]—sleeping 11 hours a day, including a two-hour afternoon nap. He did not, though, vegetate in retirement. He was not an especially influential former president, any more than he had been a forceful president, but he did keep busy.

He published his autobiography the same year he left office,[14] so he must have written at least most of it while he was still president—it is highly unlikely that he could have written the manuscript, prepared it for publication, and seen it in print all in the nine months remaining in 1929. Coolidge left most of his presidency out of his narrative—as had Grant, who had not included his presidency in his memoirs—ending it with his election in 1924.

Critics predictably proclaimed it to be a dull recitation, but it is a worthwhile book. Writers who looked at it more closely tend to agree. Coolidge biographer Robert Ferrell, for example, called it "a lithe description of a life begun close to the soil," and noted the humor in Coolidge's writing.[15] He was correct, although Coolidge had not been a farmer nor did he come from a farming family. As Ferrell himself noted, Coolidge's father had been a storekeeper and a Vermont legislator. Coolidge had been a "city man, not a country bumpkin or even a country philosopher" from the time he became an adult.[16]

Robert Sobel, Coolidge's friendliest biographer, went further. He wrote—
with some exaggeration—that "there is more about the man and his philosophy
in its mere 246 pages than in presidential memoirs three times as long." That
depends, of course, upon which other presidential memoir he means. Grant's
Personal Memoirs are much longer (not quite three times) and far surpass
Coolidge's in nearly every respect. This is no criticism of Coolidge, because
Grant's work is superb. Sobel also praised the Coolidge style, saying that it "dis-
plays a literary grace that is lacking in most such books by former presidents."[17]
Although perhaps true, few works by former presidents are of lasting value. Too
many tend to be dull and overly defensive. Those by Grant and Theodore Roo-
sevelt are among the few exceptions.

Coolidge had been frugal in his personal finances as well as with the country's and he apparently prospered from investments, so he was not in financial
difficulty even though the government had yet to provide anything for presidents in their retirements. Writing became his major occupation. He chose from
many offers and decided to write several articles for three magazines: *Cosmopolitan* (quite a different publication then from now), *Ladies' Home Journal*,
and *The American Magazine*. He also wrote for the *Encyclopedia Americana*. For
all this he was very well paid. In addition, he accepted a position on the board
of the New York Life Insurance Company, which paid little.[18]

No doubt most widely read of Coolidge's writings was a daily newspaper
column that he agreed to write for the McClure Newspaper Syndicate. This
column brought him considerable additional wealth. It appeared in some 60
papers nationwide, including in New York "the *Herald Tribune,* the leading
Republican newspaper in the country." The title of the column was "Calvin
Coolidge Says,"[19] or alternatively, "Thinking Things Over with Calvin
Coolidge."[20] Few would argue that the columns were more than flat and forgettable pieces; they were of much less interest than his autobiography. The
column lasted for only a year, 1930–1931. Coolidge himself found it too restrictive and grew tired of it.

When the Coolidges returned to Northampton, they had intended to live
in their longtime home at 21 Massasoit Street. They had been there since 1906,
and thought it would be comfortable. Hardly had a year passed when they had
to change their plans. Tourists and sightseers drove them away. They could not
sit on the front porch without cries from slowly moving or stopped cars, "There
he is!" They bought a more spacious house, "The Beeches," that they found especially congenial. Moreover, it had a large acreage with a fence and gate to keep
tourists out.[21] They moved into The Beeches, located on Munroe Street, in the
spring of 1930, and spent their remaining days there.[22]

Coolidge rarely left Northampton. He returned to Washington only once, in 1929, to attend a ceremony for the Kellogg-Briand Pact that was to outlaw war forever.

Once, also, he and Grace were the guests of William Randolph Hearst in Florida. In 1931 he traveled to Marion, Ohio, to dedicate—along with President Hoover—the Harding Memorial in Harding's hometown.[23] One bit of excitement took place in 1931 after he delivered a radio address for New York Life warning policyholders against unscrupulous agents who might try to secure commissions by persuading them to change their policies. This was unexceptional, but one Lewis Tebbetts, an insurance salesman, sued Coolidge and the company for $100,000 each, claiming that they had "slandered innocent agents." Tebbett settled out of court for $2,500 and a letter by Coolidge explaining that he "had not intended to offend him or any other agent."[24]

In the 1930s, Coolidge knew that he was a man of the past, a lonely figure, who came from an earlier reality. He told newspaperman Henry Stoddard that he "no longer fit in with these times." It was a new era in which he did not belong and he could not adjust to it.[25] When some people suggested in 1932 that he try for the presidential nomination in 1936, he scoffed at the notion.

He would not be able, he said, to figure out what to do with "these socialistic notions of government," speaking of Hoover's ideas, not those of the New Deal, which as yet remained in the future.[26] There is no indication that President Hoover ever sought his advice, or that Coolidge ever offered any. Coolidge's editor at *McClure's,* spoke of the former president's loneliness. "The failure of his successor to consult with him at all, and the consciousness that close contact of political friends with him would not be well received at the White House, made for a certain disturbance of mind," he said.[27] Coolidge did not seem to oppose the new trends; he merely recognized that he could not deal with them. He did campaign for Hoover and wrote articles on behalf of his futile effort to win re-election. It is clear, though, that Calvin Coolidge was not among the former presidents who exercised great influence.

He did not live to see Franklin D. Roosevelt inaugurated. On January 5, 1933, while Grace had gone shopping, Coolidge collapsed suddenly at home at the age of only 61. She returned home to find him dead on the floor from a heart attack.

Gifford Pinchot, Theodore Roosevelt's trusted chief forester and then governor of Pennsylvania, said that Coolidge had embodied simplicity, homely wisdom, and quiet personal courage. "As president," Pinchot said, "he typified an era. That era is passing or has passed. Coolidge will be remembered as its symbol. And his passing is the symbol of its passing also."[28] It was a perfect summation of the coming and going of Calvin Coolidge, thirtieth President of the United States.

The Coolidge funeral took place in Northampton, at the Congregational Church. He was laid to rest in Plymouth, Vermont.

HERBERT HOOVER

Iowa native Herbert Hoover brought a brilliant record and a background of success to the presidency. He was a mining engineer and businessman with great self-made wealth, having become a millionaire by age 40. He and his wife, Lou Henry Hoover, were both Stanford geology graduates who had lived and worked in China and who had mastered Chinese (they spoke it to one another in the White House when they wished to keep their conversations confidential). He had organized and administered food-distribution programs in Belgium during World War I that averted mass starvation, for which he achieved great, and well-deserved, acclaim. He also had been an outstanding cabinet member under the two preceding presidents, serving as secretary of commerce during both the Harding and Coolidge administrations.

The nation held great hopes for his administration when Hoover, with his reputation as a "wonder," became president of the United States on March 4, 1929. Hardly more than half a year thereafter the stock-market crashed. The subsequent onset of the Great Depression obscured Hoover's humanitarianism and revealed his rigid ideology as simply inappropriate to deal with the situation he faced.

Hoover left the White House a failure, widely blamed for the stock-market crash and the Great Depression. His reputation as a great humanitarian had given way to one of a cold, heartless man committed to an outdated ideology. Much of the blame was unfair. He had not caused the stock-market crash or the depression and he had worked tirelessly—if unsuccessfully—to solve the country's financial misery. On the other hand, although he was neither heartless nor unconcerned, he did subordinate his humanitarian temperament to a rigid ideology that made it impossible for him to be effective as president during the Great Depression. He believed that government aid directly to those in need would be unconstitutional and that it would be unthinkable in any case because it would "weaken character." Much of the blame was indeed unfair, but most of it he had brought upon himself.

Hoover had become president at the age of 54, leaving office at 58. Nearly two-thirds of former presidents left office in their 60s, and two (Eisenhower at

70 and Reagan at 78) at even older ages. Hoover thus was reasonably young for a former president although not exceptionally so. He lived, however, until the age of 90. That longevity, combined with his relative youth upon leaving office, meant that he had a post-presidential career of 31 years, the longest of any former president thus far. Throughout that long period he was a prominent voice in the Republican Party—and a most vehement one.

Partly because of his lengthy post-presidential career and partly because of his determination and great energy, Hoover wrote more than any other former president. After returning to California, he said that he would refrain from public pronouncements for a year. As an avid fisherman, he "fished for trout and bass from California and British Columbia to New England; for salmon in the state of Washington and New Brunswick; for big-game fish in Florida, Texas, and Lower California."[29] He also fished the Brule River in Wisconsin. Presidents Grant, Cleveland, Coolidge, and Eisenhower also fished there, encouraging local promoters to publicize it as the "River of Presidents."

The famed "First 100 Days" of the Roosevelt administration, though, had been hard for the former president. He saw New Deal activism as imposing "statism" and "socialism" on an innocent country. He wrote in letters that "February, March, and April of 1933 will someday be known as the winter of the Roosevelt hysteria." To halt the rash of failures, FDR had ordered a brief closing of banks so that they could be audited and reorganized if necessary before reopening. The closing of the banks, Hoover said, was unnecessary. "Our fight is going to be to stop this move to gigantic socialism of America."[30]

He refused to listen to the wise counsel of friends who urged thoughtful softening of his rigid views. Hoover incorporated those views in a sequel to his 1922 book, *American Individualism*. The new version, *The Challenge to Liberty*,[31] damned the New Deal as a threat to individual freedom.

Hoover's friend, Associate Supreme Court Justice Harlan Fiske Stone—who remained loyal to Hoover and who thought he should be elected president again in 1940 even though FDR elevated Stone to the chief justiceship in 1941—gently informed Hoover that he should rethink his views. He agreed with many of Hoover's criticisms, he said, but Hoover should recognize that the people govern, and they wanted reform. They expected that opposition to reform would develop and that it would be based on the assertion that reform would result in restriction of individual freedom. Hoover's work, he cautioned, would be seen in the same vein; as just another that opposed reform. He pointed to the increasing complexity of civilization in which a Jeffersonian state could no longer function. Modern problems, he said, cannot be solved by "an appeal to the eighteenth century philosophy of individualism in the abstract, for that philosophy cannot be completely adapted to the twentieth century."[32] Neither then nor later would, or could, Hoover modify his views.

Through the years Hoover's prolific writings and speeches resulted in numerous collections of his works. He published his *Memoirs* in 1951 and 1952,[33] the accuracy of which at times suffers from selective memory. Especially interesting because it is a study of one president by another was his examination of Woodrow Wilson's efforts to secure peace following World War I.[34] In his later years, Hoover worked as well on an extensive study of Franklin Roosevelt and the New Deal. According to biographer Eugene Lyons, the title was to be *Freedom Betrayed*—Hoover thought of it as his magnum opus. It appears to have been a diatribe, filled with complaints, often petty, about Roosevelt and the New Deal and allegations that they were responsible for the rise of Soviet power and the spread of communism. The ever-admiring Lyons noted, approvingly, that Hoover had "documented" Soviet gain through various agreements through which Roosevelt disposed "of the fruits of victory."[35] Lyons seems to have expected *Freedom Betrayed* to be published, but fortunately for all concerned, it has not been.

Hoover was a voice of the strong isolationist wing of the Republican Party in the 1930s. He opposed recognition of the Soviet Union and opposed entry into World War II. He argued that widespread war was unlikely. If it came, he thought it appropriate to remain out of the conflict, but to supply the Allies and assist in determining the conditions for peace afterward. The Japanese attack on Pearl Harbor, however, changed his mind and he supported an immediate declaration of war.

Hoover's post-presidential career did not entirely consist of negative criticism. He continued to remain active in charitable causes and in 1936 accepted the chairmanship of the Boys' Club of America. His energetic administration saw Boys' Clubs springing up all over the country. As war devastated much of Europe in the late 1930s, he conducted massive efforts to raise funds for food relief to Finland, Belgium, and Poland, but because of the depression along with the wartime conditions, did not meet with the success he had during World War I.

On January 7, 1944, he was himself devastated when his beloved wife, Lou, died. They had been married since 1899. The next year, his nemesis, Franklin D. Roosevelt, also died. Vice President Harry S. Truman had become president. The hostility that Hoover had directed toward Roosevelt had been returned in kind. Truman, on the other hand, "felt that Roosevelt's rebuffs to Hoover had been shameful." Truman invited Hoover to the White House for the first time since his presidency, and "one of the first things Truman did as President was to restore Hoover to political society as an informal presidential adviser."[36] For nearly the remainder of his life, Hoover actively contributed to government.

After his own retirement, President Truman described his invitation to Hoover to visit the White House. It was shortly after he had succeeded to the presidency in 1945 and Truman had become alarmed at the European food situation. "I knew what I had to do," he wrote, "and I knew just the man I wanted to help me. I had read in the Washington newspapers a small item saying that former President Hoover was in town and staying at the Shoreham Hotel." Truman picked up the telephone, he said, and asked to be put through to Hoover's room. When Hoover answered, Truman asked "How are you Mr. President?" After a pause, Truman said, Hoover asked, "Who is this?" When he answered that he was Harry Truman, Hoover responded "Oh, Mr. *President*. How are you?" Truman then said "I called to ask if you would care to come over and see your old home." Hoover replied that he did not wish to impose, but Truman said "I'd be glad to come over to see you."[37] Hoover then accepted Truman's invitation.

Truman reported that he and Hoover had "a very cordial meeting." He then broached a subject that he told Hoover was "for the welfare of the world." He spoke of starvation in Europe, "crop failures in South Africa, South America, Indonesia and other rice-raising countries," and asked if Hoover would "organize an effort to get food to all the needy, for we could not allow anyone anywhere to starve if we could possibly avoid it." Hoover, Truman said, "immediately volunteered to help," and did so. "Herbert Hoover," Truman wrote, "did a magnificent job for this country, and for other nations, in helping to prevent the starvation of millions of people. And when this work was launched and eventually taken over by the relevant government agencies, Mr. Hoover expressed a readiness to assume any other tasks I thought he could perform for the government of the United States."[38] As he always had, Hoover demonstrated his eagerness to use his considerable talents for humanitarian causes in general, and for the good of his country in particular.

In 1947 Hoover accepted appointment to head a massive study of the U.S. government and to make suggestions regarding improved organization. Republicans had taken over Congress following the results of the 1946 elections. Presidential scholars Sidney M. Milkis and Michael Nelson have written that "the Republican-controlled Eightieth Congress had appointed Hoover to head the Commission on the Organization of the Executive Branch of the Government," and that conservative leaders of the 80th Congress saw the task of the group as laying "the groundwork for an assault on New Deal programs," and hoped to "circumscribe the executive by foreclosing the possibility of another personalized, FDR-style administration." However, Milkis and Nelson wrote, Hoover had the experience to recognize the "need to fortify the modern presidency."[39] (Regardless of his ideology, Hoover was a skilled administrator and knew what was required for an administrator to be effective.)

A student of the Truman presidency, Donald McCoy, gave a different interpretation of the commission's origin. McCoy wrote that although Truman and the 80th Congress were at odds, they did agree on some domestic matters, one of which was governmental reorganization. "Truman was agreeable to having it spurred by a bipartisan commission," McCoy wrote. "Congress established and the president approved this commission in July 1947. In a brilliant stroke, Truman named former President Herbert Hoover, who had long been a champion of reorganization, as chairman of this Commission," which was to report after the 1948 elections.[40] Truman's writings in later years support McCoy's version.

Truman wrote that when first invited Hoover to the White House in 1945, he had in mind another task for the former president. That task "was to help streamline the executive departments and the new agencies that had been created to meet the various war needs. The government of the United States had grown so rapidly during the war that duplication and waste were inevitable and needed correction," Truman said. "Such a streamlining would require, of course, new statutes and Congressional action."[41] Republican leaders may well have hoped that the commission would recommend elimination of New Deal programs, as Milkis and Nelson wrote, but the choice of Hoover as its leader seems clearly to have been Truman's.

The Commission on Organization of the Executive Branch of the Government, known ever after as the Hoover Commission, was a huge undertaking.

> Hoover set up nineteen task forces to concentrate on delimited areas such as accounting, budgeting, personnel, transportation, real estate, purchasing, medical and veterans' affairs, natural resources, etc., and the machinery of the principal Cabinet departments. Over three hundred specialists were personally selected by Hoover, with the consent of the other commissioners, and attached to appropriate task forces.[42]

Hoover submitted the first of 19 sections of the Hoover Commission Report to Congress on February 7, 1949. Other sections came in at a rate of some three per week. In addition to the overall report, Hoover wrote 16 of the sections. It was certainly one of the most comprehensive governmental reports in history—Lyons called it the most comprehensive until that of the Second Hoover Commission under Eisenhower.[43]

The Report was enormously influential. Truman accepted it enthusiastically, and so did Congress. It became the basis for the Executive Reorganization Act of 1949, which authorized the president to make significant changes in many structures on his own.[44] It also resulted ultimately in the formation of a new cabinet department under President Eisenhower, the Department of Health, Education, and Welfare. Hoover also accepted appointment in 1953 to head a second Hoover Commission under Eisenhower, which aimed not only to streamline government, but to evaluate whether government should be performing certain functions, and to recommend their elimination if need be. The effect of this report was considerably less than that of the first. By the time of the second commission, Hoover was in his 80s, although he still was vigorous.

Thus, Herbert Clark Hoover, thirty-first president of the United States, had a unique career after leaving office. On the one hand, he bitterly condemned much of modern government, especially that associated with Franklin Roosevelt. On the other, as indicated, he recognized the need for a strengthened presidency. He demonstrated a dark side by his display of ill temper and his inability to put the past behind him, but nonetheless he was able to make considerable contributions to humanitarian causes, to government, and to his party. He became a conservative icon, appearing regularly at Republican National Conventions, making several "last public appearances" there. As he put it, "I outlived the bastards."

As he neared his eighty-eighth birthday, Hoover and a large contingent of friends and supporters gathered at his birthplace of West Branch, Iowa, for the dedication of the Hoover Presidential Library. He died on October 20, 1964, at the age of 90. At the time of his death he was the second oldest former president who still retained his mental faculties; only John Adams was older. Gerald Ford, who turned 90 in July 2003, may ultimately set the record for longevity. Ronald Reagan technically has lived to the oldest age of any person who has been president, but Alzheimer's disease destroyed his ability to function mentally nearly a decade before he reached the age of Hoover, Ford, or Adams. Lou and Herbert Hoover had lived their post-presidential years in Palo Alto, California (at Stanford University), and in a suite in the Waldorf Towers in New York City. Lou had been buried in Palo Alto. At Hoover's death, he was buried in West Branch, and Lou was reburied there with him.

Twelve

COLD WAR PRESIDENTS

THE PRESIDENTS WHO SERVED DURING THE HEIGHT OF THE COLD WAR were extraordinarily varied. The way each conducted himself after leaving office was also quite different, although perhaps less varied than the unique administrations themselves. Harry Truman had been feisty during and after the presidency, while Dwight Eisenhower proved cautious in both situations, although he became a bit more emboldened as a vocal hawk on Vietnam. An assassin's bullet struck down the youthful John Kennedy before he left office, denying him the opportunity to be the youngest former president—but only if he had served a single term. The incredible dynamism of President Lyndon Johnson did not accompany him into retirement, although he continued to be relatively active. Richard Nixon's retirement was in many ways an extension not only of his presidency, but of his entire political career. From the time he entered politics, he had sought time and again to redefine himself and to achieve vindication. His retirement was a continuation of his lifelong pattern; after leaving office, he persisted in his efforts to recast his image so that history would judge him favorably. Gerald Ford was a decent and unassuming man who approached his presidency thoughtfully, and who persisted in this approach in his life after the White House.

HARRY S. TRUMAN

Harry S. Truman left office on January 20, 1953, while an enthusiastic—and largely relieved—public welcomed his successor, the triumphant general with the infectious smile, Dwight D. Eisenhower. The country was weary of 20 years of upheaval, social and political reform, and war, just as it had been in 1920 when the voters put Warren Harding in the White House in a tremendous land-slide. In the 1952 elections the nation had been shocked—and perhaps con-fused—by reckless charges of communism in government from the junior senator from Wisconsin, Joseph McCarthy (as well as from lesser demagogues), and by the vitriolic nature of the campaign itself.

Although Truman had chosen not to run again and was not a candidate, there had been bitterness between him and Eisenhower during the campaign. Truman resented the Republican tactics and thought also that the general's pledge to "go to Korea" to end the war was pure grandstanding (as he had promised, Eisenhower did visit Korea, and did bring the war to a close). Vice Presidential Candidate Richard Nixon, Truman thought, was even worse. Nixon's speeches were filled with venom directed not only at the Democratic candidate, Adlai Stevenson, but also at Truman and at Dean Acheson, his secre-tary of state. "Real Democrats," Nixon snidely said, going beyond the limits of truth as well as decency, must be "outraged by the Truman-Acheson-Stevenson gang's toleration and defense of communism in high places."[1] For his part, Eisenhower thought that Truman's earthy blasts at critics—the most notorious of which was perhaps his letter attacking the *Washington Post's* music critic, Paul Hume, for his unfavorable review of presidential daughter Margaret Truman's vocal concert—failed to uphold the dignity of the office.

Truman had been especially incensed when Eisenhower revealed a petty side and refused his offer of a briefing during the campaign. After the Republican victory, however, at Truman's initiative, the two had worked together to ensure a smooth handover. Truman's innovation—especially gracious under the cir-cumstances—set a precedent for future changes in administration.

Truman may have been gracious, but it failed to mellow Eisenhower's atti-tude toward him. On inauguration day, "Eisenhower refused to do the tradi-tional thing and come into the White House to greet the outgoing president; he simply drove up in his car and sent word he was ready to go to the capitol."[2] The ride to the inauguration was not a pleasant one, but fortunately was brief. Harry S. Truman, thirty-third President of the United States, once again, as his daughter Margaret said, was simply "Mr. Citizen."[3]

The Truman presidency had been an eventful and tumultuous one. No president since Lincoln and Grant had done so much for civil rights, including desegregating the armed services by executive order. No president had striven so diligently to ensure health care for all Americans, as when Truman proposed a comprehensive health plan. No president had presided over such an enormous program of international rebuilding as the Marshall Plan. Truman had overseen the end of history's largest war, had succeeded in achieving the creation of the United Nations, had sought—often without success—to implement his "Fair Deal" (the name he applied to his program), and had managed to protect and secure Roosevelt's New Deal. After instances of corruption in the administration, fear of communism, and weariness of war and reform few presidents had left office so unpopular, but more than any other he lived to see an unparalleled reversal of his reputation that enabled him to enjoy a near-unanimous vindication of his administration.

When he left office, Congress still had not seen fit to provide a pension for former presidents or even an allowance for office expenses. Nor had it provided Secret Service protection. In contrast to most presidential families, the Trumans were of modest means.[4] Herbert Hoover, the only other former president still living, had a personal fortune that enabled him for example to live in luxury at the Waldorf Towers in New York. Of Truman's other twentieth-century predecessors, Harding and FDR had died in office. TR had an inherited estate and possessed income from his prolific writings, Wilson's second wife was wealthy, allowing them to live in an enormous mansion in Washington, D.C., and Taft had first a Yale professorship and then the position of Chief Justice of the Supreme Court to sustain him and his family in his post-presidential years. Coolidge, who lived not quite four years after he left office, likely was less well-off than the others but nonetheless also seemed free from financial worries.

The Trumans, on the other hand, had only some modest savings and Harry's tiny military pension. He had taken out a loan for an unknown amount "at the National Bank in Washington in his last weeks as President, to tide him over." In contrast to several of his fellows, particularly some successors, he vowed to do nothing that would exploit the presidential office, nor would he accept any fees that might imply product endorsement or the "commercialization" of his position.[5]

Hardly a month had gone by, however, when he signed a contract for a large sum to produce his memoirs, and his money troubles appeared to be over.[6] After working with a frustrating series of assistants[7]—at one point he inscribed "Good God, what crap," at the top of a manuscript page that one had produced—he delivered the work in July 1955. The first volume, *Year of Decisions,* came out that year; the second, *Years of Trial and Hope* came out the following year. His biographer Robert Ferrell reported that Truman ultimately received little financial return. He paid two-thirds of his royalties in income taxes and had only some $37,000 left after expenses. Ferrell also was critical of the work itself, blaming Truman's assistants.[8] Historian David McCullough, on the other hand, pointed to its value. No other president, he said, had published so comprehensive a study of his own administration.[9] McCullough quoted reviewers such as Richard Rovere in *The New Yorker* and historian Allan Nevins in the *New York Times Book Review* in support of the work's value. They "rightly treated the book as a major event," he said.[10] Nevertheless, regardless of their varied emphases, both he and Ferrell were correct. They agreed that both volumes throughout were much too uneven—as the reviewers had also noted. All remarked that the prose came to life only when the words were Truman's own. Too many people were involved, as Truman freely conceded and Ferrell stressed. Although unfortunate, the result was nevertheless valuable.

Truman's huge tax on the income from his memoirs, 67 percent, did nothing to enhance his strained relations with President Eisenhower.[11] When General Eisenhower had published his *Crusade in Europe* in 1949, the Internal Revenue Service had ruled that because he was not a professional author, he would be able to treat his earnings as capital gains. It taxed him therefore at only twenty-five percent. The Truman administration had intervened on Eisenhower's behalf. In Truman's case, however, the Eisenhower administration declined to become involved.

Truman's situation, however uncomfortable, did finally lead to a beneficial result for him and all subsequent presidents. Because of such things as a huge volume of mail that he felt obliged to answer, he requested support from Congress for his heavy office expenses. Although he did not ask for a pension, he pointed out that all five-star generals and admirals had their salaries for life plus assistants and "all the emoluments that went with their office," while presidents—their superiors—received nothing. Speaker Sam Rayburn and Senate Majority Leader Lyndon Johnson succeeded in obtaining legislation in 1958 providing former presidents with free mailing privileges, office space, staff, and a pension—at that time, $25,000 annually.[12] That amount then compared favorably with the salaries of corporate executives. It had taken the United States nearly a century and three-quarters to provide support for its former presidents.

Despite Truman's opinion of Eisenhower, he had a great respect for the office of the president. Therefore, when the president visited Kansas City, in October 1953 to speak to the convention of the Future Farmers of America, Truman called the Muehlebach Hotel where Ike was staying to indicate that he would like to come to pay his respects. An aide replied that the president's schedule was too full. Eisenhower's office later explained that "whoever answered the phone must have thought it was a crank call."[13] Truman was convinced that the snub had been deliberate. Throughout the Eisenhower administration—and even into the Kennedy presidency, Truman hoped to be asked for advice as Hoover had hoped throughout the long years of the New Deal. In neither case did such a request ever come.

Vice President Nixon rekindled Truman's hostility when he charged, in the 1960 campaign while running for president against Senator John Kennedy that if he reached the White House, the tender ears of America's schoolchildren would be protected from hearing the kind of language that Truman (who had been out of office some eight years) had used. This is especially laughable in view of the later revelations in Nixon's White House tapes that made Truman's earthy comments seem tame by comparison. Truman, however, did not laugh. He went into Nixon's own state of California to campaign against him, calling him "Trickie Dickie, the opportunist." After Nixon's loss to Kennedy and his nomination two years later for the California governorship, Truman again flew to California to condemn Nixon. "The people shut the *front* door on him," he told a group of roaring Democrats, warning them not to let him sneak in through the *back* door. The choice, he said, was between the Democrat Pat Brown, a kindly man and a good governor, and a "mean, nasty fellow."[14]

When Truman attended John Kennedy's inaugural in 1961, he "sat near Eisenhower but managed not to speak to him."[15] During the tragic days following President Kennedy's assassination, however, the two crusty old former presidents—perhaps because of the national trauma—had mellowed. Truman and his daughter Margaret had come to Washington and were staying at Blair House. After several attempts, Eisenhower managed to get a call through to him—he may have been more persistent than Truman had been in Kansas City—and asked if the Eisenhowers could pick up the Trumans and take them to the cathedral for the funeral services. Truman readily agreed. After the funeral, he asked the Eisenhowers in to Blair House for drinks. "Soon everyone was talking animatedly, and when the Eisenhowers really had to go, Truman—to the horror of the secret service—went out to the curb and talked while the car waited to take them away."[16]

Truman proved that he could mellow even with regard to one his most hated enemies, Richard Nixon. In 1964, he was in Washington at the Gridiron Dinner (an annual gathering for politicians and members of the press) when Nixon offered to bring him a drink. Truman accepted and the two chatted for a few minutes. "During the subsequent speeches Nixon related how he had gotten Truman a drink, 'and he didn't even have someone taste it before he drank it.'" After Nixon became president, he visited Truman at the Truman Library and Museum in Independence, Missouri.[17]

The Library was one of Truman's fondest achievements. He was not a scholar, but he was very well read, particularly in history, and was sensitive to the need for accurate records. He was concerned that there was no single source available that compiled a president's works—not even his public statements. In June 1957 he testified before a congressional committee on behalf of a bill (one that he had urged) to index and photocopy presidential papers.[18] As McCullough remarked, "until he raised the issue, no one had bothered to make the effort."[19] That effort succeeded. Along with the Harry S. Truman Library and Museum in Independence, the legislation regarding presidential papers was the culmination of his interest in history. Together they constitute an enormous contribution to the United States—one of the greatest by any former president.

The Library opened in 1957. Former President Hoover and Eleanor Roosevelt were there for the dedication on July 6, along with Speaker Sam Rayburn and a host of governors, members of Congress, former cabinet members, and others. Chief Justice Earl Warren gave the address. Private donations had provided the funding, and the City of Independence had donated the land. As soon as it opened, Truman moved from his office in the Federal Reserve building in Kansas City into an office suite in the Library. For years he was available there to citizens who wished to see and speak with him.

One of Truman's greatest concerns was the youth of the country. Accordingly, he spoke several times a day to school groups. He not only lectured, he answered questions. He was among our most accessible former presidents and he considered it his duty to be so. He turned away no one, even autograph seekers who simply wished to have a book signed.

Former Secretary of State Dean Acheson, who was a member of the Yale Corporation, arranged for the former president to receive a Chubb Fellowship at Yale. In 1958 the Fellowship brought Truman to Yale as an honored guest to meet with faculty and students. He spent three happy days there, charming—and impressing—students and faculty alike.[20] He remarked that it was the kind of great university that he wished he had been able to attend.

As another reflection of Truman's interest in education, in 1961 he worked on a television series dealing with the presidency. The writer Merle Miller coordinated the project, which dealt largely with the Truman administration. Truman intended the series to be an education for the country, "but more important and influential than the films that eventually resulted was the portrait that Miller would compile from recorded conversations with Truman in a book called *Plain Speaking*—a book that would not be published for another dozen years." Truman's cogent comments revealed to Miller that those who had worked with Truman on his memoirs had not served him well.[21]

On July 30, 1965, in the auditorium of the Truman Library under Truman's watchful eye, President Lyndon B. Johnson held the signing ceremony for the newly enacted Medicare Bill.[22] He did this to honor Harry S. Truman, who had been the first American president to present to Congress a message primarily devoted to health care and the first to call for appropriate legislation. The next year Truman became the proud holder of the first Medicare card and Bess received Medicare Card #2. Ironically, the bill that Truman had sought would have been considerably greater in scope than the one that Congress, nearly two decades later, finally adopted.

Truman lived for nearly two fruitful decades after he left the White House. Bess lived another decade beyond him. He lived to the age of 88, dying on December 26, 1972. She died on October 18, 1982, the age of 97. Harry and Bess are buried together on the grounds of his beloved Harry S. Truman Library and Museum in Independence.

Truman achieved much, and had paved the way for even more. Not only did his breadth of vision lead him to propose what ultimately became Medicare, but he also had been—in an act of huge political courage—the first to present a comprehensive civil rights program. In LBJ's administration, both efforts at last found success.

Notwithstanding his faults—his partisanship, his occasional pettiness, his lashing out at critics—Truman had been an outstanding president and became an outstanding former president. His accomplishments after the White House brought permanent benefits to his country, benefits for which he is too little remembered. Understandably, our attention tends to be drawn to the dramatic events of his presidency rather than to the more subtle accomplishments of his later life. But those accomplishments were substantial.

———◆———

The world, as well as America, has come to respect him and Truman was fortunate to see that respect come in his lifetime. Students and faculty at Oxford University, for example, had recognized his greatness. In 1956, when he presented himself by invitation at Oxford to receive an honorary doctorate, he found much of the ceremony to be in Latin. The dignitaries described him as "Harricum Truman." You were, they said to him, the "truest of allies, direct in your speech and your writings, and ever a pattern in simple courage." The courageous former president "burst into tears."[23] Truman set forth his consistent beliefs in his message to the assembled dons: every person was entitled to excellent health care and to education; the elderly should be free from economic worries. As he departed, glowing, from Oxford, students leaned from their windows and shouted enthusiastically, "Give 'em hell Harricum!"[24] Much that is good in America can trace its foundation to the fact that Truman had indeed had the courage, the determination, and the wisdom—both during and after his presidency—to give 'em hell.

DWIGHT D. EISENHOWER

Although riding the congenial and folksy slogan, "I Like Ike" into office, Dwight Eisenhower was an imposing presence in contrast to the down-to-earth Truman. His military achievements made him a towering figure and his election to the highest office in the land only reinforced this both during and after his presidency.

His identity as a five-star general (a general of the army), and as president of the United States continued to characterize him in retirement. Times were changing rapidly, however, and although Ike remained beloved—especially to Republicans—he rather quickly faded from the day-to-day awareness of Americans. He found contentment as he settled into the role of a gentleman farmer near Gettysburg, Pennsylvania, immediately adjacent to the historic Civil War battlefield that had become the Gettysburg National Military Park.

But contented retirement did not erase his political concerns. Although as president he had portrayed himself as above politics, leaving the political dirty work to Vice President Nixon and others, he had quickly become a dedicated partisan. Beyond mere devotion to a party, his partisanship was rather a firm commitment to his version of "modern Republicanism," accepting, although cautiously, the broad outlines of the New Deal and its principle that the government has an obligation to enhance the welfare of the people. He maintained his vigorous political interests, and throughout his retirement continued to exercise influence as an adviser to and confidant of presidents. He continued, also, to play golf and bridge with wealthy friends, from whom he gladly accepted numerous lavish gifts. He violated no law or policy. Ethics regulations were considerably less strict then.

The Eisenhowers had purchased the 189-acre site in 1950, when it was the Allen Redding Farm. Through the years it gradually grew to become "the 230 acre country estate of the thirty-fourth President of the United States." During his presidency, Ike had located his "temporary White House" there, and had used it as a retreat. He was nevertheless a serious farmer, maintaining "a show herd of Angus cattle," even while his farm was a "meeting place for world leaders." It continues today as an active farm. The National Park Service administers it, designated as the "Eisenhower National Historic Site."[25] The Eisenhowers deeded the farm to the U.S. government in 1967.

Eisenhower had been deeply depressed at the results of the 1960 election.[26] Vice President Nixon had virtually tied John Kennedy in the popular vote, losing by fewer than 120,000 votes out of slightly fewer than 70 million cast, but lost substantially in the electoral college.[27] Eisenhower strongly felt a sense of rejection at the Democratic victory. His secretary, Ann Whitman, quoted him as saying over and over that the results were a "repudiation of everything he had done for eight years."[28] Ironically, Eisenhower—and the Republicans—were the first victims of the term-limiting Twenty-second Amendment. Ike's own vengeful party during the Truman administration had pushed the unwise measure through as a posthumous, and highly partisan, slap at the late Franklin D. Roosevelt.

No less an authority than Ike's own son, John (who had served as his deputy chief of staff), has said that in spite of his age and health the old soldier would have run again if there had been no Twenty-second Amendment.[29] Considering the closeness of the 1960 election as well as Eisenhower's continuing popularity, there is little doubt that he could have won again had there been no restricting amendment. As it was, when Ike left office he was 70, the oldest person ever to be president—until Ronald Reagan became president at approximately the age Ike was when he left it.

Although he was bitter at his party's loss and unhappy with the policies of the new administration, he did not have the same animosity toward Kennedy that he had had toward Truman. Kennedy had refrained from attacking Ike personally during the campaign and he was carefully deferential toward the outgoing president. He gratefully accepted Eisenhower's offer to brief him and the two had a cordial visit.[30] He urged Kennedy to stand firm against Fidel Castro in Cuba and approved supporting guerrilla action against the revolutionary government there.

On January 17, Eisenhower gave his remarkable farewell address.[31] He pointed to a "conjunction of an immense military establishment and a large arms industry," and said they were new to this country. Although they were necessary, they created a situation that had grave implications. "In the councils of government," he warned, "we must guard against the acquisition of unwarranted influence, whether sought or unsought, by the military-industrial complex. The potential for the disastrous rise of misplaced power exists and will persist." Vigilance was more necessary than ever before. "We must never let the weight of this combination endanger our liberties or democratic processes. Only an alert and knowledgeable citizenry can compel the proper meshing of the huge industrial and military machinery of defense with our peaceful methods and goals, so that security and liberty may prosper together." It probably was the most prescient and thoughtful farewell address of any president.

As Ike watched the construction of a reviewing stand for the Kennedy inaugural, he remarked that it was "like being in the death cell and watching them put up the scaffold."[32] The Eisenhowers attended the inauguration and then slipped away for a luncheon including friends and members of his cabinet. They then were off to Gettysburg, only to discover how much they did not know about functioning outside of the capsule of the White House in modern America. For some two decades, Ike had not had to fend for himself. He had been a general, a high-ranking official, and president of the United States—all positions in which aides would rush to provide any needed service. He found that he did not know how to dial a telephone, adjust a television set, function in a retail store, pay tolls, or prepare frozen orange juice. It was frustrating until he adjusted, but Ike found a major compensating factor. For the first time in many years, he was free.[33]

Also compensating was compensation. As Eisenhower left the presidency, a special act of Congress in January—at the urging of Speaker of the House Sam Rayburn and Senate Majority Leader Lyndon B. Johnson—restored his rank as general of the army, an act that had also been accorded to Grant. He had resigned his commission in 1952 after having been elected president. The act provided that he would receive full military allowance for a five-star general in addition to his full presidential pension and allowances.[34]

Eisenhower remained active as long as his health permitted. As with most former presidents, he gave speeches, collected awards, and received numerous honorary degrees. He wrote his memoirs in two volumes—*Mandate for Change* (1965) and *Waging Peace* (1966)—and arranged for his papers to be placed in the Eisenhower Presidential Library in his boyhood home, Abilene, Kansas. As his biographer Stephen Ambrose put it, the memoirs "represented a major effort and they made a major contribution. Neither as salty nor as personal as Truman's memoirs, they nevertheless did cover all the major and most of the minor issues of the Eisenhower Administration." More successful than his memoirs was a widely reprinted collection in 1967 of down-to-earth anecdotes, *At Ease: Stories I Tell to Friends.*

As long as he was able, Ike remained an avid golfer. At the age of 77, he hit a hole in one. "He pronounced it the thrill of a lifetime."[35] Considering what he had accomplished in that lifetime, that is an indication of just how seriously he took the game.

Although Eisenhower was distressed at many of Kennedy's policies, he readily gave advice when the president asked for it. In 1963, he had the sad task of attending Kennedy's funeral. On this occasion two old antagonists—Ike and former President Harry Truman—finally developed a civil relationship.

After the funeral, Ike also met with President Lyndon Johnson in the White House. Thereafter, Johnson wrote or called Ike to discuss major decisions with him. He sought both Ike's support and his advice. "Johnson was quite sincere in his requests for Eisenhower's counsel, to which he gave great weight." Sadly, the advice that Eisenhower gave to LBJ on Vietnam was "consistently hawkish." He was supportive of Johnson's military policies, but urged him to do more. Johnson, he said, should go for victory; he should untie the hands of the generals. In 1968 when LBJ went on television to announce cessation of the bombing of North Vietnam, Ike was furious, and his "connection with the Johnson Administration came to an end."[36]

The record of Eisenhower's administration had been mixed. On the whole, it was a definite success, despite some notable failures. Ike, for example, had been tardy in moving against Senator Joseph McCarthy and he was equally tardy in moving to enforce *Brown v. Board of Education.* Also, despite his forceful actions in sending troops to Arkansas to enforce court-ordered desegregation at Little Rock High School, Ike never did speak out for racial justice, nor did he take a public position in support of the *Brown* decision. Although it was less apparent at the time than later, Eisenhower left a troubling legacy in foreign policy. His concern for economy led him to emphasize nuclear weapons over conventional forces. It also led him to countenance covert action by the CIA to undermine certain foreign regimes. Such policies caused grief in years to come, especially in Guatemala and Iran, and established dangerous precedents.

The Eisenhower administration's major successes were, however, a counterbalance to shortcomings such as these. He presided over a time of prosperity, he brought the Republican Party to accept the modern presidency, and he kept the country from war and from overt military adventurism. The influence of his retirement, by contrast, at least as it appears in retrospect, may on the whole have been detrimental. He seemed to have lost the spirit of moderation that he attempted to maintain while president.

Eisenhower had been the victim of several heart attacks, even when he was president. During the last few years of his life, his health began to decline precipitously. On March 28, 1969, he died. His widow, Mamie, lived another decade,

dying of a stroke on November 11, 1979. The Eisenhowers are buried together
in Abilene, Kansas.

Dwight D. Eisenhower was nevertheless in the news again in the spring of
2003.[37] Every state is entitled to have two statues of someone of distinction to
represent the state in the Capitol's Statuary Hall in Washington (Nevada, New
Mexico, and North Dakota thus far have only one each). The only stipulation
is that the person to be honored must be deceased. Over time the importance of
some of the figures inevitably fades or someone of much greater note overshadows older personages. Such was the case with Kansas, Eisenhower's Texas birth
notwithstanding.

So it was also with the statue of George Glick, one of the two statues representing Kansas. Glick, it turns out, was a Kansas governor, elected in 1882—
a governor of whom even most Kansans appear to be completely ignorant. No
state's statue, however, had ever been removed. Missouri, for example, has honored the great Senator Thomas Hart Benton and the distinguished Francis P.
Blair, but not its most distinguished son, Harry Truman. Powerful Kansas Republicans, though, quite understandably thought it appropriate to honor Eisenhower at the expense of Glick. The Kansas legislature agreed, as did the U.S.
Congress. Each body passed enabling legislation, and on June 4, 2003, Eisenhower's statue replaced Glick's. Glick's statue resides in the Kansas State Capitol
in Topeka.

Ike's statue is only the fourth president to grace the hall. The others are Virginia's Washington (Virginia, of course, also placed a statue of Robert E. Lee
there); Tennessee's Andrew Jackson, and Ohio's James A. Garfield. The Confederate government is well-represented, with President Jefferson Davis from Mississippi and Vice President Alexander H. Stephens from Georgia.

LYNDON B. JOHNSON

In the midst of the furor regarding the Vietnam War, Lyndon Johnson chose
to foster national unity by not running for reelection in 1968. His administration had been among the most momentous in history. Its "Great Society"
programs included the War on Poverty, Head Start, College Work Study, environmental protections, Medicare, federal aid to education, the Civil Rights
Act of 1964, the Voting Rights Act of 1965, and much more. LBJ's record
also included the Vietnam War that had seen America's consensus unravel.
His surprise announcement not to run for reelection came in a nationally
televised speech on March 31. Both Republicans and Democrats praised the

move as statesmanlike, and North Vietnam's leaders in Hanoi expressed a willingness to negotiate. Then, on April 4, a sniper killed Martin Luther King, Jr., and on June 5, another armed assassin—a displaced Palestinian named Sirhan Sirhan, in what may have been the first Arab terrorist act against the United States because of anger at U.S. policies in the Middle East—killed Senator Robert F. Kennedy.

That same month, Chief Justice Earl Warren retired from the Supreme Court, and the Senate, dominated by a coalition of Republicans and conservative Southern Democrats, refused to consider any replacement that Johnson would name. The conservative roadblock left the position vacant for months until after Richard Nixon assumed the presidency in January 1969.[38] It was the first salvo in what became a long political battle over judicial philosophy—one that continues in the twenty-first century as the second President Bush complains that Senate Democrats have blocked confirmation of some of his judicial nominations.

In August, the tumultuous 1968 Democratic National Convention brought nationally televised riots in the Chicago streets—including an out-of-control police force that itself perpetrated much of the violence. Vice President Hubert H. Humphrey, the Democratic candidate, lost a narrow race to former Vice President Richard M. Nixon in November. It was a trying year for LBJ.

On January 20, 1969, he attended President Nixon's inauguration. Then he, Lady Bird, and their daughters Lynda and Luci were guests at a luncheon in the Bethesda home of former secretary of defense and long-time presidential adviser Clark Clifford and his wife, Marny. Well-wishers lined the streets near the Cliffords' home, holding, in LBJ's words, "cheerful and affectionate signs" that he said they would always remember him. The luncheon was small. Afterward, former President Lyndon Johnson personally handed out—to Clifford, former secretary of state Dean Rusk, and advisers Averill Harriman, Walt Rostow, and William S. White—five Medal of Freedom citations that he had signed just before leaving office. From the Cliffords' they drove to Andrews Air Force Base to the waiting Air Force One that President Nixon had provided for their transportation home.[39] "Home" was in the Hill Country of Texas.

The flight took four hours. After departing the plane, LBJ spoke briefly to a large crowd at Bergstrom Air Force Base, outside Austin. After another flight, this time a brief one, they were home on the LBJ Ranch at Stonewall, Texas, near Johnson City. Lyndon and Lady Bird strolled together around the yard. In the carport, they found their bags in a "giant mound." For the first time in five years, there was no one to carry their luggage. LBJ wrote that Lady Bird looked and began to laugh. "'The coach has turned into a pumpkin,' she said, 'and the mice have all run away.'"[40]

LBJ's public life was over; he was only 60. After years in appointive office, the U.S. House and the U.S. Senate, the vice presidency and the presidency, he was a private citizen. He did not join those former presidents who sought further office. He truly was retired, although he remained active and in fact assumed management of his ranch.

But first he would relax. His daughter, Luci, remarked that she thought going back to his ranch would be like putting him in a tomb, but instead he learned to have fun; he discovered play. It "was a word that was not in his vocabulary," but he started going to horse races, taking trips to Acapulco, and enjoying life.[41] He even let his hair grow long, giving him an appearance of some of his predecessors in the nineteenth century—not to mention looking like those from the counterculture of his own day that he so resented because of their protests against his policies in Vietnam. His greatest joys were with his grandchildren.

Doris Kearns, a Harvard-educated historian and Johnson aide helping him with his memoirs and other writings, said that he did at times seem genuinely happy. "His relationship with his wife was uncommonly close. Outward signs of deep affection and love were observable on a daily level." His affection for his daughters also was obvious and each of them had "presented him with beautiful, healthy, and energetic grandchildren." In his play with those grandchildren, "Johnson exhibited the wonderful childlike qualities he himself had never lost. He could entertain them for hours with the same repetitious game long after most other adults would have lost their patience. Yes," she wrote, "there were much love and warmth and pleasure in his final years, and, at times, there seemed some truth to Johnson's claim of being happier in retirement than he had ever been."[42]

He said he was glad to be out of public life. No doubt he was, but it was not all easy; he was susceptible to great mood swings. Along with a newfound sense of freedom "came feelings of diminished stature, of grief at losing his place of centrality in the country and the world."[43] By the time LBJ retired, presidents had pensions, an office with staff, Secret Service protection and aides, and the use of a military helicopter; but it would never be the same.

In July 1969, he was an invited guest at the launch of Apollo XI. He sat in open bleachers under a blazing sun and was miserable. He told Kearns that he never should have gone, that he had wanted to be back home every minute of his stay there.[44]

Johnson had set his goals for the first few years of his retirement and they included four major public projects. First, he would produce his memoirs. He also was eager to see the LBJ Library in Austin completed to house the records of his presidency, he wanted to establish a Lyndon B. Johnson School of Public Affairs at the University of Texas at Austin, and he intended to complete a series of television interviews with Walter Cronkite for CBS.[45] None of these goals came easily.

He did complete his memoirs, *The Vantage Point,* but rarely did his wit and personality come through. Part of the trouble was his writing team and a bureaucratic desire to sanitize material. But he undoubtedly was part of the trouble too, because of his strong desire to present his best side to the public. Kearns described the real Johnson as "captious, imaginative, brilliant, and impossible." The real Johnson, though, rarely appeared in the book. Rather there was a "peculiarly colorless figure" who "plodded" through most of it. She said that "Johnson's insistence on distancing himself from the material made the book's failure inevitable."[46] Failure, however, seems to be too strong a judgment. The book is valuable as a resource, if only to serve as a comparison with other treatments of the times.

The LBJ Library was a great success. He and Lady Bird both raised and contributed large amounts of money, and "Johnson also enjoyed reviewing the architectural details of the library and consulting about the recruitment of a library staff and a faculty for the school." The Library opened on May 22, 1971, and many Washington figures came, including President Nixon. LBJ thoroughly enjoyed himself, but administrative details later, perhaps inevitably, brought frustration.[47] As long as he lived, however, Johnson enjoyed working with students and school groups and visiting with scholars and others at the Library. He addressed a major symposium there on civil rights shortly before his death.

On December 11 and 12, 1972, against doctor's orders, he drove through an ice storm to attend the conference and speak. Most of the notable civil rights activists of the 1950s and 1960s were there: Roy Wilkins, Clarence Mitchell, Whitney Young, and many others. Chief Justice Earl Warren and Associate Justice Thurgood Marshall also were there as was former Vice President Hubert Humphrey. Johnson spoke of the need to do much more to advance civil rights, and said he was ashamed that he had been able to accomplish so little in relation to the great need. LBJ said—suggesting

Lincoln's great message in his Second Inaugural—that the problem of civil rights was not a problem of one section, but of the whole country.[48]

Partly because of resentment toward the proposed war policies of Democratic candidate George McGovern and partly because Johnson recognized the horrendous difficulties of a sitting president under the circumstances, he did not criticize President Nixon during the 1972 election. He did endorse McGovern, but was lukewarm in his support. "For his troubles, Johnson got a symbolic slap in the face from Nixon."[49] Nixon in October said that he had no intention of seeking a settlement in Vietnam before the election and strongly criticized LBJ for having halted the bombing of North Vietnam in 1968.

Nixon won by a huge landslide. Although his percentage of the popular vote was somewhat less than LBJ's in 1964, he became one of only four presidents in history to reach the 60 percent figure (joining Harding and FDR in addition to Johnson). After his victory, with Watergate looming, according to presidential historian Robert Dallek, Nixon sought to intimidate LBJ into pressuring the U.S. Senate to cease its investigation of Nixonian wrongdoing. Nixon alleged that he had evidence of FBI eavesdropping on the planes that he and Spiro Agnew used in the 1968 campaign and that he would release it. LBJ in turn said that if Nixon were to do this, "he would retaliate with material from the National Security Administration files demonstrating that Nixon's campaign had illegally interfered with the Paris peace talks by convincing Saigon to stay away until after Nixon came to office." That most serious threat put a stop to Nixon's efforts to intimidate him.[50] If Johnson's allegation is true, it would be another great crime to add to those associated with Nixon and Watergate.

In December 1972, the Johnsons donated the LBJ Ranch in his birthplace of Stonewall, Texas, to the U.S. Government to become a National Historic Site. On January 20, 1973, Nixon was inaugurated for his second term. The next day, a cease-fire was announced in Vietnam. "Later that day a new Nixon plan was announced for the dismantling of the Great Society."[51] Nixon moved quickly to eliminate the centerpiece of the War on Poverty, the Office of Economic Opportunity. He also moved to shift various programs to the states and greatly restricted the War on Poverty's Community Action Program.

The day after that, January 22, the great LBJ's heart gave out and he died. He is buried in his family cemetery in the Texas Hill Country. At this writing, Lady Bird Johnson continues to reside, at the age of 90, on the LBJ Ranch. She also has a house in Austin.

Shortly before the end of his life, LBJ had said to Lady Bird that when he died, he did not want at his funeral only their friends "who can come in their private planes. I want the men in their pickup trucks and the women whose slips hang down below their dresses to be welcome too."[52] This was the real Lyndon Johnson.

Lady Bird Johnson was among the most outstanding first ladies, both during her time at the White House and after. Her relatively low profile perhaps kept her from being widely recognized as being in the same category with her relatively recent predecessors Jacqueline Kennedy and Eleanor Roosevelt, but she belongs in their company nonetheless. She sent a warm and supportive note to another outstanding first lady, Hillary Rodham Clinton, after President Clinton's impeachment. She said she had watched her on television by President Clinton's side on the South Lawn "reminding us of the country's progress in many areas such as education and health and how far we have yet to go." Then, she wrote, she learned of Hillary Clinton's role in rallying support on Capitol Hill from the Democrats. Mrs. Johnson said, "you made my day!," and said she was confident that a great many citizens felt the same way. She sent a prayer her way, she said, and also sent her cheers and admiration.[53]

Despite efforts to dismantle LBJ's Great Society, much of it continues and has become part of the generally accepted "American Way of Life." Vietnam left a scar on the country, but the blame was far from LBJ's alone. He inherited a problem and made it worse on the advice of most of the political establishment, liberals and conservatives, Republicans and Democrats. That scar, though, ultimately will fade. LBJ left much more: the Civil Rights Act of 1964, the Voting Rights Act of 1965, environmental protection, Medicare, Head Start, the College Work Study Program, consumer protections—the list is endless.

LBJ was not the most active of the former presidents, but he was productive nonetheless. Even in that role he continued to exercise his influence on behalf of racial equality. His biographer, Robert Dallek, aptly called Johnson a "flawed giant."

RICHARD M. NIXON

Richard Milhous Nixon, the thirty-seventh president of the United States, entered retirement suddenly. On August 9, 1974, not two years since he had won one of

the greatest landslide victories in American presidential history, he resigned his office. Nixon is the only president ever to do so. Had he not resigned on his own,
he would assuredly have been impeached and removed. His downfall came from
a complicated series of events. For simplicity—and we Americans always seek simplicity—these have come to be wrapped up in one simple term, "Watergate."

Nixon and his aides did everything possible to create a certain, benign
mythology surrounding Watergate. As they described it, the episode in which
White House aides directed a break-in was nothing more than a simple burglary
of the Democratic National Headquarters in the Watergate apartment complex
in Washington—a "third rate" burglary, if there is such a thing. Yet Watergate
was far more. It was, in fact, a direct attack on the constitutional system of elections—if not an attack even upon the framework of constitutional government—in this country. Using more than one burglary and a series of "dirty
tricks," the Watergate conspiracy sought—successfully, one might add—to sab-
otage the opposition party and to ensure that it would not select its strongest
candidate. It involved illegal fund-raising and payoffs, and it involved the use of
government agencies such as the Internal Revenue Service, as Nixon put it, to
"screw our enemies."

President Nixon was president no longer, but he remained on the scene for
two more decades. He wrote prolifically, some nine substantial works after leaving the presidency, always seeking vindication. To some extent he succeeded in
restoring his reputation, as was his burning desire. He became an elder states-
man in the eyes of many and a respected—if often unheeded—adviser to the
Republican Party.

When he left the White House, Nixon understandably became deeply depressed and secluded himself at his California estate, La Casa Pacifica, in San
Clemente. At the time, legal proceedings were beginning against him. President
Ford, fearing that a trial of a former president would be extraordinarily damaging to national unity and also aware that Nixon's mental state might be fragile,
without warning on September 8, 1974, approximately one month after Nixon's
resignation, went on national television and announced "a full free and absolute
pardon" for Nixon.

Historian and Nixon biographer, Stephen Ambrose, in a thoughtful comment, said that in 1974 he had been among the millions of Americans "furious
with Ford. Seventeen years later," he said, he found "the case for a pardon to be
irrefutable. All the arguments that made Ford decide to pardon as soon as possible are accurate: the last thing the country needed was to continue to be torn
apart by Richard Nixon." Moreover, if he were to be found guilty, he likely
would have been pardoned anyway. It would have been unthinkable to have a

former president serve time in prison.[54] It would be unthinkable to most Americans, although as events at the end of the century demonstrated, such a sense of moderation or propriety certainly cannot be presumed to be universal. Despite a large contingent of Nixon haters, during the Nixon travail there was evident a strong—and wise—sense that it would be destructive to waive all restraint when attacking a president; rather, regardless of the justification for the attack, it would be important also to guard against damage to the country and to the presidency itself.

Despite Nixon's apparently genuine depression, his self-serving tactics never ceased. On the day he resigned, he called his former aide, Alexander Haig, "and demanded that his papers, tapes, and other documents be sent to San Clemente immediately. The following day, Haig circulated a memorandum for the White House staff. 'By custom and tradition,' it began, 'the files of the White House Office belong to the President in whose Administration they are accumulated.'" When Ford moved into the Oval Office, he discovered that it had been "stripped clean" and in other offices there was smoke residue from papers that had been burned. A Ford staff lawyer, Benton Becker, had halted massive destruction of papers earlier and had then discovered three large military trucks waiting to take massive amounts of files from the White House. He ordered the loading halted and the Air Force colonel in charge replied that he took orders only from General Haig. Becker and the colonel immediately sought out Haig, who professed to be unaware that anything was being moved. Haig then ordered the colonel to have the trucks unloaded. Becker took no chances; as he put it, he "went outside and watched that son-of-a-bitch unload."[55] Other accounts describe this episode with slightly different details, but with the same substance. No proof has ever surfaced as to who gave the order to move the papers and tapes, but it was the beginning of a long battle for custody of the records between Nixon (and later his estate) and the government.

It was that custody battle that led to the unique status of the Richard Nixon Library. The Library, at Yorba Linda, California, is the only library devoted to a former president that is not officially a "presidential library." It receives no government funds and does not house Nixon's presidential papers, only those from before and after his presidency. There are ten presidential libraries, each operated by the National Archives and Records Administration, but Nixon's is not among them; it is in a separate category.

An article in *The New York Times* in 2002 outlined a dispute between the Nixon daughters. "Tricia Nixon Cox, who has not spoken to her sister in years," it said, "has long wanted the Richard Nixon Library and Birthplace Foundation to be controlled by family members and loyalists, while Julie Nixon Eisenhower prefers that control be exerted by a professional library staff, which would presumably be more neutral and independent."[56] The dispute, the article said, recently erupted and concluded that it was "another indication that Mr. Nixon's legacy is—well, different from those of other presidents."

So it was. Later, however, the family tension appears to have lessened. The two Nixon daughters are cooperating with former President Gerald Ford to work toward the creation of a new Nixon Presidential Library "on the site of what is now the privately run Richard Nixon Library and Birthplace." Ford, on CNN's *Larry King Live,* has "pledged his full support to correct what he considers the unfair treatment of Nixon." There are many obstacles to the project: legislation would likely be required because of the special status of the papers that resulted from the Watergate scandal, for example, as would an agreement between the National Archives and the Nixon Foundation. Julie Eisenhower nevertheless put it well when she said her father "shouldn't be outside the system."[57]

⊰⊱

Nixon in his retirement received many invitations from foreign leaders to visit and ultimately traveled abroad numerous times. He tended to be very well received in other countries. He broke his self-imposed domestic confinement when, to the consternation of the Ford administration, he visited China in 1976. The trip, however, went very well and when he returned in February, Secretary of State Henry Kissinger asked him for a written report, which he agreed to provide. As Stephen Ambrose put it, "he was on his way back."[58] Nixon brought out his massive memoirs, *RN: The Memoirs of Richard Nixon,* in 1978. They were, said Ambrose correctly, "readable if unreliable." Overall, he said, *RN* was "a classic example of Nixon at work, setting out to make everything perfectly clear, leaving everything opaque."[59] They sold well, brought him back to the headlines, and put him back in the public eye. The title was an obvious attempt to put himself in the category of presidents fondly called by their initials: TR, FDR, and of course JFK. He appeared before a national audience again in series of interviews with David Frost that were telecast after the 1976 elections.

In May 1979, the Nixons sold La Casa Pacifica to move from California. In February 1980, they settled in New York City.[60] Throughout his retirement he wrote continually and some of his works were best sellers. His rehabilitation, such as it was, would never again include law practice.[61] The Supreme Court had permitted him to resign his practice privileges. California, too, permitted him to surrender his law license—but only after admitting that he was the subject of disciplinary proceedings. New York disbarred him.

Nevertheless, he remained active—more active than ever. He gave advice on how to handle the crumbling Soviet Union. When Mikhail Gorbachev visited the United States in the spring of 1990 seeking aid for Russia, for example, President Bush the elder—along with many members of Congress—cited Nixon's arguments to justify refusing the request. On March 8 of that year, the former president spoke to the House Republican Conference, and met with Republican senators who were seeking re-election to provide them with advice and counsel. He was in demand to pose with Republican leaders for pictures. Newt Gingrich, then House Republican Whip, said the meeting with Nixon was an "extraordinary experience." Robert Dole, the prominent Republican senator and future presidential candidate, proclaimed him "rehabilitated." Ambrose remarked that Nixon was more politically involved than any former president had been since Theodore Roosevelt. One Republican Senate aide yelled with enthusiasm, "he's back." Indeed he was, Ambrose said, "and he had done it without taking 'the easy way.' There had never been a gesture of contriteness. The people yearned for him to ask for forgiveness, so that they could forgive, but he would not. Hell would freeze first."[62] It helped Nixon that he had lived so long. Not only had many of his enemies died, but so had much memory of what Watergate and its attendant misdeeds had meant.

The rehabilitation did include an interesting contribution of sorts—one unique among former presidents. In 1985, Nixon refereed a baseball umpires' strike. In addition, in 1987 he became a "foreign associate of France's Fine Arts Academy." The Nixon rehabilitation will assuredly become even less controversial as memories of Watergate continue to dim, but it was incomplete in life and will never be complete in death.[63]

That death came in 1994, on April 22, bringing to an end the tormented life of a driven man. Nixon did what he did because he was tough, "the toughest man in American politics in his day," asserted Ambrose correctly. Insults wounded him, "and he bled freely, but he always recovered." He was disciplined, well-informed, and courageously unintimidated by risk.[64] No president since Lincoln had been required to be so tough—Truman, perhaps, came closest; probably Theodore Roosevelt would have been equally tough, but was not tested politically to the extent that Nixon was.

Pat Nixon had died ten months prior to the former president, on June 22, 1993. Ambrose has written of one major change in Nixon after his presidency. "Before the resignation," he said, Nixon "had shunned any public display of affection." Afterward, however, "his concern and love" for Pat was obvious. He showed a new tenderness. "The couple had entered a new stage in the partnership, more caring, more concerned, more loving, and Nixon had been more willing to show it."[65] Perhaps if that more human part of Richard Nixon had been broader and had had a public side, the tragedy of his presidency might not have occurred. The Nixons are buried at the Richard Nixon Library and Birthplace in California.

GERALD R. FORD

On January 20, 1977, President Gerald R. Ford attended the inauguration of his successor, President James Earl Carter. The Fords then departed for their home in Rancho Mirage, California. They also maintained a residence near Vail, Colorado.

Ford had been elected to the House of Representatives from Michigan in 1948 and had spent his life since then in public service. He had considered himself to be a creature of the House with a goal of someday becoming speaker. He had not aspired to the presidency, but his life took a dramatically different turn from what he had expected. Vice President Spiro T. Agnew suddenly resigned from the troubled Nixon administration. The resignation was part of a deal to avoid spending time in jail resulting from charges of financial wrongdoing when he had been county executive of Baltimore County and later governor of Maryland. Previously it had been impossible to fill a vacancy in the vice presidency except in the regular presidential/vice presidential election. The new Twenty-fifth Amendment had become part of the Constitution in 1967, however. It had the strong support of President Johnson, whose experience without a vice president caused him to be concerned about presidential succession. Under its provisions, President Nixon nominated House Minority Leader Ford to fill the vacancy. After confirmation by both houses (the Senate, alone, confirms other appointments), Gerald Ford took the oath of office on December 6, 1973 and became Vice President Ford. Although he did not become speaker of the House, in an ironic twist, as vice president he was President of the Senate.

Lightning in Ford's case struck twice. Less than a year after he became vice president, President Nixon himself resigned. Thus on August 9, 1974, Ford became the thirty-eighth president of the United States—the only president never to have been elected either as president or vice president.

Initially, Ford had decided that he would not run for his own term in 1976, but in 1975 he announced that he had changed his mind. He faced a challenge from within his own party from former California Governor Ronald Reagan, who was the favorite of the Republican right wing. After a bruising, and damaging, struggle at the Republican convention Ford emerged as the nominee. The election was hard-fought and the results were close, but Carter had won a clear-cut victory. Gerald Ford would leave office after having served 895 days as president. His was not the briefest presidency—William Henry Harrison, James A. Garfield, Zachary Taylor, and Warren G. Harding, all dying in office, served shorter periods than Ford—but his time had been brief.

Despite the brevity of his term, Ford succeeded in restoring integrity to the White House following the tumultuous Nixon years. He worked to soothe the country that was reeling from Watergate and a unique presidential resignation. He also adopted activist policies, both in foreign and domestic affairs (such as in civil rights and energy); he was no Whig president.

Regardless of gibes from comedians and political opponents, Ford was capable and energetic. He was a fiscal conservative, but he was a moderate by temperament and policy. As such, he was concerned regarding the extremist forces that were working to dominate American politics. As president and as former president, Ford has worked to encourage moderate policies.

In 1982, for example, in response to the growing power of the religious right in politics, Ford participated in a program sponsored by liberal television producer Norman Lear's People for the American Way. He joined with numerous celebrities and other political figures such as Barry Goldwater and Lady Bird Johnson, appearing in a two-hour "musical and dramatic salute to American freedom" filmed before a live audience. ABC broadcast the program nationally on March 21. Ford also worked with People for the American Way on their "I Love Liberty" contest. Some 35,000 school children entered drawings, stories, and the like, competing for $500 savings bonds. Accompanying the bonds as prizes to the winners were letters from Ford and a certificate bearing his signature and that of Lady Bird Johnson. Presentations took place in Los Angeles at the NEA Convention on the Fourth of July.

Some unique negotiations took place during the 1980 Republican National Convention with the new Republican candidate, Ronald Reagan, that attested to Ford's continuing political significance after leaving office. In response to an offer by Reagan, former President Ford considered accepting the vice-presidential nomination to be Reagan's running mate.[66] Former presidents such as Grant had considered running again; Van Buren, Fillmore, Cleveland, and Theodore Roosevelt actually did so, but in this instance, a former president actually considered running again not as president, but as vice president.

Perhaps Ford's commitment to public service and his concern for the country entered into his consideration of this proposal that other former presidents might have found insulting. There is no doubt that Ford had little confidence in Reagan's ability to make sound presidential judgments. In his memoirs, for example, Ford wrote of Reagan's "penchant for offering simplistic solutions to hideously complex problems," and of Reagan's "conviction that he was always right in every argument; he seemed unable," wrote Ford, "to acknowledge that he might have made a mistake." Ford also commented on the likelihood that Reagan would be unwilling or unable to devote sufficient time and energy to the presidency.[67] With specific regard to Social Security, Ford recognized as preposterous Reagan's desire to "plow those funds into the stock market," and said, correctly, that it was "proof" that Reagan "didn't understand the complicated problems" of Social Security.[68] Although this is speculative, it seems probable that Ford thought his presence in the administration could help to serve as a check on these perceived inadequacies of Reagan's.

When Ford insisted on the authority to exercise certain powers—powers that would have made him virtually a co-president—the Reagan forces balked and Ford rejected the idea. In fairness to Reagan, it would have been unwise and possibly damaging to the presidency for any president to agree to such a power-sharing arrangement. Regardless of the merits of the proposal, though, it would have been a fascinating historical development for the vice presidency to be occupied by a former president.

As the Fords settled into retirement, Ford accepted membership on several corporate boards. More important, perhaps, have been his numerous educational activities. He has lectured widely and participated in many seminars and public discussions regarding Congress and the presidency. Since the dedication in 1981 of the Gerald R. Ford Library in Ann Arbor, Michigan, and the Gerald R. Ford Museum in Grand Rapids, Ford has hosted dozens of conferences on public policy.

He remains a staunch Republican, but not a fierce partisan. He has warned his party that it damages itself with its recent uncompromising opposition toward abortion and that it must embrace affirmative action more fully. For a quarter century after leaving the presidency, he has spoken out on policy matters.

On October 4, 1998, he published an op-ed piece in *The New York Times* calling for censure, not impeachment, of President Clinton. He took care to point out that he was most concerned about preserving respect for the institutions of government. On December 21, 1998, after the House impeached President Clinton, Ford joined with former President Jimmy Carter in another op-ed piece in *The Times,* once again calling for censure, rather than conviction and removal from office. The former presidents stressed the need for action to be truly bipartisan and said that the time had come "to put aside political differences and plant seeds of justice and reconciliation." Presidents Ford and Carter had written words of wisdom, but they fell on deaf ears.

On August 8 of the same year, Ford wrote yet another op-ed piece in *The Times*. His alma mater, the University of Michigan, was defending itself against a lawsuit alleging that its affirmative-action policies were inappropriate. Ford strongly argued the need for an inclusive America and defended affirmative action and the University of Michigan. Two years later, on July 31, 2000, Ford cooperated with former Republican presidential candidate Robert Dole to endorse President George W. Bush's selection of Richard Cheney as his vice presidential running mate. Ford, in defending Cheney, was defending a former member of his own administration. Ford and Dole characterized Cheney as extraordinarily able and trustworthy. As the new administration of George W. Bush got underway, Ford complimented the president on his handling of the presidency. He warned, however, about relying entirely on the Republican Party's "hard-core right wing."[69]

In August 1999, President Clinton presented former President Ford with the Medal of Freedom for his services to the country during his presidency. The following October, Gerald and Betty Ford received the Congressional Gold Medal for "dedicated public service and outstanding humanitarian contributions."[70] Perhaps most significant of all, on May 21, 2001, the John F. Kennedy Library presented to Gerald Ford the 2001 Profile in Courage Award for the most controversial act of his presidency, and of his career, the pardon of former President Richard Nixon.

In 2002, at the age of 89, Ford published an op-ed piece in the *Washington Post*. Although he had strong concerns about reproductive cloning, he said, the situation was different with regard to therapy. He strongly opposed congressional action against all cloning. Those in need, he argued, "deserve the finest treatment imaginable by the world's best scientists," and a ban that included therapeutic cloning would prevent them from getting it. He spoke out against proposed legislation that was not "locking the lid on Pandora's box," but rather was "slamming the door to lifesaving cures and treatments merely because they are new."[71]

As probably his final act of official public service, Ford joined with former President Jimmy Carter to co-chair the National Commission on Federal Election Reform. The Commission was appointed to review the nation's electoral procedures and recommend reforms to prevent a repetition of the Florida fiasco of 2000. In July 2001, the Commission issued its report to a flurry of news coverage. It called for comprehensive reform to provide accuracy and fundamental fairness. President Bush accepted the report, and without endorsing any specific recommendation said that it could lead to meaningful reform. Several members of Congress reacted immediately and introduced various bills to achieve those reforms. As this is written, in late 2003, there has been little or nothing heard of electoral reform since that time.

———◆———

The former president became 90 on July 14, 2003, and Betty Ford is younger by approximately five years. Both have had some health difficulties, as would be expected at their ages. They have lived long and productive lives and their many contributions will last long after they are gone.

Thirteen

JAMES EARL CARTER, JR.

Nobel Laureate

IT IS COMMON TO HEAR THE REMARK THAT ALTHOUGH JIMMY CARTER MAY NOT have been the best of presidents, he is the finest former president the United States has ever had. This reputation did not come easily. Carter was thoroughly unpopular when he left office and was shattered by the recognition that in the election of 1980 he "had lost to a man he thought immoral to the core." He felt that Ronald Reagan was unprincipled, insincere, and hypocritical, and that he had "ridden into the White House" on dangerous themes: "abhorrence of government, xenophobia, and massive tax cuts." Looking back on his presidency, Carter in 1995 said that "allowing Ronald Reagan to become president was by far my biggest failure in office."[1] He has spent the rest of a long post-presidential career attempting to make up for that failure.

When the Carters returned to their home in Plains, Georgia, they had more to contend with than brooding over the results of the election. They had put their assets, chief among them the Carter Peanut Warehouse, into a blind trust. They discovered not only that the warehouse was bankrupt, but that they were in debt by some one million dollars.

They sold the business, "signed lucrative book contracts, thereby assuring their financial security," and settled down into their new lives.[2] One frequently overlooked feature of the Carters' retirement is their prolific writing—which has not been primarily political—and their status as best-selling authors.[3] Rosalynn Carter has written four books, including a highly successful autobiography; Jimmy Carter has written eighteen, also including an autobiography and most recently a well-received novel; jointly they have authored two. Their subjects range from guides for caregivers to the mentally ill to childhood reminiscences, explorations of religious faith, and even—in Jimmy Carter's case—a children's book and a book of poetry.

Carter scholar Douglas Brinkley has said that among presidents, "besides Carter, only John Quincy Adams and Abraham Lincoln were in communion with the poetic muse"—other presidents, of course, most notably Theodore Roosevelt, were avid readers if not authors of poetry; TR, in fact, read poetry (along with other works) in several languages, including some esoteric and archaic ones. Carter's volume of poetry, *Always a Reckoning*,[4] is a slim volume containing 51 poems. Brinkley wrote—the extent to which this is a tribute is a matter of taste, but certainly it could be worse—that Carter's poems were "an amalgam of Carl Sandburg at his worst and Rod McKuen at his best." They ranged widely, he said, "from boss politics, possum hunting, and barefoot fishing to the plight of the homeless and familial relationships."[5] Brinkley commented further that the volume, "to the surprise of literary critics," became a *New York Times* bestseller, that Carter came to be in demand by poets' groups, that some of his poems appeared in respected literary journals, and even that some poets—among them Joseph Brodsky, who said that Carter wrote with "professional competence"—spoke favorably of the former president's work. The novel, *The Hornet's Nest*, is a tale of the Revolutionary War in Georgia.

For a while, the Carters kept a low profile, but this could not continue long for the restless, energetic, and determined former president. In April 1982 he received appointment as University Distinguished Professor at Emory University, and began planning for a policy research center there.

At the same time, Carter also worked toward establishing the Jimmy Carter Library and Museum and the Carter Center. The Center opened first, in October 1986; the Library followed in January 1987. Even before the Center officially opened, it began to host symposia on such topics as arms control negotiation, health policy, and natural resources.

From the beginning, Carter envisioned the Carter Center as a "duplicate Camp David in Atlanta . . . as a neutral forum within which hostile groups could meet to explore common approaches to problems." According to Rosalynn, the idea for the Center came to her husband about a year after he left the presidency, during a restless night in January 1982. Carter's goal was peace; he "wanted to be a peacemaker, even if it meant inviting African warlords or

Latin American despots to Atlanta."[6] The Center has been a great success in dealing on a case-by-case basis, one at a time, with various problems around the world—especially with regard to such issues as health care (especially in impoverished countries), peacemaking, agricultural development (again, especially in impoverished countries), and hunger.

The Center has served as Carter's base as he has engaged in projects around the world. One of the most prominent has been his effort to eradicate the guinea worm in various African countries and in Pakistan. The worm produces "a debilitating condition that had maimed and crippled some 5 million people a year." The victim—all of whom are human; the worm seems to infest no other creature—ingests the larvae in contaminated water and a worm grows within the body to a length of two to three feet over the course of a year. Ultimately it burrows near to the skin and grows there before bursting through a blister to the outside, usually on or near the feet, causing intense pain. Carter speculated that guinea worm infestation had troubled humanity since ancient times and that it might be what the Bible calls the "fiery serpent" that afflicted the Israelites on the shore of the Red Sea. The solution to the problem is clean water; even filtered water will screen out the larvae.[7]

⸻❖⸻

Some of the very qualities that impeded Carter's performance as president came to be advantages in his new, much less political, role. He immediately began employing his engineering background in approaching problems, determining what needed to be done, and forging ahead regardless. His projects took him constantly around the world—he surely is the most traveled former president in history.

One must concede that even after his presidency Carter's fervor at times has been a double-edged sword. As a deeply religious man—yet one whom the religious right rejected when they gave their support instead to Ronald Reagan, a divorced former actor who restored to the White House the hard liquor that Carter had banned—Carter reacts quickly to perceived slights to religion. When Iranian leader the Ayatullah Khomeini issued the *fatwa* condemning author Salman Rushdie to death for insulting Islam in his 1988 novel *The Satanic Verses,* Carter shocked many friends and supporters—and received praise throughout the Arab world—for criticizing Rushdie in a *New York Times* op-ed piece at the same time that he deplored the death sentence. He noted that "It's not right to ridicule another person's religion."[8] To be sure; but it also is not conducive to civilized living to issue a death sentence on the basis of the mere use of words, especially words in a work of fiction.

In this instance, Carter's judgment failed him. To say that condemning Rushdie to death is wrong, but in the same article to point out that Rushdie should not have written what he did, is a clear instance of blaming the victim—and of minimizing the right of free expression. Rushdie's book may well have been "provocative." Carter's reasoning, though—implicitly that Rushdie "asked for it"—was perilously close to that of the person who says that rape is of course wrong, but that it would not happen if women did not wear "provocative" clothing or "ask for it." In either case, such reasoning is wrong. Carter's overall record, though, more than overshadows such lapses.

A brief selection of his many activities is sufficient to demonstrate the remarkable nature of Carter's post-presidential agenda. In 1989, he and a team made several visits to Panama to prepare to observe elections that were to take place there in February 1990. Although the voting had been conducted in a reasonably fair fashion, the Manuel Noriega government quickly began to report false figures. Carter denounced the election as a fraud and discredited the results. Also in 1990, he led a team to observe elections in Nicaragua. Astonishing most observers, the vote turned the leftist government of Daniel Ortega out of office and Ortega accepted the results. After several trips to Haiti, Carter and his team monitored Haitian elections that became that unfortunate country's first fair contest. In February 1991 the Carters attended the inauguration there of the democratically elected President Jean-Bertrand Aristide.

And so it has gone—and continues to go. The Carters have observed elections countless times around the world. They have journeyed to troubled areas, working for peace. A recent example came during the unrest in Venezuela in 2002. Carter undertook a peace mission to counsel President Hugo Chavez at the president's own invitation. After demonstrations against Chavez became serious, an army coup removed him from office. In response to counter demonstrations, loyalist troops reinstated him on April 14. Carter arrived July 6. Later, he said he told Chavez, the elected leader, to adopt policies to reconcile with the 35 percent of the people who "despise him."[9]

Most visible to Americans—and most well received—has been the Carters' work with Habitat for Humanity, a nonprofit organization that builds homes for the poor. Members devote regular time to projects, actually working themselves to help build houses. Habitat has expanded with projects around the world. In 2002, for example, a brief news item reported that Carter was in South Africa, where he laid bricks and worked with concrete to build low-income housing. He was, said the item, one of 4,500 volunteers there under the auspices of Habitat to build 100 homes in Durban. The report indicated that since its founding in 1976, Habitat had built "more than 100,000 homes in sixty countries."[10] In 1986, the Carters began, with Habitat, a Jimmy Carter Work Project that meets for one week each summer in a different location. There, the Carters help to build homes from the ground up.[11]

What is less visible, but no less important both in actuality and symbolically, has been Carter's private human-rights activities. He employs his prestige as a former president of the United States to communicate directly with foreign rulers to halt torture and to release political prisoners. In this regard, Carter has worked closely with Amnesty International. Historian Douglas Brinkley, a keen student of Carter's post-presidential career, has written that, although it is impossible to be precise regarding numbers, "from 1981 to 1997 Carter was directly responsible for the release of approximately 50,000 political prisoners whose human rights had been violated." Carter did this, Brinkley said, "without fanfare or media hoopla."[12] No autocratic leader has been immune from Carter's efforts.

More broadly, the Carter Center has incorporated human rights as an "umbrella concept" under which all of its programs operate. It has monitored human-rights violations around the world, regardless of ideology or politics. Brinkley has credited Carter with being the one American political figure who has done more for human rights both at home and abroad than any other, except perhaps for Eleanor Roosevelt.[13]

In 2002, Carter made one of the most dramatic journeys of his post-presidential career. Cuban leader Fidel Castro had invited the former president, who is enormously popular in Latin America, to visit Cuba. *The New York Times* on March 26 reported that the Bush administration was likely to approve the trip and it did so. Press Secretary Ari Fleischer commented that "President Bush would urge Mr. Carter to press the Castro government for democratic reforms."[14] Carter's five-day trip began on May 12. Castro permitted Carter to inspect biotechnology centers that some American officials believed harbored facilities for concocting biological weapons. He offered to let Carter choose technical experts to accompany him.[15] Carter reported that it was unlikely that Cuba was developing anything substantial and Secretary of State Colin Powell agreed, although both noted also that Cuba did have the capability.[16]

Most remarkably, Carter received a petition while he was in Cuba with the names of 11,000 dissidents and pro-democracy advocates,[17] and he was permitted to address the Cuban people on live national television. He spoke in Spanish and mentioned the petition.[18] In addressing the Cuban people, he called both for the United States to end its sanctions against Cuba, and most tellingly, he challenged Castro to "allow elections to bring broad reforms in political rights and castigated the socialist system for denying basic freedoms." *The New York Times* reported that Castro "sat impassively in the front row" while Carter spoke. Carter, said the *Times,* was "the most prominent American political leader to visit Cuba since Mr. Castro took power in a 1959 revolution. The uncensored transmission of a speech on Cuban soil by such an influential American has no precedent under the Communist government."[19] Carter, upon returning home, reported directly to the American people in an op-ed piece in the *Washington Post.*[20]

Despite such a breakthrough, there were the predictable jeers from the right. Fred Barnes of *The Weekly Standard* said that it was a myth that Carter was a great former president and called him a menace.[21] A syndicated columnist, Jonah Goldberg, accused Carter of calling "the United States a liar," because he contradicted a lower-level State Department assertion that Cuba had biological weapons. As noted, Secretary of State Powell agreed with Carter. Goldberg pontificated that the former president may have "done yeoman work as a homebuilder for the American poor," but "is something of a joke as an international figure."[22]

Regardless of that columnist's opinion, every year for many years it was no joke that Jimmy Carter had been nominated to receive the Nobel Prize for Peace. In 2002, he finally became a Nobel Laureate. He received the award on December 10. The Norwegian Nobel Committee selected him because of "his decades of untiring effort to find peaceful solutions to international conflicts, to advance democracy and human rights, and to promote economic and social development." The news media in the United States were full of items about Carter's prize. A number of them also noted an implicit criticism in the Norwegian Committee's Citation of President George W. Bush—some of them condemned it. The offending passage, in its entirety, said: "In a situation currently marked by threats of the use of power, Carter has stood by the principles that conflicts must as far as possible be resolved through mediation and international cooperation based on international law, respect for human rights, and economic development."[23] Taking offense at such mild language reflected the furor that the Bush administration was attempting to encourage among the public prior to its preemptive strike at Iraq. Those who protested too much should have remembered that the award was, after all the Nobel *Peace* Prize. What other language was the Committee to have selected, if "peace" were to have any meaning at all?

In the course of his brief acceptance lecture, Carter said, "I am not here as a public official, but as a citizen of a troubled world who finds hope in a growing consensus that the generally accepted goals of society are peace, freedom, human rights, environmental quality, the alleviation of suffering, and the rule of law."[24] As he concluded, he noted that "war may sometimes be a necessary evil. But no matter how necessary, it is always an evil."[25] Carter was speaking as one with an impressive background: not only as a former president of the United States, but also as a military professional and a graduate of the U.S. Naval Academy. He had more actual military service than any twentieth-century American president except for Dwight Eisenhower. He was the third of those presidents, following Theodore Roosevelt and Woodrow Wilson, to win the Nobel Peace Prize.

——❖——

Jimmy Carter thus "reinvented" himself, as a *Washington Post* article discussing a PBS documentary on the former president put it.[26] "He could have gone down in history as a failure," said Adriana Bosch, who produced the film. "His nature is such that he wasn't going to sit and do nothing. This Nobel Peace Prize, he got it for himself."[27] He did so by devoting his enormous energy to improving the world. Among former presidents of the United States, very few—John Quincy Adams comes readily to mind along with William Howard Taft, Theodore Roosevelt, and no more than two or three others at most—can rival Jimmy Carter in their post-presidential contributions to their country.

Fourteen

FROM REAGAN THROUGH BUSH TO CLINTON

A Study in Contrasts

THE PRESIDENTS WHO BROUGHT THE TWENTIETH CENTURY TO A CLOSE RANGED from the oldest who ever held the office to the first who had been born after World War II. They included two of the most adept in using the media, Reagan and Clinton. It was during this time that the Soviet Union began to crumble and then vanished, bringing the Cold War to an end. It was during the Reagan and Bush administrations that the deficit soared to unprecedented heights, only to have been conquered by the century's end—the more optimistic observers thought it was gone forever as the century closed with a level of prosperity that was unique in all of human history.

Although perhaps there still is not sufficient distance from Ronald Reagan's presidency to evaluate it dispassionately, there is no doubt that Reagan was one of the most significant presidents in a century of significant presidents. The long-term effects of his administration may in fact make him one of the most significant—for good or ill—in the history of the country.

The contrast of the visionary Reagan with Vice President George Bush could hardly have been more marked. Bush followed Reagan to become the first sitting vice president to be elected directly to the presidency since Martin Van Buren in 1836. In spite of Bush's victory—a victory that not only was personal but also a public tribute to Reagan—Bush by his own statement had trouble with "the vision thing."

No lack of vision troubled Bill Clinton. Visionary ideas permeated his tumultuous presidency. He consistently confounded his fervent and bitter enemies and demonstrated a determination and toughness in facing adversity that only Lincoln and Nixon could equal. Like Lincoln, but unlike Nixon, he consistently reflected that vision while fending off his troubles.

If it is too early to evaluate Reagan's presidency, it certainly is too early to evaluate Clinton's retirement. As for the retirements of Reagan or Bush, neither stands out as being especially significant when contrasted with those of other presidents. This in all probability reflects their ages. Reagan, at nearly 78 when he left office, was by far the oldest person ever to be president. His tragic submersion into the depths of Alzheimer's Disease made it impossible for him to be an active former president for more than a short time after he departed the White House. Bush, at 68, only ten years younger when he departed office, would have been the second oldest president if he had served another term. There is no doubt about Bush's mental capacities, which remain keen, and his physical vigor also appears be extraordinary, given his age. Nevertheless, his post-presidential years have not been especially notable except for his having become, along with John Adams, the father of another president. Clinton, on the other hand, only 46 when he took office, was the third youngest of the presidents (only Theodore Roosevelt at 42 and John Kennedy at 43 were younger).

After two terms as president Clinton was only 54, which is uncommonly young for a former chief executive. Among two-term presidents, only TR was younger; at 50, he still holds the record. Pierce, at 52, and Polk and Fillmore at 53 were younger, but they each served only one term. Cleveland was only 51 (almost 52) when he first became a former president after his initial term, but after his second—which was non-consecutive—he was two weeks short of his sixtieth birthday. Journalist Jonathan Alter wrote that Clinton was "the youngest, most kinetic and intellectually alive ex-president since Teddy Roosevelt."[1] Age alone, of course, is not an infallible guide as to what will happen in a former chief executive's post-presidential career. TR, Cleveland, and Fillmore remained active; Pierce and Polk ("Young Hickory") did not—Polk, in fact, died within three months of leaving office. The chances are good, though, that Clinton will have by far one of the more significant post-presidential careers—for one thing, his enemies contribute to his visibility by continuing to attack him almost as if he still were in office.

RONALD W. REAGAN

Ronald and Nancy Reagan happily attended the inauguration of George Bush as the forty-first President of the United States on January 20, 1989 (he actually was the fortieth to hold the office, but it is customary to count Cleveland twice). The same day, they left to return to their home in Bel Air, California.[2] Reagan was the second president—and the second Republican—to come under the restrictions of the Twenty-second Amendment and be denied the opportunity to run for a third term.

Still energetic at the age of 78, however, Reagan did not stay put long. He soon journeyed with Nancy to Europe. On June 14, he presented the Winston Churchill Lecture in London to the English-Speaking Union, and the following day he received an honorary knighthood from Queen Elizabeth II. On June 15 he attended celebrations in Paris commemorating the one-hundredth anniversary of the completion of the Eiffel Tower.

In July, while on a vacation in Mexico, the former president fell from a horse and received what he thought were mere bruises and superficial injuries. In September, however, he visited the Mayo Clinic for what he publicized as a "routine physical," which disclosed that he had fluid on his brain—apparently a result of the fall. One week later, on September 15, he underwent brain surgery at St. Mary's Hospital in Rochester, Minnesota, to have the fluid drained.

For the next four years, as Reagan gave numerous speeches and appeared at public ceremonies, which he relished, a catalogue of his activities would fill several pages. On November 15, he visited the White House to see the presentation of his official presidential portrait. In July 1990, he presented an address at the dedication of the Richard Nixon Library and Birthplace in Yorba Linda, California. On the one-hundredth anniversary of former President Eisenhower's birth, he gave an address at the Eisenhower Boyhood Home in Abilene, Kansas. In September, he visited several European countries again, and participated in various ceremonies. On February 4, 1991, he escorted former British Prime Minister Margaret Thatcher on a tour of the yet-to-be-finished Reagan Presidential Library in Simi Valley, California; and on March 23, he toured the same facility with President Lech Walesa of Poland. On November 4, he attended the Library's formal dedication. In 1992, he gave an address at the Hoover Presidential Library in West Branch, Iowa, and on August 17, he addressed the Republican National Convention in Houston. On January 13, 1993, outgoing President George H. W. Bush presented Reagan with the Presidential Medal of Freedom. On April 27, 1994, Reagan attended former President Richard Nixon's funeral at the Nixon Library and

Birthplace. On May 4, he joined with former Presidents Ford and Carter to send a letter to all members of the House of Representatives urging support for the banning of assault weapons.

Some of Reagan's activities in those years, though, brought him criticism. On October 28, 1989, the Reagans completed a nine-day visit to Japan. He was there as the guest of the Japanese government and the Fujisankei Communications Group—which paid between $6 and $8 million to bring the Reagans to the Far East. Of that amount, $2 million went to Reagan directly for two speeches and some public appearances. While he was there, he expressed support for the proposed purchase of Columbia Pictures by the Sony Corporation, a Japanese company.[3] This was at a time when there was strong criticism in the United States of Japanese investment in American industry, particularly those companies dealing with communication. At the same time, reports indicated that Reagan aides were discussing a $1 million donation by Sony to the Reagan Library. Reagan even remarked that a Japanese takeover of the film studio might result in improvements. "I just have a feeling that maybe Hollywood needs some outsiders to bring back decency and good taste to some of the pictures that are being made," he observed.[4]

Amid the criticism, there also were words of praise. One Peter B. Gemma, Jr., a contributing editor to *Conservative Digest,* wrote an op-ed piece in *USA Today* commending Reagan.[5] How could the critics still be after Reagan, he wondered, "sniping at his heels," when Reagan had been out of office for a year? Gemma obviously wrote before Bill Clinton left office. He said that according to press reports "joyous crowds" greeted the Reagans in Japan, and that any "petty political sniping President and Mrs. Reagan must endure for the moment is inconsequential in light of their legacy of leadership." History, he said, would honor Reagan's eight years in the White House, but that it was "nice to see him get some of that credit right now."

Other reports, although noting that the Japanese government gave the Reagans a lavish welcome, said that the Reagan visit had been "largely ignored by the press."[6] Japan's government did award the former president its highest honor, the Grand Cordon of the Supreme Order of the Chrysanthemum, but the *Christian Science Monitor* wrote that "between the relentless efforts of Mr. Reagan's aides to keep him away from the press and the exclusive coverage rights of the Japanese media conglomerate which invited the Reagans, the visit has had little visibility."[7] A *Boston Globe* editorial said that Reagan's critics castigated him "for his selling of the American presidency, saying that they could not imagine Dwight Eisenhower or Franklin Roosevelt taking $2 million from a foreign company for two speeches." Such critics, said the editorial, did not "perceive Reagan's uniqueness." His "presidential style was that of a performer who presided over the government. He once said that being president was not very different from acting in pictures. They give you the script, he explained, you stand on the chalk marks, and you deliver your lines to the camera." Reagan's "lucrative jaunt was consistent with his ideals," and with those of his Japanese sponsors. "Reagan never hid his devotion to unfettered free enterprise."[8]

Reagan has his detractors and his fervent supporters. All agree, however, that his illustrious career is over, and that he is experiencing a sad ending—one not yet reached. Ronald Reagan as of this writing is 92 years old, surpassing John Adams's record as the president who lived to the oldest age. On November 5, 1994, Nancy and Ronald Reagan issued a final letter to the American public. The former president revealed that he had recently been diagnosed with Alzheimer's Disease. He said that he and Nancy had decided to make the news public. He said that he wished that there were some way that he could spare Nancy from the painful experience that she would have to endure, but that he knew she would face it with faith and courage.

She has done so, continuing to protect and care for Ronald Reagan as she has always done. Even the harshest Reagan foe must feel more than a touch of regret at such an end to his memorable life and must feel admiration for Nancy Reagan's dedication and fortitude. In a sense, John Adams retains the record as the oldest living president (although Gerald Ford likely will surpass it). Adams died at 90 with his mental faculties intact. In a biological sense, Ronald Reagan has lived beyond that age, but the real Ronald Reagan died years ago, not abruptly but very much in the sense of General Douglas MacArthur's old soldier, just fading away.

GEORGE H. W. BUSH

George Bush, the patrician forty-first president of the United States, lost the presidency to a young upstart from an "insignificant" small Southern state, Arkansas. He was bitter at the loss, as were many Republicans, but was gracious, as many Republicans were not. The outgoing president and Barbara Bush received the incoming Clintons warmly at the White House on January 20, 1993, inauguration day.[9]

Some Republicans, in fact, were never to accept Bill Clinton's legitimacy. After all, Republicans had a "lock" on the presidency—they were destined to win it, even if some cruel trick of fate directed that Democrats always would control the House of Representatives. Carter, of course, had taken the presidency, but that was merely a reaction to Watergate. The GOP white knight on a shining horse, Ronald Reagan, had unseated the Georgian interloper, and with Reagan enshrined and succeeded by Vice President George Bush all was right with the world.

That world crumbled when Bill Clinton defeated George Bush. Of course, many of the True Believers themselves had turned their collective backs on that very George Bush. After all, he was no Ronald Reagan (nor a Robert E. Lee). He may even have been one of those who restrained him and would not "let Reagan be Reagan!" But now the unthinkable had happened. Another interloper had upset their ordered world. They found it difficult to believe—and impossible to accept.

For his part, however, Bush took the loss with his characteristic dignity. He displayed his sense of style by leaving a gracious note in the desk for incoming President Clinton. "I don't want to be overly dramatic," he said, "but I did want him to know that I would be rooting for him."[10] The Bushes attended the Clinton inaugural, flew by helicopter with Vice President Dan Quayle and his wife Marilyn to Andrews Air Force Base, and then flew on to Houston. They settled in and waited for their home in the fashionable Tanglewood area to be completed.

❦

George Bush has not been the most visible of former presidents. The Bush Presidential library website has no chronology of his activities, and an archivist there indicated in June 2003 that he had done little politically. In general, she said, he confined himself to giving speeches and doing charity work, particularly at the University of Texas's M. D. Anderson Cancer Center in Houston. At times, however he has made headlines.

In 1997, on March 25, the 72-year-old former president became the only president, or former president, in U.S. history to make a parachute jump. He jumped from an airplane flying over Arizona at 12,500 feet—a higher altitude than private aircraft customarily fly—free fell for some 8,000 feet, and then landed safely at the Army's Yuma Proving Ground. Journalist Hugh Sidey reported that Bush later "had the glow of a man fulfilled." It was the fulfillment of a promise that he had made to himself as a young naval pilot in World War II.

Bush had been on a bombing raid on Chi Chi Jima, a Japanese-occupied volcanic island in the Pacific. Surface fire hit his plane, a Grumman Avenger, and forced an evacuation. He said that he had given the order to bail out, and one crew member did, but his parachute failed to open. The other did not respond. Assuming that the silent crew member had been killed, Bush jumped. He parachuted safely into the water, inflated a life raft, and waited to be picked up. Other planes from his squadron watched him and relayed his position to an American submarine, the *USS Finback*, which rescued him. The bodies of the other two crewmen were never recovered. As he descended, he promised himself that one day he would parachute from an airplane for fun.[11]

To celebrate his seventy-fifth birthday, in 1999 Bush repeated the feat. He landed "on the lawn in front of his presidential library at Texas A&M University in College Station, Texas, about ninety miles northwest of Houston."[12] When asked if this would be his last jump, Barbara Bush replied, "You bet," but then relented, and suggested that he might do it again when he becomes 80.

On October 20, 1998, President Clinton signed into law an Intelligence Authorization Act that designated the headquarters of the Central Intelligence Agency as the George Bush Center for Intelligence. President Bush, a former director of Central Intelligence, was present at the dedication ceremonies on April 26, 1999, along with Barbara Bush and other dignitaries.[13] Bush gave a brief address on the occasion. A Nimitz class aircraft carrier, CVN–77, scheduled to be launched in 2009, also will bear President Bush's name. Assuming that the vigorous former president is still alive at that time, he will join a select few living persons whose names ships in the U.S. Navy bear.[14]

As with any former president, Bush has received many awards. Among them is the Joseph Prize for Human Rights from the Anti-Defamation League. Bush received the award on February 8, 2002, in recognition of his efforts as president on behalf of Ethiopian Jews. His direct intervention resulted in "Operation Solomon," that rescued some 15,000 Jews from Ethiopia in less than 24 hours. Bush said of the airlift that he knew he had been doing the right thing.[15]

On the lighter side, Bush appeared—or at least his voice was heard—in a touring stage production of *The Will Rogers Follies* in 2003. On Broadway the production used Gregory Peck's voice as "the legendary producer Flo Ziegfeld, who is heard but never seen. For the summer tour starring Texas native Larry Gatlin," it was George Bush's voice that represented Ziegfeld's.[16] Very likely this is another unique accomplishment for a president or a former president, since President Reagan's professional theater career ceased before he became president.

Most important, of course, is Bush's influence on policy. He is only the second person in the history of the United States to have his son become president. As such, Bush might be expected to have more political influence than most former presidents do.

The popular view is that he does have such influence. Walter Scott, in his "Personality Parade" column in the Sunday supplement *Parade Magazine,* for example, answered a question in 2002 asking who the most influential former presidents were. He cited two—either ignoring or being unaware of such things as, for example, John Quincy Adams's distinguished career in the House of Representatives, Grover Cleveland's reelection to the presidency after a term as a former president, and William Howard Taft's post-presidential career as Chief Justice of the U.S. Supreme Court. First, Scott named Jefferson, saying that he had been so powerful as to have "hand picked" his successors Madison and Monroe. This certainly exaggerates Jefferson's influence. Scott then picked Bush as his other most powerful former president. "Bush has exerted his influence more indirectly," Scott wrote. "Working through his trusted associates Dick Cheney and Brent Scowcroft," he asserted, "Bush virtually directed his son's Presidential campaign and helped select his Cabinet. Cheney," he said, "remains the primary political link between the Bushes."[17] This may be correct, or it may be wildly exaggerated. Scott, of course, is no authority; in this instance, though, no one else really knows either except the people who themselves are involved. One obvious difficulty with Scott's assertion regarding Vice President Cheney is that Cheney has become a full-fledged hawkish unilateralist. Such a position seems inconsistent with the more moderate and internationalist record of the senior Bush.

Almost all assertions regarding the effects of the father-son relation upon the presidency of the second Bush are pure speculation. An example appeared in *The New York Times* in 2002. The younger Bush had rebuked Israeli Prime Minister Ariel Sharon for military action in the West Bank. The action, he had said, was "not helpful." Within three weeks, though, "Bush reversed course, describing Mr. Sharon as a democratically elected leader who was legitimately 'responding to the will of the people' for more security." The new statement came after consultation with the National Security Council "and, presumably, private discussions with his father, the former president, who spent the Easter weekend at his son's 1,600-acre ranch." The two Bushes appeared in public only at church, and said nothing. "The former president's private counsel to his son, if there was any, is a subject none of his aides will discuss and most insist it is a mystery to them too."[18]

Bush has been extremely careful, at least in public, to maintain a considerable distance from his son's presidency. The elder Bush has indicated—and quite appropriately so—that the president must make his own decisions. At all costs, both Bushes wish to avoid giving the impression that the younger Bush must rely upon his father and is not up to the job. This was especially true early in the second Bush's administration.

Later, the younger Bush did send his father as his personal representative to London to a memorial service for the British citizens who had lost their lives at the World Trade Center on September 11, 2001. By that time, with the overwhelming display of support from the public, George W. Bush may have become sufficiently secure to make use of his father's experience.[19] To date, however, this seems to be the exception rather than the rule.

The Bushes are sensitive to any speculation regarding a Bush dynasty, which they deny strongly. The elder Bush dismisses it as "this legacy crud."[20] Loyalty is such a prime Bush trait, especially loyalty within the family, that there is reason to believe that Bush the father would be more likely to remain silent even about policies he considers unwise than to do anything that might cast doubt upon or raise questions about his son's judgment.

The younger Bush's most momentous decision, of course, has been the decision to engage in the 2003 Iraq War. Hugh Sidey reported in *Time* magazine that the former president said to him in an interview that the decision regarding war must ultimately be made by only one person, the president. In a revealing comment, Sidey wrote that Bush, who would turn 80 in 2003, was not concerned with the "rightness of the cause in Iraq." Rather, he was a father who saw his son "on a lonely and difficult march."[21]

Bush—if *The New York Times* was correct—did play a major role in foreign policy early in his son's administration. The younger Bush in 2001 "had taken a hard line as president on relations with North Korea," alarming many experts who considered the approach to be counterproductive and possibly dangerous. According to this account, the elder Bush wrote to his son a memo "forcefully arguing the need to reopen negotiations with North Korea, according to people who have seen the document." The administration then announced that it would open discussions with North Korea, and the memo's content seems to have been "largely incorporated into the decision."[22]

The record fueling speculation regarding the effect of Bush upon Bush is, however, decidedly mixed. In 2002, for example, General Brent Scowcroft, who had been George H. W. Bush's national security adviser and had held the same post under President Ford, wrote an op-ed piece in the *Wall Street Journal* urging that there not be a unilateral decision to go to war in Iraq. He urged that any action be taken through the United Nations.[23] Other advisers to the elder Bush took similar public positions. These public expressions generated speculation that the elder Bush might be communicating with his son through his former advisers.

For a time, the administration of George W. Bush did attempt to work through the UN. Scowcroft then wrote another op-ed piece, this time in the *Washington Post,* praising that approach.[24] Subsequently, however, finding resistance in the UN, Bush went ahead regardless. He did succeed in securing Britain's cooperation, but made it clear that support from other countries was desirable, but not essential. Thus, if the first President Bush had been trying to send a message to his son—and it certainly would have been an indirect way to go about it, when each had access to a telephone—it was singularly ineffective.

On the other hand, a "longtime friend" friend of the Bushes said that "his father is not the kind of guy who's calling him and saying, 'Hey, Georgie, you ought to be doing this." He said that he had been in the room with the president "when he's talked to his dad and mother, and the calls are 90 percent family."[25] Columnist Elisabeth Bumiller reported in *The New York Times* that Bush father and son speak by telephone about twice a week. The conversations "began last summer," she said (2002), "when a series of former advisers to the forty-first president wrote opinion articles that warned about President Bush's approach to action against Iraq." Subsequently, the younger Bush pushed "the speculation even further when he referred obliquely at the U.N. to an assassination attempt against his father, saying that 'in 1993, Iraq attempted to assassinate the emir of Kuwait and a former American president.'" An administration official later said that obviously it would not do to personalize the situation. "In fact," though, wrote Bumiller, "only the two men know for sure how much the father is influencing the son," but, she said, all aides are convinced that it is not much.[26]

She pointed out that the question ultimately will have to be answered by historians. Engaging in speculation herself, she surmised that they will conclude that hostilities against Iraq will be seen as "the son's phase II to the father's beginning." She quoted the prominent Yale historian John Morton Blum—who actually taught George W. Bush at Yale—as believing that the current President Bush sees action against Iraq "as a continuation" of his father's policies, "not as an avenging" of his defeat.

Bumiller is correct that questions regarding George H. W. Bush's influence on his son cannot be answered except ultimately by historians. Undoubtedly, he has a channel of influence that exceeds even those of most former presidents. Personality and family dynamics, however, may preclude him from exercising that influence except in the most indirect way. Bush takes his role as father seriously, as he should. He took his role as president seriously, also. Whether he takes his role as former president as seriously as he takes his role as father—that is, whether for the good of the country he would attempt to pressure his son to reverse a policy he saw as unwise even at the expense of the son's independence—is the question that for now cannot be answered. Until recently, all evidence has suggested that he is unlikely to bring strong pressures on his son regarding policy.

Then, however, a dramatic development caused speculation that the former president had cast off his restraint, and was sending a pointed—and public— message of criticism to his son and successor. Early in October 2003, the Bush Presidential Foundation announced that on November 7, former President Bush would give the 2003 George Bush Award for Excellence in Public Service to none other than Senator Edward Kennedy, a vocal critic of George W. Bush's policies in Iraq.

Syndicated columnist Georgie Anne Geyer wrote that the award would be "nearly as astonishing" as if Vice President Cheney were to give his "Favorite Foreigners Citation to the French."[27] She argued that "the ideological rift between father and son has been growing ever since George W. began focusing on Iraq"—an "obsession," she called it, with unilateralism and preemption. She said that the son had ignored the father's objections, and had in fact adopted policies designed to counter, "or even to wipe out, his father's entire political legacy." She charged that the son had "replaced his father's courtesy and good graces with an almost proud rudeness and scorn for others." She wished, she said, that the senior Bush would "drop his polite reticence and tell us what he and the team of his presidency really think about what is happening in America today."

Certainly, historians will be the final judges about the effect of former President Bush upon his son's policies. It may be, though, that Geyer is correct; that we will not after all have to wait for the historians' judgment to determine that, despite his best efforts, former President Bush had little influence after all.

WILLIAM JEFFERSON CLINTON

Bill Clinton unquestionably was a colorful president. Equally without doubt, his presidency was one of the most controversial of all time. This resulted less from the things he did than from the ferocious zeal of his political enemies on the one hand, and from the frenzied media that publicized every allegation about Clinton—documented or unsubstantiated; plausible or preposterous— on the other. Of course, Clinton did hand his opponents and the media a great deal of ammunition, but it was nothing compared to what they added on their own.

Despite all the furor, Clinton left office as a popular president. The country was more prosperous than it had ever been, unemployment was low, and the stock market was booming. Astonishing all observers, the Clinton administration had even eliminated the chronic budget deficit, leaving a huge surplus to its successor.

Clinton was the first Democratic president to be affected by the ill-conceived Twenty-second Amendment that limits a president to two elected terms. In the late 1940s, congressional Republicans took their spite out upon the memory of the late President Franklin D. Roosevelt and his four electoral victories by proposing the unwise amendment adopting term limits. They not only were going against the considered judgment of the Founders who had explicitly rejected such limits, but their petty posthumous slap at FDR soon came to haunt them in the cases of Eisenhower and Reagan.

So the Twenty-second Amendment for nearly a half century had worked to the Republicans' disadvantage. No Democrat had completed a second term since its provisions became effective. Finally, however, the Amendment worked to favor the Republicans, since Bill Clinton could not run again. There is little doubt that he would have done so if it had not been for the Amendment. Considering the 2000 election, which had no truly attractive candidates and which ended virtually in a tie, there is every likelihood that the popular Clinton—by any measure the most skillful campaigner in American politics of his day— could have won reelection.

As it was, he attended his successor's inauguration and then had to decide what to do with the rest of his life. Even as he left office, Clinton in a sense had accomplished something—at least vicariously—that no other former president had ever done. First Lady Hillary Rodham Clinton had taken her seat as a newly elected U.S. senator.

The Clintons had previously established a residence in New York City for his retirement. In the November election, Hillary Clinton had become the first woman senator from New York. She was the first former first lady to run for office and the only former first lady—and in fact sitting first lady—ever to become a member of Congress. For a brief period between the time when the new Congress convened on January 3, 2001 until the inauguration of the new president on January 20, Hillary Clinton was *both* first lady and U.S. senator. Since "first lady" is an informal title and not an official position, there was no question about holding two "offices" simultaneously.

For the first few months after he left office, Clinton continued to dominate the headlines. It was a source of frustration to the new administration that when the new President Bush and Clinton gave speeches on the same day, Clinton tended to get the attention. Bush, of course, is a notoriously poor speaker, but the reason for this probably was the public's lingering fascination with Clinton. The events of September 11, 2001, changed this dynamic. As great national trauma overwhelmed the country, the image of Bush changed abruptly. No longer was he an inexperienced president of questionable legitimacy and dubious competence. Almost overnight he had become a leader; a president who was firm and resolute. Clinton, to be sure, did not fade into the background, but he no longer dominated as he had before and Bush no longer had to compete for media coverage.

Somewhat more than a year after he left office, *Newsweek* published an interview with Clinton by Jonathan Alter. Alter reported that the former president had given nearly 200 speeches in 30 countries in the previous 14 months.[28] Staff in his Harlem office indicated that about 40 percent of his speeches are for pay. Considering Clinton's speaking fees and the frequency of his talks, Alter calculated that the figures "would drive the Clinton haters nuts." Including his $12 million book deal, which Alter called the "largest in world history," he estimated that Clinton would earn some $40 million in his first two years out of office.

Both Clintons received lucrative contracts to produce their memoirs. Hillary Clinton's was $8 million. A *New York Times* article in 2002 correctly speculated that hers would be on time or early, and that his would be delayed. Simon and Schuster released Hillary Clinton's *Living History* in late spring, 2003, and it immediately jumped to the best-seller lists. Predictably, some of television's conservative commentators sniffed that she had not "revealed the truth" about Whitewater. As a matter of fact, she had: There was nothing to it. Bill Clinton's book, as of this writing, is still underway.

To some extent, of course, Clinton has been forced to devote himself to making money. He left office with millions of dollars of legal expenses left over from the impeachment and trial and from the numerous lawsuits against him.

He told Alter, though, that he hoped within five years to "be in public service full time."[29] He told the same thing to James Fallows, who interviewed him for *The Atlantic Monthly*. Fallows noted that Clinton had never been motivated greatly by money. Even as things stand at the moment, he spends some half of his time on public service, "which ranges from charitable and international work to fundraising for his party."[30]

Alter interviewed Clinton just a month after "the eight-year, $73 million Whitewater investigation—which eventually led to impeachment—turned up no evidence of criminal wrongdoing by the Clintons." The interview confirmed all over again, Alter said, Clinton's "contempt for prosecutors and the press" (which, typically, buried the exonerating story after hyping the charges for years). He reported that Clinton "hasn't the slightest doubt that he's the victim of a GOP attack machine that announced on Capitol Hill its intention to impeach him long before he gave them the Monica Lewinsky story to exploit."[31] One of those who sought to impeach Clinton before the Monica episode was Bob Barr, who then was a member of the House of Representatives. Barr later was one of the House impeachment "managers," and still later was voted out of office. In an amusing—and astonishing—display of chutzpah, Barr on March 17, 2002, filed suit in U.S. District Court against former President Clinton, Clinton's former aide James Carville, and *Hustler* Magazine for "causing him emotional distress during the Clinton impeachment!"[32]

The same Bob Barr had requested an investigation by the General Accounting Office of charges that members of the Clinton administration had vandalized the White House as Clinton left office. In June 2002, the G.A.O. issued its report. *The New York Times* described the report under the misleading headline: "White House Vandalized In Transition, G.A.O. Finds." To be sure, the report did describe some pranks ("W" keys missing from keyboards, etc.). Much of the damage, though, was normal wear and tear, and the pranks were far from unique. "The accounting office said similar pranks were reported in prior transitions, including the one from Mr. Bush's father to Mr. Clinton in 1993," the *Times* noted. "We were unable to conclude," the report's writers commented, "whether the 2001 transition was worse than previous ones."[33] It likely will be some time yet before the furor over the Clinton presidency subsides.

❦

The most thoughtful look at Clinton as a former president—and one of the most insightful essays about any president's post–White House career—was

Fallows's *Atlantic Monthly* interview in March 2003. It looked at Clinton's life as precedent-setting for the long-lived and vigorous former presidents who likely will be increasing in number. James Fallows who had himself been an aide to President Carter, gave his piece the meaningful title, "Post-President for Life." Clinton, he said, continually campaigns, working the crowd, speaking with small groups, meeting people. At one time this would have been "part of his thirty-year campaign for electoral approval. Now he does it because he likes to."[34]

Fallows described Clinton's enormous popularity around the world. In many countries, he wrote, Clinton was much more popular than that nation's own leaders. A flood of news reports over the months supports Fallows's comment. Yet at home, his position remains ambiguous.

America, Fallows said, in Carter and now Clinton, has two very active former presidents. Clinton excels anyone in modern politics in his ability to speak "with equal poise to people at every level of class, education, and sophistication." To Clinton's critics, he said, this verifies the former president's chameleon-like character, but Fallows thought rather that it demonstrates "a combination of emotional and intellectual acuity that other people would copy if they could." Fallows predicted that Clinton's post-presidential career will be like his presidency, "noisy and controversial," and that it also will create "both admirers and contemptuous detractors."[35] Clinton's major task, he surmised, would be to discipline himself, to focus his almost limitless energies into a few channel rather than dissipating them into too many.

Clinton hopes to write not merely his memoirs, but other works, as Jimmy Carter has done. Nearly every person over 50, he told Fallows, should write whether or not there is any intention of publication. "You need to think about what really meant something to you," he said. "Who did you really love? Who really made you what you are?"[36] Additionally, he is putting energy and prestige into the effort to control AIDS around the world. "He has joined Nelson Mandela in leading an international effort to improve the medical infrastructure of affected countries, so that drug companies and donors in the developed world won't feel they're throwing their money away if they send aid." He has engaged in a number of other international humanitarian efforts as well. Peru's Hernando de Soto, a well-known writer and economist, met with Clinton to exchange ideas and discuss reforms. He "suggested that Clinton's appeal in the Third World was so broad that he could serve as a younger, more engaged, successor to Nelson Mandela."[37]

In the meantime, of course, Clinton spreads himself thin—as do the rumors about his intentions. In 2003, paired with his former opposing presidential candidate Bob Dole, Clinton began to appear on the CBS news magazine, *60 Minutes.* He and Dole engaged in a comment/response format. He was not the first former president to do television commentary, though. That distinction goes to Gerald Ford, who provided analysis for NBC during the 1980 presidential campaign.[38] Also in 2003 there was gossip that Clinton might run for mayor of New York. The rumors were strong enough to surface in *The Washingtonian* and in *The New York Times,*[39] but Clinton has not endorsed any movement to put him in city hall. At the same time, however, he did speculate that it would be well to revise the Twenty-second Amendment. Without going so far as to suggest repeal, he proposed that it be modified to prohibit more than two consecutive elected terms, so that a former president could return and run again.[40] It takes little effort to imagine the kind of rumors—and for some, anguish—that such a suggestion coming from Bill Clinton could generate.

As Fallows put it, one thing Clinton could do is to "help show the way for youngish ex-presidents of the future." When the two discussed the possibility of an "expanded corps of active ex-Presidents," the idea excited Clinton, who said that they should organize to determine what they might do together. One thing would be, he said, to "organize really constructive debates about our honest disagreements—in a respectful way, so America could hear them." A handful of former presidents with no vested interests, he thought, "might be able both to do things together and sort of edify the American people about how to handle our differences."[41] The way in which people respond to such ideas, Fallows said, essentially determines how they react to Bill Clinton. For his part, he said, he has seen so much of the effort that Clinton has invested in good causes, and has heard so much of his accomplishments that he had come to believe him. "Because of his youth, vigor, talent, and restlessness, he is sure to mark new parts of the political and social landscape as appropriate for post-presidential involvement. The less cynical our expectations about him," Fallows said, "the more valuable his effect is likely to be."

Bill Clinton not only is our newest former president, but also the one with the greatest potential for accomplishment of any since Theodore Roosevelt. At the moment, Jimmy Carter is our most distinguished former resident of the White House. With regard to post-presidential accomplishment, only a handful of others can be considered alongside him. Clinton, as of this writing, has been out of office not yet three years. Carter, at that stage in his post-presidency, was writing in virtual seclusion. If Clinton can harness his talent and energies as Carter came to do, he could well surpass even Carter as our most distinguished former president. An old saying is that the best revenge is living well. In Clinton's case as with Carter's, all things considered, the best revenge likely would come less from doing well than from doing good.

SOME CONCLUDING THOUGHTS

FORMER PRESIDENTS OCCUPY A MOST UNUSUAL POSITION IN THE AMERICAN political system. To some extent there are similarities between the status of a former president and that of first lady. As President Clinton said, a former president no longer has power, but he does have influence. The same is true of the first lady. The similarity, though, ends there. There is a considerable difference in accountability. The first lady exercises her influence largely through the president and the president is accountable. If a former president chooses to do so, under certain circumstances he (or someday, she) may be able to exercise a significant effect upon public policy without such direct accountability.

It is rare for any figure to have so much influence without considerable public scrutiny. Former presidents may regain a measure of true power by being elected to office or by accepting formal appointment. With a renewed official position would come accountability.

A former president may also choose to exercise influence by working openly and in public. Former President Theodore Roosevelt did so when he urged President Wilson to enter World War I. He continued to do so when he worked to mitigate the effects of Wilson's harsh crackdown on civil liberties. Former President Carter has chosen to influence world leaders in the cause of peace. Openness brings its own accountability.

The former president who prefers to work without fanfare, however, can often remain a substantial force behind the scenes. For example, few people were aware of the effect that former President Eisenhower may have had on the Vietnam policies of the Kennedy and Johnson administrations. True, Kennedy and Johnson were themselves accountable for their policies, but their relationships with the former president were an unknown quantity. The nature of the relationship between a president and first lady may be unclear, but the relationship itself is an obvious one. The open closeness of such a relationship creates a certain accountability. This may not be the case when a former president is working without the knowledge of the public.

Today, the role of former President Bush is largely a mystery. He is in a position to have more influence than other former presidents, because of his familial relationship with the current president. The extent of this influence, or if in fact he is exercising influence, is unknown.

There have been a number of suggestions for making use of the expertise of former presidents. One of the more common is to create a seat for each one in the Senate, perhaps a non-voting position. There has been less attention to the desirability of encouraging some sort of accountability. The notion that former President Clinton discussed—creating a council of sorts for active ex-presidents to encourage national discussion regarding the serious issues of the day—could be a step in the right direction.

At the moment, the United States has an unusually large number of living former presidents. Presidents Reagan, Carter, Ford, Bush, and Clinton are still alive, and the latter four are still active. With increasing longevity and improvements in health care, the prospects for having several active former presidents at any given time are good. Even disregarding the issue of accountability, it would be fascinating and instructive for the United States to experience regular sessions of thoughtful discussions among a group composed of figures such as Presidents Bush, Carter, Clinton, and Ford.

NOTES

INTRODUCTION

1. Quoted in James Fallows, "Post-President for Life," The Atlantic Monthly (March 2003), p. 63.
2. Thomas A. Bailey, "The Post-Presidential Glow," in *Presidential Greatness,* New York: Appleton-Century, 1966, pp. 112–114.
3. Marie B. Hecht, *Beyond the Presidency,* New York: Macmillan, 1976.

CHAPTER ONE

1. Sidney M. Milkis and Michael Nelson, *The American Presidency: 1776–1998,* 3rd ed., Washington: Congressional Quarterly Press, 1999, p. 85.
2. Clinton Rossiter, *The American Presidency,* 2nd ed., New York: Harcourt, Brace and World, 1960, p. 232.
3. Douglas Southall Freeman, *Washington,* Richard Harwell Abridgement, New York: Simon and Schuster, 1968, p. 710.
4. James T. Flexner, *Washington: The Indispensable Man, Boston:* Little Brown, 1974, p. 360.
5. Ibid., p. 362.
6. John Ferling, *John Adams: A Life,* Knoxville: University of Tennessee Press, 1992, p. 418.
7. Freeman, p. 712.
8. See, for example, Willard Sterne Randall, *George Washington: A Life,* New York: Henry Holt, 1997, p. 496.
9. Richard Norton Smith, *Patriarch,* Boston: Houghton Mifflin, 1993, p. 324.
10. David McCullough, *John Adams,* New York: Simon and Schuster, 2001, p. 510.
11. Ibid.
12. Ibid., p. 516.
13. Ibid., p. 519.

14. Stanley Elkins and Eric McKitrick, *The Age of Federalism,* New York: Oxford University Press, 1993, p. 605.
15. Randall, p. 498.
16. See, for example, Freeman, pp. 741ff.

CHAPTER TWO

1. David McCullough, *John Adams,* New York: Simon and Schuster, 2001, p. 564.
2. Ibid., p. 558.
3. Ibid., pp. 564–565.
4. Joseph J. Ellis, *Passionate Sage: The Character and Legacy of John Adams,* New York: W. W. Norton, 1993, p. 19.
5. Ibid., p. 20.
6. McCullough, p. 565.
7. Ibid., p. 549.
8. Ibid.
9. John Ferling, *John Adams: A Life,* Knoxville: University of Tennessee Press, 1992, p. 404.
10. Lynne Withy, *Dearest Friend: A Life of Abigail Adams,* New York: The Free Press, 1981, p. 281.
11. Ibid., p. 280.
12. Ibid., p. 283.
13. Forrest McDonald, *The Presidency of Thomas Jefferson,* Lawrence: University Press of Kansas, 1976, p. 139.
14. Ibid., p. 159.
15. Merrill D. Peterson, *Thomas Jefferson and the New Nation: A Biography,* New York: Oxford University Press, 1970, p. 920.
16. Ferling, p. 417.
17. Quoted in Ellis, p. 55.
18. Ibid.
19. Ellis, p. 67.
20. Ibid., p. 68.
21. McCullough, p. 593.
22. Ferling, p. 422.
23. Ellis, pp. 61–68; quotations on pp. 61–62.
24. Ferling, pp. 428ff.
25. McCullough, p. 596.
26. Ibid.
27. Herbert Sloan, "Presidents as Historians," in Richard Alan Ryerson, ed., *John Adams and the Founding of the Republic,* Boston: Massachusetts Historical Society, 2001, p. 268.
28. Ferling, p. 425.
29. Noble E. Cunningham, Jr., *The Presidency of James Monroe,* Lawrence: University Press of Kansas, 1996, p. 107.
30. McCullough, p. 631.

31. Peterson, p. 926.

32. McCullough, pp. 544–545.

33. John Chester Miller, *The Wolf By the Ears: Thomas Jefferson and Slavery,* Charlottesville: University of Virginia, 1991, pp. 270–271.

34. Ibid., p. 618.

35. Ibid., p. 928.

36. See Lester J. Cappon, ed., *The Adams-Jefferson Letters: The Complete Correspondence Between Thomas Jefferson and Abigail and John Adams,* vol. II, Chapel Hill: University of North Carolina Press, 1959, pp. 390–391.

37. See Max J. Skidmore, *Legacy to the World: A Study of America's Political Ideas,* New York: Peter Lang, 1998, pp. 95–98.

38. Jefferson to Adams," October 28, 1813, in Cappon, p. 390.

39. See "Adams to Jefferson," November 12, 1813, in Cappon, pp. 392–394.

40. Hannah Arendt, *On Revolution,* New York: Viking, 1965, p. 252.

41. Adrienne Koch, *The Philosophy of Thomas Jefferson,* New York: Columbia University Press, 1943, pp. 162–165.

42. Richard K. Matthews, *The Radical Politics of Thomas Jefferson: A Revisionist View,* Lawrence: University Press of Kansas, 1984.

43. Arendt, pp. 258–259.

44. Ibid., p. 257.

45. Drew R. McCoy, *The Last of the Fathers,* Cambridge: Harvard University Press, 1989, pp. 27–29.

46. Peterson, pp. 929–930.

47. Ibid.

48. James F. Simon, *What Kind of Nation,* New York: Simon and Schuster, 2002, pp. 266–267.

49. Ibid., pp. 261–293; quotations from p. 263.

50. Ibid., p. 264.

51. Peterson, p. 988.

52. Ralph Ketcham, *James Madison: A Biography,* Charlottesville: University Press of Virginia, 1990, pp. 620–621.

53. Cappon, p. xxv.

54. Ibid., p. xxvii.

55. McCullough, p. 605.

CHAPTER THREE

1. Ralph Ketcham, *James Madison: A Biography,* Charlottesville: University Press of Virginia, 1990, pp. 603–604.

2. Garry Wills, *James Madison,* New York: Times Books, 2002, pp. 154–155.

3. Drew R. McCoy, *The Last of the Fathers: James Madison and the Republican Legacy,* Cambridge: Harvard University Press, 1989, pp. 9–10.

4. Irving Brant, *The Fourth President: A Life of James Madison,* Indianapolis: Bobbs-Merrill, 1970, p. 197.

5. Wills, pp. 36–37.

6. McCoy, p. 73.
7. Ketcham, p. 620.
8. Ibid., pp. 630–631.
9. Brant, p. 607.
10. Ibid.
11. Robert Allen Rutland, *James Madison: The Founding Father,* Columbia: University of Missouri Press, 1987, pp. 242–243.
12. McCoy, p. 236.
13. Ketcham, p. 622.
14. Ibid., pp. 621–622.
15. Ibid., p. 646.
16. Rutland, p. 245.
17. Ketcham, p. 658.
18. Rutland, p. 246.
19. John Chester Miller, *The Wolf by the Ears: Thomas Jefferson and Slavery,* Charlottesville: University of Virginia, 1991 (originally published in 1977 by The Free Press).
20. McCoy, p. xiii.
21. Ibid., pp. 1–6.
22. Garry Wills, *A Necessary Evil: A History of American Distrust of Government,* New York: Touchstone Edition, 2002, p. 149
23. Merrill D. Peterson, *Thomas Jefferson and the New Nation,* New York: Oxford University Press, 1970, p. 986.
24. Wills, *A Necessary Evil,* p. 150.
25. Ibid., pp. 150–152.
26. McCoy, pp. 139–140.
27. Rutland, p. 242.
28. See McCoy, pp. 116–125; quotation on p. 125.
29. Ibid., pp. 73–74.
30. Ibid., pp. 85–87.
31. Brandt, p. 644.
32. Ketcham, pp. 620–621; see also McCoy, pp. 31–32.
33. Merrill D. Peterson, *The Jefferson Image in the American Mind,* New York: Oxford University Press, 1960, p. 136.
34. Quoted in McCoy, p. 33.
35. Marie B. Hecht, *Beyond the Presidency: The Residues of Power,* New York: Macmillan, 1976, pp. 196–197.

CHAPTER FOUR

1. Paul C. Nagel, *John Quincy Adams: A Public Life, A Private Life,* Cambridge: Harvard University Press, 1997, p. 328.
2. Robert V. Remini, *John Quincy Adams,* New York: Times Books/Henry Holt, 2002, p. 127.
3. Ibid., p. 328.

4. Leonard Falkner, *The President Who Wouldn't Retire*, New York: Coward-McCann, 1967, p. 7.
5. William Lee Miller, *Arguing About Slavery*, New York: Alfred A. Knopf, 1996, p. 6.
6. Nagel, pp. 330–333.
7. Quoted ibid., p. 336.
8. Ibid., pp. 337–338.
9. See Leonard L. Richards, *The Life and Times of Congressman John Quincy Adams*, New York: Oxford University Press, 1986, pp. 39–54.
10. Nagel, p. 340.
11. Richards, p. 3.
12. Nagel, pp. 341–345.
13. Quoted ibid., p. 345.
14. Ibid., pp. 346–348.
15. Nagel, p. 355.
16. Falkner, p. 265.
17. Ibid., p. 266.
18. Remini, p. 144.
19. Falkner, pp. 266–267.
20. Ibid., pp. 297–299.
21. Nagel, p. 356.
22. Ibid., p. 359.
23. Ibid., pp. 371–372.
24. This account of the *Amistad* case is taken largely from Richards, pp. 135–139; see also Nagel, pp. 379–381, and Miller, pp. 399–408ff.
25. Richards, p. 137.
26. Ibid., p. 138.
27. Ibid., p. 139.
28. Ibid.
29. Nagel, p. 388.
30. Ibid., pp. 402–403.
31. Ibid., pp. 418–419.
32. Richards, p. 145.

CHAPTER FIVE

1. Robert V. Remini, *Andrew Jackson*, New York: Harper Perennial, 1999, p. 146.
2. Quoted ibid., p. 219.
3. Ibid., p. 220.
4. Ibid., p. 222.
5. Ibid.
6. Ibid., p. 224.
7. Wilson Sullivan and Robert A. Rutland, "Martin Van Buren: The Red Fox," in Michael Bechloss, ed., *American Heritage Illustrated History of the Presidents*, New York: Crown Publishers, 2000, p.123.

8. Ibid.
9. David C. Whitney, *The American Presidents,* Garden City, NY: Doubleday, 1969, p. 87.
10. Sullivan and Rutland, p. 123.
11. See Norma Lois Peterson, *The Presidencies of William Henry Harrison and John Tyler,* Lawrence: University Press of Kansas, 1989, pp. 103–105.
12. Richard M. Pious, "John Tyler: Tenth President, 1841–1845," in James M. McPherson, ed., *To the Best of My Ability,* New York: Society of American Historians/Agincourt Press, 2001, p. 82.
13. See Dan Monroe, "Lincoln the Dwarf: Lyon Gardiner Tyler's War on the Mythical Lincoln," *Journal of the Abraham Lincoln Association* 24:1 (Winter 2003), pp. 32–42.
14. Ibid., p. 32.
15. Ibid., p. 42.
16. Sam W. Haynes, *James K. Polk and the Expansionist Impulse,* New York: Longman, 1997, p. 190.
17. Paul Bergeron, *The Presidency of James K. Polk,* Lawrence; University Press of Kansas, 1987, p. 257.
18. Ibid.
19. Ibid., p. 260.

CHAPTER SEVEN

1. Jean Harvey Baker, "Millard Fillmore," in James M. McPherson ed., *To the Best of My Ability: The American Presidents,* New York: Society of American Historians/Agincourt Press, 2001, p. 98.
2. Elbert B. Smith, *The Presidencies of Zachary Taylor and Millard Fillmore,* Lawrence: University Press of Kansas, 1988, p. 249.
3. Ibid., p. 251.
4. Robert J. Scarry, *Millard Fillmore,* Jefferson, NC: McFarland, 2001, pp. 264–265.
5. Smith, p. 252.
6. Ibid., pp. 252–253.
7. Scarry, p. 278.
8. Smith, p. 253.
9. Scarry, p. 284.
10. See Robert Rayback, *Millard Fillmore,* Buffalo: Henry Stewart for the Buffalo Historical Society, 1959, pp. 403ff.
11. Smith, p. 254.
12. See Yanek Mieczkowski, *The Routledge Historical Atlas of Presidential Elections,* New York: Routledge, 2001, pp. 49–51.
13. Smith, p. 254.
14. See ibid.
15. Scarry, pp. 320–321.
16. Smith, p. 255.

17. See Larry Gara, *The Presidency of Franklin Pierce,* Lawrence: University Press of Kansas, 1991, p. 179.
18. Ibid., p. 178.
19. Marie B. Hecht, *Beyond the Presidency,* New York: Macmillan, 1976, p. 20.
20. Ibid., pp. 19–20.
21. Gara, p. 179.
22. Ibid., p. 180.
23. Joel H. Silbey, "Franklin Pierce," in Alan Brinkley and Davis Dyer, eds., *The Reader's Companion to the American Presidency,* Boston: Houghton Mifflin, 2000, p. 175.
24. Gara, p. 180.
25. See Philip Shriver Klein, *President James Buchanan,* University Park: Pennsylvania State University Press, 1962, p. 402; see also Elbert B. Smith, *The Presidency of James Buchanan,* Lawrence: University Press of Kansas, 1975, p. 190.
26. Klein, p. 409.
27. Smith, p. 195.
28. Klein, p. 408.
29. Ibid., p. 420.
30. See George Ticknor Curtis, *The Life of James Buchanan: Fifteenth President of the United States,* vol. 1, New York: Harper and Brothers, 1883, pp. 17–18 (there is a reprint: Freeport, NY: Books for Libraries Press, 1969).

CHAPTER EIGHT

1. See, for example, Jean Edward Smith, *Grant,* New York: Simon and Schuster, 2001, pp. 427–429.
2. Hans L. Trefousse, *Andrew Johnson: A Biography,* New York: W. W. Norton, 1989, pp. 355–358.
3. Ibid., p. 363.
4. See ibid., pp. 364–372; quotation on p. 372.
5. Ibid., pp. 373–379.
6. Ibid., p. 377.
7. Smith, pp. 585–586; see also the Grant Project, Ulysses S. Grant Association/Southern Illinois University, *http://www.lib.siu.edu/projects/usgrant/.*
8. For an excellent discussion of the allegations of corruption, see Frank J. Scaturro, *President Grant Reconsidered,* Lanham, Maryland: Madison Books, 1999, chapter III.
9. Ibid., pp. 36–40.
10. Jeffry D. Wert, "James Longstreet and the Lost Cause," in Carl Gallagher and Alan T. Nolan, eds., *The Myth of the Lost Cause and Civil War History,* Bloomington: Indiana University Press, 2000, pp. 129–130.
11. Lloyd A. Hunter, "The Immortal Confederacy: Another Look at Lost Cause Religion," in Gallagher and Nolan, pp. 205–206.
12. See Janny Scott, "History's Judgment of the 2 Civil War Generals is Changing," *New York Times on the Web* (September 30, 2000).

13. Smith, pp. 606–607.
14. Frank Scaturro, Grant Monument Association, http://saints.css.edu/mkelsey/granthist5.html.
15. Smith, p. 607.
16. Ibid., p. 608–609.
17. Ibid., p. 610.
18. Ibid., p. 611.
19. Ibid., p. 612–613.
20. See ibid., pp. 615–616.
21. Ari Hoogenboom, *The Presidency of Rutherford B. Hayes,* Lawrence: University Press of Kansas, 1988, pp. 197–198.
22. Julia Dent Grant, *Personal Memoirs,* quoted in Smith, p. 616.
23. Smith, pp. 622–623.
24. Ibid., pp. 624–625.
25. Ibid., p. 627.
26. Julia Dent Grant, *The Personal Memoirs of Julia Dent Grant,* John Y. Simon, ed., New York: G. P. Putnam's Sons, 1975.
27. Hoogenboom, p. 223.
28. Marie B. Hecht, *Beyond the Presidency,* New York: Macmillan, 1976, p. 211.
29. Ibid., p. 222.
30. Hans L. Trefousse, *Rutherford B. Hayes,* New York: Times Books/Henry Holt, 2002, pp. 133–134.
31. Ibid., p. 137.
32. Hecht, p. 124.
33. Ibid., p. 139.
34. Hoogenboom, p. 123.

CHAPTER NINE

1. Thomas C. Reeves, *Gentleman Boss: The Life of Chester Alan Arthur,* New York: Knopf, 1975, p. 180.
2. Justus D. Doenecke, *The Presidencies of James A. Garfield and Chester A. Arthur,* Lawrence: University Press of Kansas, 1981, p. 76.
3. Henry F. Graff, *Grover Cleveland,* New York: Times Books/Henry Holt, 2002, p. 97.
4. Louis W. Koenig, "Grover Cleveland: the Law Man," in Michael Beschloss, ed., *History of the Presidents,* New York: American Heritage, 2000, p. 291.
5. Graff, pp. 99–100.
6. Ibid., p. 132.
7. Ibid., pp. 134–135; see also pp. 132–136.
8. See Homer E. Socolofsky and Allan B. Spetter, *The Presidency of Benjamin Harrison,* Lawrence: University Press of Kansas, 1987, p. 207.
9. Ibid., p. 208.

CHAPTER TEN

1. Kathleen Dalton, *Theodore Roosevelt: A Strenuous Life,* New York: Alfred A. Knopf, 2002, p. 268.
2. Ibid., p. 344.
3. Louis Auchincloss, *Theodore Roosevelt,* New York: Times Books/Henry Holt, 2001, p. 110.
4. Nathan Miller, *Theodore Roosevelt: A Life,* New York: William Morrow, 1992, p. 500.
5. Dalton, pp. 359–360.
6. See Miller, pp. 508–511.
7. Ibid., p. 362.
8. Dalton, p. 378
9. Ibid., p. 366.
10. John A. Gable, *The Bull Moose Years: Theodore Roosevelt and the Progressive Party,* Port Washington, NY: Kennikat Press, 1978, pp. 9–10.
11. Quoted ibid., p. 11.
12. Paolo E. Coletta, *The Presidency of William Howard Taft,* Lawrence: University Press of Kansas, 1973, p. 159.
13. Henry F. Pringle, *Theodore Roosevelt,* Norwalk, Conn: The Easton Press, 1988 [1931], p. 562.
14. See Yanek Mieczkowski, *The Routledge Historical Atlas of Presidential Elections,* New York: Routledge, 2001, pp. 85–87.
15. Pringle, p. 561.
16. Gable, pp. 81–83.
17. Mieczkowski, p. 86.
18. Dalton, pp. 520–521; see also Gary Murphy, "'Mr. Roosevelt is Guilty': Theodore Roosevelt and the Crusade for Constitutionalism, 1910–1912," *Journal of American Studies,* 36 (2002), pp. 441–457.
19. Theodore Roosevelt, *Theodore Roosevelt: An Autobiography,* New York: Charles Scribner and Sons, 1913.
20. See Dalton, pp. 428–439; Miller, pp. 535–538.
21. See Dalton's excellent treatment of TR and World War I, pp. 443–505.
22. Miller, p. 544.
23. Dalton, p. 448.
24. Ibid., p. 474.
25. Miller, pp. 554–555.
26. Dalton, p. 487.
27. See ibid., pp. 478–480.
28. Ibid.
29. Ibid., pp. 490–491.
30. William H. Harbaugh, *The Life and Times of Theodore Roosevelt,* rev. ed., New York: Oxford University Press, 1975, p. 428.
31. Gable, p. 250.

32. Edward J. Renehan, Jr., *The Lion's Pride: Theodore Roosevelt and His Family in Peace and War,* New York: Oxford University Press, 1998, pp. 174–175.
33. Hermann Hagedorn, "Theodore Roosevelt: A Biographical Sketch," in Hermann Hagedorn and Sidney Wallach, eds., *A Theodore Roosevelt Round-Up,* New York: The Theodore Roosevelt Association, 1958, p. 51.
34. Pringle, p. 603.
35. Cooper, p. 259.

CHAPTER ELEVEN

1. Paolo Coletta, *The Presidency of William Howard Taft,* Lawrence: University Press of Kansas, 1973, p. 230.
2. Michael Harwood and John Milton Cooper, Jr., "William Howard Taft: Reluctant Leader," in Michael Beschloss, ed., *History of the Presidents,* New York: Crown Publishers, 2000, p. 335.
3. Kendrick A. Clements, *The Presidency of Woodrow Wilson,* Lawrence: University Press of Kansas, 1992, p. 84.
4. Ibid., p. 190.
5. David C. Whitney, *The American Presidents,* Garden City, NY: Doubleday, 1969, p. 235.
6. Coletta, p. 238.
7. Whitney, p. 235.
8. Harwood and Cooper, p. 335.
9. Mark C. Carnes, "William Howard Taft," in James M. McPherson, ed., *To the Best of My Ability,* New York: Society of American Historians, 2001, p. 194.
10. Alan Brinkley, "William Howard Taft," in Alan Brinkley and Davis Dyer, eds., *The Reader's Companion to the American Presidency,* Boston: Houghton Mifflin, 2000, p. 314.
11. Sidney M. Milkis and Michael Nelson, *The American Presidency,* 4th ed., Washington: CQ Press, 2003, pp. 255–256.
12. Quoted in Robert Sobel, *Coolidge: An American Dilemma,* Washington: Regnery, 1998, p. 390.
13. Milkis and Nelson, p. 258.
14. Calvin Coolidge, *The Autobiography of Calvin Coolidge,* New York: Cosmopolitan Book Corp., 1929.
15. Robert Ferrell, *The Presidency of Calvin Coolidge,* Lawrence: University Press of Kansas, 1998, p. 201.
16. Ibid., pp. 204–205.
17. Sobel, p. 403.
18. Ibid., pp. 403–404.
19. Ibid., pp. 405–406.
20. Ferrell, p. 202.
21. Ibid., pp. 199–200.
22. Sobel, p. 407.
23. Ferrell, pp. 202–204.

24. Sobel, p. 408.
25. Ferrell, p. 204.
26. Sobel, pp. 410–411.
27. Ibid., p. 408.
28. Ibid., pp. 414–415.
29. Eugene Lyons, *Herbert Hoover: A Biography*, New York: Doubleday, 1964, p. 324.
30. Martin L. Fausold, *The Presidency of Herbert C. Hoover*, Lawrence: University Press of Kansas, 1985, pp. 240–241.
31. Herbert Hoover, *The Challenge to Liberty*, New York: Scribner's, 1934.
32. Fausold, pp. 242–243.
33. Herbert Hoover, *Memoirs of Herbert Hoover*, 3 vols., New York: Macmillan, 1951–1952.
34. Herbert Hoover, *The Ordeal of Woodrow Wilson*, New York: McGraw-Hill, 1958.
35. Lyons, p. 437.
36. Michael Beschloss, *The Conquerors*, New York: Simon and Schuster, 2002, p. 221n.
37. Harry Truman, *Mr. Citizen*, New York: Bernard Geis Associates, 1960, pp. 118–119.
38. Ibid., pp. 120–121.
39. Milkis and Nelson, p. 295.
40. Donald R. McCoy, *The Presidency of Harry S. Truman*, Lawrence: University Press of Kansas, 1984, pp. 96–97.
41. Truman, p. 121.
42. Lyons, p. 398.
43. Ibid., p. 400.
44. Milkis and Nelson, p. 295.

CHAPTER TWELVE

1. Robert H. Ferrell, *Harry S. Truman: A Life*, Columbia: University of Missouri Press, 1994, p. 931.
2. Ibid., p. 379.
3. Ibid., p. 380; *Mr. Citizen* also became the title of a book by Truman in 1953, issued in several editions.
4. See David McCullough, *Truman*, New York: Simon and Schuster, 1992, pp. 928–929.
5. Ibid.
6. Ibid., p. 932.
7. See Ferrell, p. 386; see also McCullough, pp. 937–938.
8. Ferrell, pp. 386–387.
9. McCullough, pp. 936–937
10. Ibid., pp. 948–949.
11. See ibid., p. 963.
12. Ibid., pp. 963–964.
13. Ibid., p. 936.

14. Ferrell, p. 392.
15. Ibid., p. 390.
16. Ibid., p. 391.
17. Ibid., p. 392.
18. Harry S. Truman, *Mr. Citizen,* New York: Bernard Geis Associates, 1960, pp. 240; 257–260.
19. McCullough, p. 962.
20. Ibid., pp. 964–965.
21. Ibid., p. 977.
22. See Max J. Skidmore, *Medicare and the American Rhetoric of Reconciliation,* Tuscaloosa: University of Alabama Press, 1970, p. 95.
23. Ferrell, pp. 395–396.
24. McCullough, p. 957.
25. See the web site at *http://www.nps.gov/eise/home.htm* of the Eisenhower National Historic Site.
26. Stephen Ambrose, *Eisenhower: Soldier and President,* New York: Simon and Schuster, 1990, p. 529.
27. Yanek Mieczkowski, *The Routledge Historical Atlas of Presidential Elections,* New York: Routledge, 2001, p. 117.
28. Ambrose, p. 529.
29. Michael R. Beschloss, *Mayday: Eisenhower, Khrushchev, and the U–2 Affair,* New York: Harper and Row, 1986, p. 3; quoted in Sidney Milkis and Michael Nelson, *The American Presidency,* 4th ed., Washington: CQ Press, 2003, p. 344.
30. Ambrose, p. 531.
31. Available at http://mcadams.posc.mu.edu/ike.htm, which is the source of these quotations.
32. Ambrose, p. 539.
33. Ibid., p. 540–541.
34. Ibid., p. 535.
35. Chester J. Pach, Jr., and Elmo Richardson, *The Presidency of Dwight D. Eisenhower,* rev. ed., Lawrence: University Press of Kansas, 1991, p. 236.
36. Ambrose, pp. 558–563.
37. See Matt Stearns, "Ike Finally Takes Residence in the Capitol Rotunda," *Kansas City Star* (June 5, 2003), p. A3.
38. See LBJ's own description of these events in Lyndon B. Johnson, *The Vantage Point: Perspectives of the Presidency, 1963–1969,* New York: Popular Library, 1971, pp. 538–550.
39. Ibid., p. 567.
40. Ibid., p. 568.
41. Robert M. Dallek, *Flawed Giant: Lyndon Johnson and his Times, 1961–1973,* New York: Oxford University Press, 1998, p. 604.
42. Doris Kearns, *Lyndon Johnson and the American Dream,* New York: Harper and Row, 1976, pp. 356–357.
43. Dallek, p. 605.
44. Kearns, pp. 358–359.
45. Dallek, p. 607.

46. See Kearns, pp. 354–357.

47. Dallek, p. 609.

48. Ibid., pp. 620–621.

49. Ibid., p. 618.

50. Ibid., pp. 618–619.

51. Kearns, pp. 365–366.

52. Quoted in Douglas Brinkley, *Unfinished Presidency: Jimmy Carter's Journey Beyond the White House,* New York: Penguin, 1999, p. 39.

53. Hillary Rodham Clinton, *Living History,* New York: Simon and Schuster, 2003, p. 491.

54. Stephen A. Ambrose, *Nixon, vol. 3, Ruin and Recovery 1973–1990,* New York: Simon and Schuster, 1991, pp. 461–462.

55. Ibid., pp. 449–450.

56. Robert F. Worth, "Presidential Libraries: Mines or Shrines?," *The New York Times* (April 24, 2002), p. G6.

57. Phil Willon, "Nixon Daughters Campaigning to Bring Father's Papers Home," *Los Angeles Times* (January 1, 2003), part 2, p. 6.

58. Ambrose, *Nixon,* p. 493.

59. Ibid., pp. 516–517.

60. Ibid., pp. 529–530.

61. See ibid., p. 498.

62. Ibid., pp. 572–573.

63. Joan Hoff, *Nixon Reconsidered,* New York: Basic Books, 1994, pp. 343–344.

64. Ambrose, *Nixon,* p. 583.

65. Ibid., p. 499.

66. Yanek Mieczkowski, *The Routledge Historical Atlas of Presidential Elections,* New York: Routledge, 2001, p. 131.

67. Gerald R. Ford, *A Time to Heal: The Autobiography of Gerald R. Ford,* New York: Harper and Row, 1979, pp. 294–295.

68. Ibid., pp. 364–365.

69. Helen Thomas, "Ford Gives Good Advice," *Seattle Post-Intelligencer* (June 8, 2001), B7.

70. Gerald R. Ford's Recent Activities," *http://www.ford.utexas.edu/grf/grfnow.htm,* retrieved June 8, 2003.

71. Gerald R. Ford, Curing, Not Cloning," *Washington Post* (June 5, 2002), p. A23.

CHAPTER THIRTEEN

1. Douglas Brinkley, The Unfinished Presidency: Jimmy Carter's Journey Beyond the White House, New York: Penguin, 1999, p. 3.

2. Burton I. Kaufman, *The Presidency of James Earl Carter, Jr.,* Lawrence: University Press of Kansas, 1993, p. 211.

3. For a list of their books, see "Books Written by President and Mrs. Carter," Jimmy Carter Library and Museum, http://carterlibrary.galileo.peachnet.edu/library/carterbi.phtml.

4. Jimmy Carter, *Always a Reckoning*, New York: Times Books, 1995.
5. Brinkley, p. 439.
6. Ibid., pp. 76–77.
7. Ibid., pp. 222–224.
8. Ibid., p. 253.
9. Associated Press, "Carter Arrives in Venezuela on Peace Mission," *Kansas City Star* (July 7, 2002), p. A16.
10. Associated Press, "Carter in South Africa," *Kansas City Star* (June 4, 2002), p. A8.
11. Brinkley, pp. 254–255.
12. Ibid., pp. 212–214.
13. Ibid., p. 211.
14. Christopher Marquis, "Bush Is Likely to Approve Carter Trip to Cuba," *New York Times* (March 26, 2002), p. A6.
15. David Gonzalez, "Castro Says Carter Can Inspect Biotechnology Centers," *New York Times* (May 13, 2002), p. A3.
16. David Gonzalez, "Carter and Powell Cast Doubt on Bioarms in Cuba," *New York Times* (May 14, 2002), p. A3.
17. David Gonzalez, "Cuban Dissidents Put Hope in a Petition and Jimmy Carter," *New York Times* (May 14, 2002), p. A3.
18. David Gonzalez, "Castro's Door: Both Open and Closed," *New York Times* (May 16, 2002), p. A10.
19. David Gonzalez, "Carter Addresses the Cuban Nation and Urges Reform," *New York Times* (May 15, 2002), p. A1.
20. Jimmy Carter, "Open New U.S.–Cuban Relations," in *Kansas City Star* (June 3, 2002), p. B5.
21. "Judging Carter," *Kansas City Star* (May 19, 2002), p. A2.
22. Jonah Goldberg, "Hyping Jimmy's Cuba Tour," *Kansas City Star* (May 19, 2002), p. B9.
23. "Citation," in Jimmy Carter, *The Nobel Peace Prize Lecture*, New York: Simon and Schuster, 2002, pp. x-xi.
24. Ibid., p. 15.
25. Ibid., p. 20.
26. Patricia Brennan, "The Reinvention of Jimmy Carter," in the *Kansas City Star* (November 11, 2002), p. E1.
27. Ibid., p. E5.

CHAPTER FOURTEEN

1. Jonathan Alter, "Citizen Clinton Up Close," *Newsweek* (April 8, 2002), p. 37.
2. Much of the information on Reagan's retirement comes from the "Ronald Reagan Post-Presidential Chronology," at http://www.reagan.utexas.edu/resource/handout/Postpres.htm, available also through a link from the Reagan Presidential Library.
3. Steven R. Weisman, "Sony Discussing Contribution to Reagan's Library," *The New York Times* (October 29, 1989), Section 1, Part 1, p. 4.

4. David Hoffman and Fred Hiatt, "Reagan Seeks Sony Donation," *The Washington Post* (October 28, 1989), p. A1.

5. Peter B. Gemma, Jr., "Reagan's Japan Trip is Well-Deserved," *USA Today* (October 25,1989), p. 10A.

6. Elisabeth Bumiller, "In Japan, Hail to the Reagans: A Nostalgic Welcome for the $2 Million Man," *Washington Post* (October 24, 1989), p. C1.

7. Daniel Sneider, Reagan has a Ball, But Gets Little Play in the Japanese Press," *Christian Science Monitor* (October 26, 1989), p. 3.

8. "The Great Communicator Abroad," Editorial, *Boston Globe* (October 29, 1989), A30.

9. Hillary Rodham Clinton, *Living History,* New York: Simon and Schuster, 2003, p. 124.

10. Herbert S. Parmet, *George Bush: The Life of a Lone Star Yankee,* New York: Scribner's, 1997, p. 510.

11. See Hugh Sidey, "The Presidency: Bush's Final Salute: The Ex-President Closes the Book on a Terrifying World War II Experience," *Time* (April 7, 1997), at http://www.cnn.com/ALLPOLITICS/1997/03/31/time/bush.html.

12. Ex-President Bush Makes Birthday Parachute Jump," *CNN.Com* (June 9, 1999) at http://www.cnn.com/ALLPOLITICS/stories/1999/06/09/bush.skydive/.

13. See "The George Bush Center for Intelligence," at the CIA website, http://www.cia.gov/cia/information/bush.html.

14. See, "USS George H. W. Bush (CVN–77), at http://www.wikipedia.org/wiki/USS_George_H._W._Bush.

15. "ADL Presents President George H. W. Bush with Joseph Prize for Human Rights," Anti-Defamation League Press Release at *http://www.adl.org/presrele/mise_00/4038_00.asp.*

16. "On Stage," *Kansas City Star* (June 23, 2003), p. D3.

17. Walter Scott, "Personality Parade," *Parade Magazine* (June 16, 2002), p. 2.

18. David E. Sanger, "Hard Choices for Bush," *The New York Times* (April 1, 2002), pp. A1, A5; quotations from p. A5.

19. Max J. Skidmore, "Presidents After the White House: A Preliminary Study," *White House Studies* 2:3 (2002), p. 248.

20. Maureen Dowd, "This Dynasty Stuff," *The New York Times* (May 1, 2002), p. A23.

21. Hugh Sidey, "Former President George H. W. Bush: 'the Decision on the War . . . Must be Made by One Personæthe President,'" *Time* (March 9, 2003), available at http://www.time.com/time/nation/article/0,8599,430687,00.html.

22. Jane Perlez, "Fatherly Nudge May have Shaped a Shift on North Korea," *The New York Times* (June 10, 2001), p. Y8.

23. Brent Scowcroft, "Don't Attack Saddam," *Wall Street Journal* (August 15, 2002), p. A12.

24. Scowcroft, "An Effort to Match in the Middle East," *Washington Post* (November 21, 2002), p. A41.

25. Elisabeth Bumiller, "White House Letter: Did President 43 Say to 41, 'You Be Dad, I'll Be Son'"? *The New York Times* (September 16, 2002), p. A14.

26. Ibid.

27. Georgie Anne Geyer, "Bush Sr.'s 'Message' to Bush Jr.," *Boston Globe* (October 18, 2003), available at: http://www.boston.com/news/globe/editorial_opinion/oped/articles/2003/10/18/bush_srs_message_to_bush_jr/.

28. Alter, p. 36.

29. Ibid., p. 42.

30. James Fallows, "Post-President for Life," *The Atlantic Monthly* (March, 2003), p. 64.

31. Alter, p. 37.

32. Clinton Critic Files Lawsuit, Alleging Harm by Magazine," *Kansas City Star* (June 14, 2002), p. A17.

33. Robert Pear, "White House Vandalized In Transition, G.A.O. Finds," *The New York Times* (June 12, 2002), p. A16.

34. Fallows, p. 61.

35. Ibid., pp. 62–63.

36. Ibid., p. 72.

37. Ibid., pp. 72–73.

38. Jonathan Alter, "The Bill and Bob Show," *Newsweek* (March 17, 2003), pp. 42–43.

39. Joyce Purnick, "Envisioning a Clinton At City Hall," *The New York Times* (June 12, 2003), p. A29.

40. Howard Fineman, "Clinton: Want Me Back?," *Newsweek* (June 9, 2003), p. 12.

41. Fallows, p. 73.

INDEX